FROM POVERTY
TO DIGNITY

CHARLES HAMPDEN-TURNER

ANCHOR BOOKS

ANCHOR PRESS/DOUBLEDAY

GARDEN CITY, NEW YORK

1975

From Poverty to Dignity was originally published in a hardcover edition by Anchor Press/Doubleday in 1974. This edition is published by arrangement with Anchor Press/Doubleday.

Anchor Books Edition: 1975

There are ideas and ways of thinking with the seeds of life in them, and there are others, perhaps deep in our minds, with the seeds of a general death. Our measure of success in recognizing these kinds, and in naming them making possible their common recognition, may be literally the measure of our future.

Raymond Williams, *Culture and Society 1780–1950*

Contents

Preface and Acknowledgments

Acknowledgments are very difficult for me because I lose track of literally hundreds of influences upon me. Moreover as a synthesizer who crosses disciplines and political alignments I often find myself associating persons who have no desire to be joined, and who retort that on the contrary they are quite *different*.

Almost by definition original ideas in politics must borrow from the right as well as the left. I regard myself as "radical" in my willingness to alter root conceptions and make hopefully novel syntheses, but not as the kind of radical who takes current left-wing rhetoric to its farthest logical extremity.

My preferred definition of radicalism has caused great strain and misunderstandings. Many who supported me when I began this work later moved into vehement opposition with severe economic sanctions. Community Development Corporations which I describe and advocate in this book are just such a synthesis between business corporations (right) and community change agencies (left). Similarly my strategy for "social marketing" is a synthesis between commercial advertising (right) and Movement politics (left). It has amazed me how much tension and ambivalence such "mongrel" conceptions produce as each polar camp seeks to purify itself. Even supporters of these conceptions are often found, on closer examination, to be secretly ashamed of that ingredient borrowed from the other camp.

For example we produced a magazine-cum-catalogue, half mail order, half manifesto. We poured our souls into the manifesto and thousands wrote in to purchase copies. Alas, the commercial ingredient resembled a policy of public penance for American consumers, so that few readers could bring themselves to atone by actually *ordering* the products in the catalogue.

Despite all storms and stresses I subscribe to none of the pretentions of being "above" right and left. My hope is to make the left a better place for political imagination and to show that the synthesis—not the ingredients—is what counts. Nor can I pretend to have been abandoned when I consider the long list of persons who stuck with me.

To Gar Alperowitz I am indebted for introducing me to the whole context of community development. Sandy (Christopher) Jencks was an immediate and greatly valued supporter of the idea of social marketing. (His own Educational Voucher plan borrows similarly from opposite ends of the political spectrum.) Sandy, Bob Lifton, Rollo May, Chris Argyris and Jonathan Kozol joined to sponsor me for a John S. Guggenheim Fellowship. I thank the foundation, and to my sponsors I am indebted for ideas, influence and friendship besides.

Other valued companions in adversity include Harvey Cox, Milton Kotler, Christian Bay, "Ping" Ferry, Elliot Sclar, Matt Edel, Mike Brower, Martin Duberman and Dick Wakefield. Without the help of key members of the movement for community development I could not have finished this. Bernard Gifford, ex-president of FIGHT was especially supportive, as were De Forest Brown, Tom Morse, Stuart Lichtman, Lou Ramirez, Cecil Butler and Phil Lo Presti. With great understanding they tolerated my mental "juggling" with issues which were, for many of them, matters of sheer survival.

To members of the New World Coalition who labored to give social marketing its first concrete trial my sincere thanks, especially to Terry Rode, Dick Steckel and Jerry Pyle. My editor, Bill Whitehead, and my copy editor, St. Clair Sullivan, must have been driven to the verge of compulsive neatness in order to compensate for the ill-kempt nature of my manuscript, and only Bill has stood between me and a Micawberish fate.

Finally my wife Shelley has *not* read proofs or typed drafts with wifely resignation. Nor has she tolerated any moody behavior on my part. She is an architect, not my handmaiden. We are both so liberated from chores that the house is really a mess.

The Wright Institute
2728 Durant Avenue
Berkeley, California 94704

Introduction

Perhaps for the first time in her history America faces problems of admitted urgency, yet seemingly beyond her powers to resolve. The smug optimism of the fifties, the moral crusading of the mid-sixties have given way to fundamental doubts about the conscience, the viability, the social processes and the institutions of this country. A small but influential segment of the population even questions the fitness of our system to survive.

Over the years, rhetoric has become curiously detached from social reality. Our TV sets and national media have vibrated with declarations of peaceful intent, with outraged exposures of hunger in America, with solemn promises of aid to the afflicted. On the level of verbal argument the reformers always seem to be winning, as thousands sign pledges, hundreds of thousands march and agreements are publicly signed . . . but then nothing really happens. The bombing of the near helpless becomes a way of life. The rhetoric bounces and echoes among the concrete walls and glass of towering buildings, which seem to insulate their occupants from the voices in the streets.

Revolution has been likened to a long period of gestation, climaxed by the birth of a new order. Yet America's pregnancies prove to be hysterical ones. The mountain belly of moralization labors convulsively to bring forth wind and then subsides.

It will be the theme of this book that what is frustrating our attempts to turn rhetoric into reality is the lack of an adequate theoretical framework with which to fuse competing perspectives towards human development. But even if such perspectives could be reconciled, poor Americans lack—and here I refer to the economically and culturally "poor"—the *institutional means* for empowering their perspectives. Because a citizenry can more readily change its social opinions than its social structures, and because the "early changers" are usually those in the less structured situations, we now face a dilemma in which those with the most humane sensibilities are, as yet, without effective institutions, while many "effective" institutions remain insensible. That political and social events seem gripped by bureaucratic imperatives and do not answer to humane helmsmen, is perhaps attributable to this lag between a new consciousness and designing ways to effect its beliefs. This book is intended as a contribution towards this necessary restructuring.

FROM POVERTY TO DIGNITY

CHAPTER 1

The Empowerment of the Poor: Ten Principles of Human Development

. . . while the clenched fist is a necessary symbol, the clenching ought never to be such that the hand cannot open, and the fingers extend, to discover and give shape to the newly forming reality . . .

Raymond Williams, *Culture and Society*

Since the Spanish Civil War poor people and other protestors have periodically symbolized their determination by raising their hands in a clenched fist. Extend and separate your fingers and they become more agile, sensitive, vulnerable and feeling. Close your hand and the fingers overlap, are compressed, protect and turn in upon each other, give mutual warmth and/or grip some implement with a common determination.

The principles of human development are like these fingers—sometimes appearing separate (though not in reality separable) and at other times closed tightly, fused for strength and virtually indistinguishable. It is this capacity for closure that the poor have to achieve. Partly because human solidarity is one of the very few resources they have, and partly because the dominant culture is individualistic, analytic, categorical and divisive in its operations and is forever prying the fingers apart into powerless, open vulnerability, before crushing the hand with powerful blows or breaking each finger.

Before proceeding, let me insert a note on terms such as "black" and "poor." Books on the subject of poverty are becoming unreadable because of the grammatical participation of every conceivable victim in the subject matter of each sentence. To say "he" without "she," "black" without Chicano or Puerto Rican, to say "ghetto" without "barrio" is to court the anger of the forgotten group. In this book I attempt to solve social and stylistic problems alike by speaking of "the most oppressive situation," which I regard as being poor and black, whether female or male. I am unable to say which gender is more oppressed, so therefore I shall attempt to use an equality of pronouns. None of this is to deny that certain conditions apply exclusively to certain groups, or to imply that the condition of lighter complexioned minorities is of less concern to me; rather it is hoped that proposals to solve the severest oppressions can be modified in the reader's mind to suit the less severe situations. In the meantime the term "Black Americans" should be taken to designate those subject to color prejudice and sometimes to class prejudice as well, while "poor" refers to those discriminated against on economic grounds, and sometimes on the basis of color as well.

Let us now turn to some principles of development.

1. *The principle of FREE EXISTENCE . . . the poor denied the right to originate*

"Free EXISTENCE" is far more than a vague rhetorical affirmation. Existence comes from the Latin *ex-istere*, to stand out. Although people are bombarded daily with inducements, threats, predigested "news," so that they learn not just about events but how to think about events, they yet retain the capacity to choose some communications in preference to others, to label and attach symbolic meanings to incoming information, and to weave this symbolic inventory into a great number of creative combinations. Finally, they can take such self-wrought syntheses and *thrust them out* (EX-IST) into their human environment, to give themselves and their environment meaning. This is what is meant by freedom, individual or collective.

To start with a definition of freedom is likely to cause dismay to many of the science-minded. Have I not abandoned thereby the search for lawful principles and scientific regularities? Not necessarily at all. Take linguistics, for example. Here numberless kinds of meaningful sentences can be generated within the rules of grammar and linguistic usage. Freedom can adhere in the continual recombination of finite and lawful elements. It can adhere in a unique act or expression whose underlying form and preconditions are rule-bound. It is not necessary to be a cultural absolutist *or* a cultural relativist, or to choose between many of such competing polarities. A cultural expression may have universal and particular aspects. Creative acts may in *some* respects be similar to all other creative acts.

If one assumes that all men need to EX-IST and do so in modest or greater proportions as their environment and development allow, then it becomes apparent that a major impediment to the self-assertion of the poor is that their environment is labeled, organized and spoon-fed to them by persons who do not share their economic, ethnic or cultural experience. Indeed, to be "poor" is to be regarded as generally incapable of originating significant thought or action of any kind. The poor having "failed," therefore more "capable" persons must decide for them. Alas, such judgments are self-fulfilling in the most disastrous way, for the less people steer themselves and the more they stagger at others' commands, the less "capable" will they appear, especially to those who program them. Dominant groups in society can no more EX-IST and interpret on behalf of the poor than a restaurateur can digest my luncheon on my behalf and serve me the repellent results. Just as the body thrives on reconstituting the foods it eats, the mind and nervous systems develop psycho-socially by reorganizing

received information and communicating such transformations to others. One way to persuade Black Americans to re-
constitute received information is to condemn it as "evil,"
"racist" and culturally worthless. We deprecate such extremist responses with pained expressions, while totally
failing to see their vital function in persuading blacks to
exist for themselves. Here, for example, is one of their
spokesmen,

> The American Negro, caught in social situations from which
> he cannot readily depart, retreat, or advance, resembles Jean
> Paul Sartre's existential man who is "condemned to be free."
> What we are up against is the fact that Western civilization
> is intellectually, spiritually and morally bankrupt. It is a civili-
> zation that is no longer able to originate creative ideas in
> social thinking . . . In this sense, white America has inher-
> ited a racial crisis that it cannot handle and is unable to create
> a solution that does not do violence to the collective white
> American racial ego.[1]

You cannot, Harold Cruse is saying, develop by a system
and set of rules that are stacked against you and have lost
their generative powers.

The major myth that bids each individual surrender his
personal and cultural EXISTENCE in favor of "The American
Way" is the idea of the melting pot.

> America never was the all-white nation that the national
> psychologies pretend. America is and always was multi-
> racial, multi-national and culturally pluralistic. People who
> try to deny this fact with talk about Americans all speaking
> the same language or sharing the same "customs" are merely
> propagating the myth about "assimilated Americanism."[2]

Although I feel, as I must, that the lack of creativity and
moral bankruptcy of whites in America has some personal
exceptions, the case for poor minorities existing for themselves instead of waiting for a white Godot seems overwhelming. For whatever the merits of WASP culture, its
value structures, even where developmental, principally

benefit their originators rather than minorities on whom they are "traded down." A rule-maker is his own yardstick. Even the bed of Procrustes probably fitted *that* gentleman perfectly; only strangers were stretched and lopped until they fitted. Cruse asks rhetorically,

> For whom and in whose interest, does the cultural apparatus exist in America? Does it exist for the social edification, the spiritual uplift, the cultural development, solvency and morale of all the diverse groups in America? Or does it exist solely, and disproportionately, for the social supremacy, the group narcissism, and the idealization of the white Anglo-Saxon Protestant minority?[3]

Especially for Black Americans there are even more urgent reasons to resynthesize white definitions. Such definitions may not be just sterile culturally or inappropriate for certain groups, but quite deliberately oppressive and destructive. Poor Americans have to do more than "turn off" or contradict unsuitable or destructive communications. They must also avoid the pitfall of taking each destructive epithet and asserting its opposite: for example, that black men are really superior, that God is black and expelled white devils . . . etc., as James Baldwin put it.

> One had the choice of acting just like a nigger or *not* acting just like a nigger—and only those who have tried it know how impossible it is to tell the difference.[4]

Simple negation is not the same as free EXISTENCE, argues James Turner, rather blacks must mold a *new* image of the dominant group and its utterances, avoiding "counter contrast conceptions" and "opposite Negroes."

> The essential concern becomes not free *from* what, but free *for* what. There is a radical conception in process that has Black men redefining themselves and, of necessity, reevaluating the white man. The objective of this process is to wrest the Black man's image from white control; its concrete mean-

ing is that white men should no longer tell Black men who they are and where they should want to go.[5]

The concrete, lived experience expressed as the consciousness of the poor is the *root* of all conception and subsequent abstraction. In this sense the principle of existence is radical (radix = root). Such radicalism requires neither violence nor the taking of every proposition to some ultimate extreme. It requires that the poor, and especially poor minorities, have the right to reorganize their existence from the roots up, and that the dominant white society respond to such new conceptions. The principle of EXISTENCE is one with creativity, radical resynthesis and cultural renewal.

2. The quality of PERCEPTION . . . seeing contradictions

One cannot define the development of PERCEPTION apart from that of EXISTENCE. They are like the fingers on our hand, which function together. The act of PERCEPTION includes construing, defining, choosing. There is no *at*tention without *in*tention—and those who insist upon their immaculate perception will suffer a diminished self-awareness as they force their preferred conceptions upon others, whether in the name of revealed religion or objective truth.

We focus on certain facts to the exclusion of others, arbitrarily choosing a "ground" against which to see a "figure"; even the pupils of our eyes expand quite involuntarily to let in what we like and what interests us and to close out much of what we dislike and what bores us.[6]

A quarter will appear larger to a child from a poor home.[7] Some 30 per cent of black children in Roxbury identified a bear as a rat.[8] Even if it could be established by the Latter Day Empiricists that we all can come to see the same objects and label them "correctly," the configuration and visual organization *among* the objects would still differ.

There is great *definitional power* as well as creativity in the right to label reality and have that label stick. "The Negro problem," "right to work laws," "ghetto violence," "separatist thinking," "culture of poverty," "extremism," "socialized medicine" are all examples of opprobrious labeling which has helped to stall much-needed responses to the plight of the poor. Stokely Carmichael and Charles Hamilton quote a classic expression of this point in *Black Power*:

"When I use a word," Humpty Dumpty said in a rather scornful tone, "it means just what I choose it to mean—neither more nor less."

"The question is," said Alice, "whether you can make words mean so many different things."

"The question is," said Humpty Dumpty, "which is to be the master—that's all."9

It is not just the explicitly political labels that wrest from poor people their rights to live by what they see, but the implicit "politics" of would-be helpers who proclaim their good intentions or scientific neutrality. Virtually all middle-class helpers define the problems of poverty and race relationships according to their own expertise and specialty, with the result that the minds of those poor that heed them and their communities are fragmented into as many pieces as there are specializing professionals and agencies —and that's a lot of fragments! The alienated bureaucracies of welfarism and social research, which with all their knowledge and money have never succeeded in coordinating themselves, drop their steely lattice of departments upon the ghettos, cutting poor communities and the minds of bewildered clients into a mass of little pieces, like vegetables beneath a dicer.

Poverty becomes a "mental health problem," a "nutritional problem," a "housing problem," a "transportation problem," economic, financial, moral, educational prob-

lems, etc. Actually there are few groups who do *not* want
to get in on the act. Thus poverty has been ascribed to
"ignorance in the area of Home Economics," and (a real
piece of Victoriana, this one) "lack of knowledge about
the merits of physical exercise."[10] After all—if there is
money in poverty wars—why should not Phys. Ed. and
Home Ec. experts get their share?

Even the liberal proponents of enlightened attitudes towards Black Americans may require some redefinition. For
example, Gunnar Myrdal's classic of sociological relevance
An American Dilemma saw the condition of blacks as a
reaction to the contradiction within the American Creed,
just as Western sociologists in general tend to see man as
determined by the structure and function of his social
system. Ralph Ellison objected:

> Are American Negroes simply the creation of white men, or
> have they at least helped to create themselves out of what
> they found around them? Men have made a life in caves
> and upon cliffs, why cannot Negroes have made a life upon
> the horns of the white man's dilemma? . . . Much of Negro
> culture might be negative, but there is also much of great
> value, of richness which, because it has been secreted by
> living, has made lives meaningful.[11]

There are actually two dialectical components in the
kind of PERCEPTION required for development. There is the
capacity to see what *is* and the imagination and creativity
to see potentials and ideals within the status quo and
within oneself that could transform the situation. It is this
tension between "is" and "ought," this capacity to "hold
two opposed ideas in one's mind at the same time and still
retain the ability to function" that brings home to the poor
the contradictions in which they are caught.

Research on the perceptual growth of black ghetto children points up this interdependence of knowing and
changing reality. The research confirmed Piaget's notion of
perceptual growth via a series of widening conceptual cir-

cles. Young people come to know their family, their street, their community, city, state, nation and world in that order. Many ghetto adolescents, especially those with harsh experiences, were found to be "fixated" at street and family levels, with scant knowledge of the "wider circles" of community and city.[12]

This strongly suggests that transition from smaller circles to wider ones is a function of the relationship between a street and its community, a community and its city, a city and Washington, etc. Wherever such relationships become an experience of personal degradation, wherever well-meaning "scientists" strip the poor of their value-ladened visions of how their community "ought" to control their city, then neither awareness of contradictions nor the will to resolve them can develop.

Yet where we respect the perceptual constructions made by the poor or their spokesmen, we also cede them the right to encounter us on *their* agendas, and play on their "home ground." Political and social power moves from perceptual definition to action and accrues to those who combine and hold both initiatives.

3. *The strength of* IDENTITY . . . *the rooted and changeable self*

It could be supposed that a nation that celebrates individualism might contribute significantly to the growth of human IDENTITY. That this has not happened, at least among poor minorities, suggests that crucial aspects of IDENTITY formation have been ignored.

Here we will make two crucial distinctions within the concept of IDENTITY: (a) those aspects of IDENTITY that maintain an inner continuity and sameness, and (b) those aspects in which IDENTITY changes, accumulating new characteristics and strengths over time.[13] The two dimensions support one another, for without the theme of continuity, changes and developments could not be cumulative and would lack an organizing principle—a core around which new aspects of the self are synthesized.

For the poor and especially Black Americans it is the core of inner continuity, the sense of cultural and historical movement through time which has been lethally assaulted. This has occurred, first, by denying roots and origins; second, by undermining of a "black" self-acceptance based on these roots; third, by a definition of success that emphasizes triumph *over* ethnic backwardness; and, fourth, by an ethic of "color blindness" that falsely avers that "it makes no difference." With rootedness and continuity undermined, the changeable aspects of the self simply cannot develop, however much the virtues of this change may be extolled.

Black Americans did not immigrate to America. They were uprooted, chained down aboard the *Good Ship Jesus* and other vessels and sold in random lots that did not even respect family and kinship. Today they face depictions of Africa in the mass media where only wild animals are treated with respect. Harold Cruse bids us compare the racist clichés of the film *King Solomon's Mines,* the bathos of *Green Pastures* and other specimens of American niggerphilia with the simple beauty and dignity of *Heritage* by Countee Cullen.[14] The opening verse reads,

> What is Africa to me
> Copper sun or scarlet sea
> Jungle tar or jungle track
> Strong bronzed men,
>   Or regal black
> Women from whose loins
>   I sprang
> When the birds of Eden sang?
> One three centuries removed
> From the scenes his
>   fathers loved,
> Spicy grove, cinnamon tree,
> What is Africa to me?

With firm roots built upon a basic acceptance of oneself, one's skin, appearance, ethnicity and heritage it is possible to grow into the future. W. E. B. Du Bois expressed this "credo":

> Especially do I believe in the Negro Race, in the beauty of its genius, the sweetness of its soul, and its strength in that meekness which shall inherit this turbulent earth.

> I believe in pride of race and lineage itself; in pride of self so deep as to scorn injustice to other selves; in pride of lineage so great as to despise no man's father; in pride of race so chivalrous as neither to offer bastardy to the weak nor beg wedlock from the strong. . . .[15]

Written in 1904, this credo anticipates a growing conviction by modern psychiatrists that acceptance of others is based firmly upon an acceptance of oneself.

Existential literature has argued that these two aspects of human identity, the rooted-unchangeable and the emergent-transcendent, are, in the very glaringness of their contrast, mutually enhancing. It is the absurd limits of the human condition that makes so admirable the capacity to go beyond them. Similarly, the very stigma that blackness constitutes in a white society makes more magnificent the affirmation of that stigma, in a way that breaks the stranglehold of racist expectation and which transforms the manner in which blackness is regarded. One snatches meaning from the face of bigotry.

This triumph is not *over* blackness as one might conquer a "dark" habit or private vice, but *through* blackness. The difference is crucial, sociologically as well as psychologically. To triumph through blackness is to involve one's community, family and lineage in an extension of black consciousness moving through time, while to triumph over blackness detaches the minority individual from his community as surely as it detaches the changeable, bleachable self from its black roots, and trains it to applaud the American Way.

When Althea Gibson says, "I am not a black tennis player, I am a tennis player," she is partaking of that curious liberal delusion, the ethic of color blindness. Skin color, texture of skin and hair, it is argued, are utterly superficial marks. We should look at the "whole man"—an entity presumably lurking within, bodiless, skinless and hairless.

That intimate and extended knowledge of another can make his or her pigmentation into a surface characteristic, that a white person, given time, can love a black person and vice versa, is not so much false as irrelevant. For it is in the fleeting, instrumental relationships, which are constantly being formed, broken and reformed that black people suffer. Any barrier to the smoothness of such relationships, any added anxiety that might delay by as much as an hour the making of a deal or a swift rapport can become a permanent handicap to those of minority color. As our society "speeds up" we perforce prejudge others, and may not even have the opportunity to check on our first impression. This first "impression of blackness" is quite crucial to a comprehension of racist dynamics.

Hence the liberal ethic of color blindness has limited applications outside the love nests of interracial couples. The attempt "not to notice" color is patently absurd.

Differences in color are extremely intrusive upon consciousness. One does *not* have to be taught in order to fear pigmentation totally different from one's own, as we shall see presently. So far from blackness being a thing to forget, it is a key to understanding and resolving the contradictions afflicting black people. It is an issue that holds scores of other problems in its thrall. On this issue *black people are greater experts than the "experts,"* so that they should assume the initiative and define social problems. For, as we have seen, nearly all experts, the writer included, define problems so that there is a role for themselves in their solution. One might as well be straightforward about it.[16]

4. COMPETENCE . . . *a synthesis of powers*

According to the late R. W. White the central theme of human motivation is to experience oneself as competent.[17] The sense of "adequacy," "potency" or "self-esteem" is echoed by numerous psychologists and theorists on human development.

The call for black and poor power is a devastatingly authentic statement of this basic issue. Some black clergymen affiliated with the National Council of Churches put it as follows:

> The conscience of black men is corrupted because having no power to implement the demands of conscience, the concern for justice in the absence of justice becomes a chaotic self-surrender. Powerlessness breeds a race of beggars. We are faced with a situation where powerless conscience meets scienceless power, threatening the very foundations of our Nation.

> . . . without the capacity to participate with power, i.e., to have some organized political and economic strength to really influence people with whom one interacts, *integration is not meaningful.*[18]

The full fury of racism has always been reserved for black assertion and potency. Black mistresses were acceptable because a woman was thought to "surrender" in love to a man, and be "ruined" *by* him, while adding to his reputation for virility. Early attempts by black men to court white women were met with lynching. Lynch mobs have cut off the genitals of their victims and stuffed them down their throats, not, I suspect, because all the motivation is basically sexual, but because the sexual potency of blacks was the one area of potential COMPETENCE which was usually inaccessible to control by white repression. This omission leads to all manner of white phobias concerning "primitive passions."

Hence the only "COMPETENCE" conceded to Black Americans are the forbidden kinds of power: sexual, violent, secret and illegitimate—precisely those "dark powers" whites fear within themselves. What is required for psycho-social development is the broadest possible synthesis of competences, including political, economic, moral, persuasive, benefactory, physical, technical and organizational COMPETENCE. A major theme of this book will be that all these kinds of COMPETENCE *must be integrated and fused* if poor people are to develop. An unbalanced situation, for example, moral strength and physical weakness, only conjures up its reverse in the opposing force, moral weakness and physical strength, so that "powerless conscience meets conscienceless power."

It has been the historical tragedy of many black attempts to advance that different kinds of competence have been sought, not as components of a whole, but as alternatives. Booker T. Washington urged economic self-help instead of civil rights and political agitation. W. E. B. Du Bois became so engrossed in his dispute with Washington that economic advancement became identified with "accommodationism" as legal and political rights once more came to the fore. After years of bitter civil rights struggle, some desegregation and the death of Martin Luther King, there dawned a realization with which Booker T. might have agreed.

> We found we had nothing, nothing really for millions of black people, who could vote all day long and still be hungry, and go and order a hamburger . . . but not have the money to pay . . .[19]

Even Black Power has proved a very ambiguous slogan, containing, as Harold Cruse has observed, the same historically one-sided definitions of COMPETENCE. Thus Julian Bond has defined Black Power as "a natural extension of the work of the civil rights movement." Floyd McKissick sees it "as a new thrust which seeks to achieve economic power and develop political movements." Ralph Edwards defines it as "defensive violence." Roy Innis "as the acceptance of values meaningful to ourselves." Cruse himself has no doubts: "(It is) *nothing but the economic and political philosophy of Booker T. Washington given a 1960's militant shot in the arm and brought up to date*" (italics in original).[20]

Although Martin Luther King has been unfairly accused of flaunting powerlessness rather than competence, he was in fact concerned with *moral* COMPETENCE and *persuasive* COMPETENCE. He also saw that the poor must have something to give, some *benefactory* power, and their witness in demonstrations was intended as a gift towards the renewal of America's values.

Ron Karenga is an advocate of the cultural components of COMPETENCE: art, theater, letters, music and dance. Black people must first become a *cultural nation,* and on that foundation, insulated from white beguilements, build economic and other institutions.[21] Cruse comes the closest to advocating a synthesis of competences; like Karenga he sees black culture as an organizing principle and the hidden source of strength.

> The historical truth is that it was the Afro-American cultural ingredient in music, dance, and theatrical forms (the three forms of art in which America has innovated) that has been the basis of whatever culturally new and unique that has come out of America. Take away the Afro-American tradition of folksongs, plantation minstrels, spirituals, blues, ragtime, jazz styles, dance forms and the first Negro theatrical pioneers in musical comedy of the 1890's down to Sissle and Blake of the 1920's, and there would be no jazz industry involving publishing, entertainment, recording; there would have been no Gershwins, Rodgers and Hammersteins, Cole Porters or Carmichaels or popular song tradition—which is based on the Negro blues idiom. There would have been no American musical comedy form—which is America's only original contribution to theatre; there would have been no foxtrot—which has formed the basis for American ballroom dancing.[22]

But Cruse is under no illusion that Black Americans can dance or sing their way into power. It is the cultural *apparatus* that contains economic, cultural, persuasive, moral, political, technical and benefactory powers.[23]

To move on the cultural front, as a means of developing a variety of related competences, is also to move against "the weakest sector of the American capitalist free enterprise front." Cruse has this advice for the black leader:

> He should take to the rostrum and assail the stultifying blight of the commercially depraved white middle class who has poisoned the structural roots of the American ethos. He should explain the economic and institutional causes of the American cultural depravity. He should tell black America how and why Negroes are trapped in this cultural degeneracy, and how it has dehumanized their essential identity, squeezed the lifeblood of their inherited, cultural ingredients out of them and then relegated them to colonial slums.[24]

5. *Authentic and intense COMMITMENT . . . participation of the whole*

The test of social action is whether, in fact, one's true EXISTENCE, PERCEPTION, IDENTITY and sense of COMPETENCE has been COMMITTED through the act. In other words, if the COMMITMENT is both *authentic* and *intense,* it will include all four principles of development discussed so far and will contribute to their testing. This idea is similar to that of praxis, the word-deed. The poor, along with those—like myself—who would seek alliance with them, need to test our ideas in action. Only through such COMMITMENT, with the emotion aroused through real involvement, can we learn to reconcile head with heart, mind with body, and discover the fusion of abstract values and concrete experiences.

To act in real life situations so as to experience the consequences is fundamental to psycho-social learning. It could be as important to social progress as hypothetico-deductive methods have been to the physical sciences. However, the use of laboratory methods and simulations in *social* affairs eviscerates our experience of its *authenticity* and *intensity* to give us a "science" of Man the Pretender.

For black and poor people it is especially vital that they act, and be seen to act, from deepest conviction, for the dynamics of oppression include the requirement that they collude with oppressors in accommodating "cheerfully" to unjust relationships.

> We wear the mask that grins and lies
> It tides our cheeks and shades our eyes
> The debt we pay to human guile
> With torn and bleeding hearts we smile
> And mouth with myriad subtleties
>
> We smile, but, O Great Christ, our cries
> To Thee from tortured souls arise
> We sing, but oh the clay is vile
> Beneath our feet, and long the mile
> But let the world dream otherwise
>   We wear the mask.[25]

There can be no liberation without *demonstration*, literally "showing what you mean." King explained from his Birmingham jail:

> We merely bring to the surface the hidden tension that is already alive. We bring it out into the open, where it can be seen and dealt with. Like a boil that can never be cured so long as it is covered up, but must be opened with all its ugliness to the natural medicines of air and light, injustice must be exposed, with all the tension its exposure creates, to the light of human conscience and the air of rational opinion before it can be cured.[26]

King clearly believed in the curative powers of American Air, which proved more fetid, perhaps, than he originally supposed. While he understood, brilliantly, the necessity for authentic witness and emotive communication, he seemed to believe that exposure was sufficient and from then on semi-mystical forces, "air" "light" and "conscience," would begin to "cure." They didn't.

The danger, especially for middle-class rebels, is that demonstration falls in love with its own expressiveness. Frustrated from achieving its aims for long periods of time, the *protest itself* becomes a "thing of beauty," an exercise in romanticism, a celebration by existential heroes of their own heroic utterances as they become immersed in their own moral aura. It is never made clear exactly who will translate abstract moral concern into concrete details—perhaps some working-class or lower-middle-class functionary. It is hardly surprising, therefore, that the latter groups often go sour on moral crusaders, and listen with some appreciation to diatribes against "pointy heads."

6. SUSPENSION and RISK . . . *the politics of the body*

When a man commits himself to action, his personal COMPETENCE, PERCEPTION and IDENTITY are exposed before others, and he must be prepared to modify the synthesis of what he believes in the light of their reactions to his COMMITMENT. But since his COMPETENCE includes an ordered and purposive structure of meanings, the modification cannot take place without a temporary SUSPENSION, so that new meanings can enter his "open" mind, and the totality can be reordered.

This SUSPENSION involves RISK, because any new information may permanently alter, contradict or even destroy the way in which a man conceives of himself. Such existential risk taking should not be confused with economic or physical risks which may or may not be present. Existential risk taking requires *moral* courage. I discover that I am valuable and meaningful to the Other, only by risking the discovery that I am worthless and meaningless. To suspend one's assumptive world in the process of encountering another is to be *un*prejudiced. Prejudice (literally, "judging before the event") is tantamount to a failure to suspend prejudgments during the course of encounters. The non-risking, unsuspended person cannot discover his mistaken prejudgment.

RISK and self-SUSPENSION produce tension. Racism is, in part, an incapacity or refusal to tolerate the tension necessary to falsify prejudgments. Prejudgments are themselves an armor against painful tension. None of this is intended to reduce the entire phenomenon of racism to psychological mechanisms. The larger social system may require life-styles in which prejudgments are inescapable, may exacerbate tensions and falsely attribute blame.

A very common way in which the tension between black and white, between poor and affluent, is mismanaged is to abbreviate tense encounters by increasing unilaterally the tension felt by one party to the interaction, typically the black and poor. The latter then back away from an argument—not because they agree but because disagreement is too painful. Actually tension is only painful when increased beyond a certain level. Tension in very low amounts is usually called "boredom." In moderate amounts it is experienced as "excitement," and in strong amounts it is called "anxiety." The consequences of tension for pleasure-pain can be represented by the bell-shaped curve illustrated below, with "pleasure" at the summit, and boredom and excitement at either end.

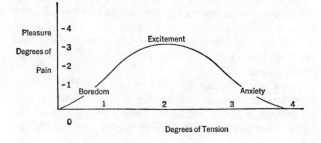

Clearly the maximization of "excitement" depends upon the capacity to *hold tension at a moderate level* for much of the time. We are now able to postulate what happens when black and white, poor and affluent confront one another. First, both feel their tension increase, with the result that "excitement" shades over into "anxiety." Simultaneously both struggle to control their tension and to reduce anxiety. Where one is stronger than the other, the stronger *will attempt to control his own tension by controlling the other*, and is likely to see the other in terms of the anxiety within himself, that is vaguely menacing, "dark," subversive, irrational, physical, phobic, etc. The weaker party to the interaction may lapse into apathy or "boredom"—that is, he may deliberately choose a "low tension strategy" partly to mollify the stronger, but also to keep a wide margin between himself and the anxiety condition into which the stronger will try to push him at the slightest provocation.

Usually the poor can be made anxious and thus induced to discredit themselves, through "excessive" remonstration, tears, apathy, addiction, silence, depression, flight or aggression. The poor being more desperate, having fewer verbal, legal and other resources, and lacking the state's recourse to legal coercion, are routinely panicked and then punished for panicking. The teen-ager shot for running from a policeman, or beaten for "resisting arrest," or locked up for not finding the appropriate words that would have cleared him of suspicion, is trapped in a vortex of anxiety the moment authority snarls. Little wonder, then, that he turns to the artificial risks of drugs or the numbers game, or that he will attempt by "criminal" violence to control his own tension in a manner similar to the "legal" violence visited on him.

What especially ails the poor and black is the difficulty they have in holding their tension at the optimal level of excitement, a level essential for social learning and for initiative over one's own life. James Baldwin, even with the advantage of his extraordinary articulateness and middle-class status, reports,

> But I didn't expect what I found in the South, either. . . . I felt I was walking on this rug, this wall-to-wall carpet. Beneath it is a complex system of wires, and one of those wires, if you step on it, will blow up the whole house . . . and everybody in the South knows where that wire is except me. . . . Every time I open my mouth I'm wrong. The way I look at people is wrong. The way I sound is wrong. I am obviously not only a stranger in town, I'm an enemy. I've arrived with a bomb because I'm black from America in America.[27]

Of all black leaders it was Martin Luther King who seemed to grasp intuitively the importance of teaching a moral courage that RISKS and SUSPENDS. Coming from an intensely verbal and particularistic culture, the South, where racism flaunted itself openly through daily encounters, wherein blacks were threatened by hundreds of social signs and verbal stratagems, King saw that the counter-strategy was to control one's anxiety through remaining *as relaxed and flexible as possible*. Not only might this non-violent SUSPENSION be self-fulfilling by disarming or at least inhibiting authoritative violence, but it could totally reverse the usual trick by which authorities panic the poor into "immoral" behavior. If anyone lost their cool it would be the authorities—and although their rage could be deadly, this might, with sufficient publicity, be turned to *their* social disgrace. In this event, the surviving demonstrators would experience their own power to maintain social poise in the face of threat, while white "masters" threw a public tantrum, pushed *by blacks* into that "uncontrollable anxiety condition" which victims know so well.

One of the most successful of modern psychotherapies is closely analogous to these tactics. In the systematic desensitization of anxiety, the overly anxious person trains himself to relax. With each relaxation the object or person towards which he feels such exaggerated dread is brought closer. Once the phobic object, say a cat, is sitting on the patient's lap, while he still relaxes, he is cured of his dread. Ways of inducing relaxation include going limp, and, especially with children, warmth and embraces from trusted persons. Such methods reduce all tension where the object is, in fact, harmless, or they reduce the excess tension where normal tension, e.g., "excitement," is needed to function—as in self-assertion.[28]

It could be objected that the authority that oppresses poor people is less phobic than real in its menace. Even so, specific dangers are easier to deal with than the vaguely menacing and omnipresent "wired carpet" on which poor minorities tread so warily. None of this implies a blanket endorsement of non-violent demonstration techniques. They are, at best, an imperfect and vulnerable growth dynamic. They contain, however, most important components necessary for psycho-social development, which are sadly underestimated today.

7. BRIDGING the DISTANCE . . . racial and attitudinal divides

I have argued that tension is an inevitable part of daily life, especially in interpersonal relationships, and that it shades over into strong anxiety when blacks meet whites or the poor meet the affluent. But why is this? One answer is that the DISTANCE between classes and between those of different color is so wide as to require *greater* SUSPENSION and RISK. It is more hazardous to commit oneself authentically to someone distant from one's own values, needs, background and experience. To the extent that black is "unlike me," my personal experience has not taught me how to engage him or her.

Clearly the idea of DISTANCE and the necessity to BRIDGE it are tightly interwoven with our other principles. The poor and the black can only avoid the strain of wide distances and enjoy distances equivalent to those bridged by whites if the bulk of their interaction is with those of the *same class and color*. Yet this is difficult where money, jobs, status, etc., are all on the other side of the divide. What we force poor minorities to do is strain every nerve and resource to reach across this distance to us. Then we under-reward them significantly for the extra effort.

There is some dispute as to whether differences in color, or whether differences in opinion and life-style constitute the distance that makes people anxious. One researcher showed that a white racist would rather remain in a room with a black person who agreed with him, than a white who disagreed with him.[29] Another showed that white and black teen-agers who were in fact very similar in taste and background did not perceive the similarity except among those of their own color.[30] A third survey showed that black students could correctly predict the attitudes of prejudiced white students, but not the attitudes of unprejudiced whites.[31] All this seems to suggest that differences in skin color *warn of impending disagreement and misinvolvement*. Black skin is a signal to a white person, and vice versa, that the subject will not successfully reach an understanding with the "different" person. Such a warning may be true or false; the point is that it can be costly to find out, and it may take anxious effort just to try.

So far from anxiety about DISTANCE having to be taught, the evidence from anthropology suggests a primordial fear of marked differences among numerous races. Anthropologists have reported that young children may scream the first time they see a black or white face, and dark children have been observed to suffer shock when first observing a white person stripped to the waist. They thought only his face was pale—hence "paleface."[32] It seems that we start with our own self and reference group as examples of normality.

In light of such findings it is difficult to argue that anx-

iety about racial differences is irrational. Many people
fail to understand their anxiety and invent racist theories
of innate inferiority that attempt to make sense of the
anxiety they feel. Such myths are contrary to fact, but
they do represent attempts to account for genuine feelings of fear and pain. One can delegitimize all such myths
without doing anything at all to combat the simple fact
that a face of a different color *does* signal the imminent
onset of anxiety, and *does* enable the individual to predict
the likelihood of misinvolvement. In short, there is a logical connection between perceived DISTANCE and the possibility of a less than pleasant experience.

The problem is compounded when a black face also permits a white person to predict someone of a different class.
It happens to be true that many Black Americans are also
poor or working-class. Since the vast majority of Americans
seek friends and enjoyment among those of similar education, similar age, and similar socio-economic group,[33] it is
hard to accuse of bigotry the lower-middle-class white who
correctly draws the inference that the increase of black
persons in his neighborhood means that its class composition is changing and that it is going to be harder for him
to establish rapport with his neighbors. Such a man simply
cannot afford the "enlightenment" of an Ivy League academic who encounters blacks who have been pre-screened
for class, intelligence and culture compatible with his college. The "already found" and certified black person is
ironically in greater demand than his white equivalent.
Remove the difficulty of the original discovery and you
have an easy symbol of your tolerance. In fact, there is
evidence that class and color difference produces considerably more rejection than do black and white differences
within the middle class.[34]

I have come close to saying that black and white an-
tipathies are understandable and reasonable, but it is not
quite that simple. While wide DISTANCES are harder to
BRIDGE, the rewards for succeeding may be considerably
greater than the BRIDGING of shorter DISTANCES between

those of very similar background. By definition a creative discovery combines matrices of thought or meaning, previously considered DISTANT from each other. Fresh information, new perspectives and creative combinations are simply not possible for those unwilling to encounter life-styles at variance with their own.

Here we encounter a most formidable difficulty. It is necessary to "leap the abyss" in order to learn. Every attempt to do so risks falling into the depths. How peculiarly unfortunate it is that blackness with all its cultural associations *has come to represent falling itself.* Instead of Black Americans being appreciated as a unique culture with saving knowledge upon the far side of a cultural divide, they are feared as inhabitants of the Pit itself. The temporary undoing that we feel within ourselves while trying to understand strangers has become associated with the "outer darkness" of being permanently undone.[35]

Two strategies have arisen to deal with the problem of DISTANCE and the need to BRIDGE it. The first, that of the civil rights movement, emphasizes the extent to which the DISTANCE is exaggerated by superficial aspects, such as skin color, and urges blacks to appeal, to conform to, and to personify those aspects of the American tradition which are most noble, e.g., dialogue, equality, liberty, tolerance, individuality, etc. By such methods DISTANCE will be shortened and black and white understanding will be fostered, and "men will be judged not by the color of their skins, but the content of their characters."[36] The dormant goodness within the white system can be evoked.

The second strategy, which can be broadly identified with the Black Power movements, argues that the DISTANCE is real and not a matter of appearance, that Black Americans gain power and confidence by intensive interaction with each other, rather than with whites, that if the DISTANCE between whites and blacks is worth BRIDGING, this will only be so when each side of the bridge has its own firm foundations, so that there is something substantial for whites to discover when they reach blacks and something substantial for blacks to represent when they reach whites. Whites are not seen as having the answer within their political traditions, or a readiness for action that needs only to be evoked by appeal and demonstration. Rather, white society is seen to have lost its way. Blacks need independence (a better word than separatism), according to Malcolm X,[37] in order to save themselves. To this independence whites can relate if they wish.

It is this second approach which comes closer to the general thrust of my argument, although many of the values which King died for can be included. A strong black culture with institutions to protect its integrity is essential. Because white society controls most of the wealth and the incentives, there may never be a shortage of blacks willing to scramble over barriers, but as long as this scramble resembles a bridge with one-way traffic from blackness to whiteness, it is unrealistic to expect from whites a fraction of the effort to understand black points of view, from which it appears so many of their own wish to flee. No one in his senses builds a bridge over an abyss unless that bridge leads somewhere. That is the challenge for Black Americans and the organized poor, to lead somewhere, to ex-ist as a group and a culture.

8. *SELF-CONFIRMATION and SELF-TRANSCENDENCE . . . reasons for living*

To achieve SELF-CONFIRMATION is to have one's EXISTENCE, PERCEPTION, IDENTITY, COMPETENCE, etc., fulfilled through the understanding, appreciation and acknowledgment of others. It is closely akin to self-actualization and self-fulfillment. To have some part of one's competence pass from one's own consciousness to dwell in and enrich the life of one's group or the culture that has confirmed one is to experience SELF-TRANSCENDENCE. This can be an ecstatic experience of oneness, a glorious reunification with one's sisters and brothers. Often sneered at, and as often counterfeited, dreamed of in mass movements and present in regression as well as growth, it is nonetheless a powerful dynamic.

SELF-CONFIRMATION is also close to the idea of fate control. To be confirmed as one anticipated, is to gain control not necessarily *over* but *through* others. One makes the impact on one's environment that was intended. The Coleman Report, which attempted to account for scholastic success in terms of school expenditures, social class and race, found that no variable was as important as fate control.[38] If middle-class students faired better than most of the poor, the greater control experienced over their destinies bore the strongest relationship to greater success.

So when we ask how "overly differentiated" groups like Black Americans and Chicanos can survive when the DISTANCE to whites is so great, and the uncertainty of reaching them is so high, the answer must be that they get their confirmation from each other, and fate control must be structured into their own institutions. (We shall discuss in later chapters how these institutions are to get funds in the first place.)

Studies of adolescents of different ethnicities in American high schools have shown that their sense of COMPETENCE (or self-esteem) is not a function of the prestige of that ethnic group in the culture at large. WASP children thought significantly less of themselves, on the average, than did Jewish children. COMPETENCE was a function of the quality and constancy with which the children were confirmed by family and friends.[39] Children outnumbered in their neighborhoods by others of different ethnicity, color and religion tended to think less of themselves than those in local majorities. Those remembering "traumatic rejection" by other groups also thought less of themselves (except Jews, who appeared to have tightened their bonds following such rejections and to have more than compensated one another *within* their group for any suffering outside).

The problem for all minorities of color is that, while a psychic strength can be generated among sisters and brothers, decent wages, national reputations and public recognition are the monopolies of the white world. Hence for thousands of talented blacks, white recognition is a pursuit of loneliness, gaining them occasionally public recognition ("You're a credit to your race"), but not *private* or *intimate* confirmation. And no one knows that better—or says it better—than James Baldwin. In the midst of literary lionization he is in some ways quite alone.

> If I can't, for example, go home and get drunk with my brothers, or sit around with my brothers and sisters and just do nothing—you know, fry chicken or eat some watermelon or play some music—if I can't find myself with people who know enough about me to correct me, who are not intimidated by whatever it is the world thinks I am, or whatever I may think I am, if you don't find the people who know enough about you to do that, then you are very quickly lost and you become a kind of walking cauldron.[40]

There are unintentional indications of Baldwin's alienation in this passage. His nostalgia is curiously stereotyped —music, watermelon, fried chicken. His culture is a kind of unchanging rest stop in a changing world, where he "tanks up" with affection, "to be loved, baby, hard, at once, and forever, to strengthen you against a loveless world."[41] But you cannot reify black culture in this way if the culture itself is to develop.

There is the added problem for Baldwin that with all his fame and reputation he cannot stop his own brothers from being beaten on a Harlem street. That's individualism for you! Sick with this realization he once made the mistake of seeking solace among his white associates.

> One of my brothers was in trouble and I was at this cocktail party and a very famous American intellectual . . . said to me, "What are you crying about, Jimmy? You've made it." I could not believe I heard him. Made what? . . . I walked out and I never went back and I never will.[42]

It is not surprising, therefore, to find that while white upward mobility brings some reduction in the number of psychosomatic symptoms and anxiety attacks, black upward mobility brings a significant increase of such symptoms. When we consider that the anxiety and despair among many groups of poor blacks has been found in the past to be severe, and that the individual escapee from poverty who struggles away from his brothers up a career ladder only worsens his anxiety, then we begin to understand the unenviable choice of collective poverty or "personalized" loneliness which is forced upon blacks by our system. In a very real sense most of the black middle class has been lured away from the black under class to serve as "integration mascots" in corporate front offices. Like lonely meteors from another world they burn up in our atmosphere.

What happens is that "color blind" confirmation by whites of the individualized black only succeeds in flaying his skin, scalping him and uprooting him. "You did it all *yourself*," he is told, and finds himself used as an example to stop his own brothers from complaining. Margaret Mead has characterized the trap of "white acceptance" thus:

> We'll deny your hair, we'll deny your skin, we'll deny your eyes. We deny you when we accept you; we deny the ways in which you are not exactly like us, by ignoring them.[43]

The imperative need for solidarity among black and poor people derives not only from the doubtful kinds of support they receive from whites but also from the fact that only a minority of whites express any sympathy at all! Over 50 per cent of white respondents regard blacks as having as good or better chances than they do.[44] As one observer has remarked, the real American Dilemma is that most Americans *see no dilemma at all*—just a few troublemakers.[45] After all that has been filmed, found, written and vowed on the subject of racial justice it says something for the sheer impermeability of racial barriers that not yet have a majority of whites been convinced sufficiently to express concern, much less take action.

Consider twenty strangers in a corporate office. Two are black. Two are poor whites. Sixteen are Middle Americans. Barring unusual clashes of personality the Middle Americans will have fifteen relationships which they can form swiftly and easily. They will have only four difficult and anxious relationships. But the Black Americans and the poor whites have only *one* easy relationship each, sixteen which are difficult and anxious, and two rather doubtful friends who may join with the majority against them. If people develop as the result of successful relationships, it is easy to see how gravely disadvantaged the minority is in such assimilated conditions.

What leaders of the poor have been saying is that the "two blacks" and the "two poor whites" need the very strongest of brotherhoods to withstand what they suffer in the other relationships. Even the courage to leap the very widest distances between the races and to encounter affluent whites as equals, requires all the self-confidence and skill which only intensive group experiences can generate.

9. *Dialectic leading to* SYNERGY

The analysis becomes more complicated here, so the reader should be prepared. SYNERGY comes from the Greek *synergia*, a working with. Elements are synergistic when their individual action contributes to the enhancement of other individual elements and the whole so formed. Crucial to the dynamics of co-operative life is an understanding of synergistic processes. Yet, as I shall argue in Chapter 3, habits of thought in the West have crippled all but the most primitive forms of mutuality. In order to gain an understanding of SYNERGY and its developmental capacity we have to break some of these habits, starting right here.

First, we have to part with the notion that all terms, concepts and goals must be clarified by assigning to them single, discrete definitions that demarcate them from other goals, and that "rigorous thinking" will countenance no deviation from one-dimensional ideas and objectives. Second, we must question the assumption that co-operation ensues when all persons agree upon a common goal, purged of an ambiguity which is believed to be the source of misunderstandings. Third, we have to question the whole "possessive metaphor," whereby people have or hold a belief as if it were a physical thing, while social scientists do their best to "physicalize belief objects" as if they were things external to people. Fourth, we must dispute the entire polarity of conflict vs. collaboration—that is, the belief that one moves *away from* conflict, e.g., wanting something different, *towards* collaboration, wanting the same thing. Finally, we have to reconsider the idea that co-operation is achievable by simple effort of "good will" and "rationality" rather than having to be initially *designed into* a system. Let me show how the concept of SYNERGY contradicts these basic assumptions.

SYNERGY is destroyed by the creation of a vocabulary of discrete meanings, because so-called ambiguous words may also be "junction words," that hold together a convergence of *different* needs of different participants. It is because participants *differ* in their wants and satisfactions that they can co-operate in multi-faceted objectives, wherein the objective itself is multi-dimensional. Actually, if people wanted exactly the same thing and that thing was finite and physical, the resulting scarcity would immediately drive them into competition. And this is what happens. Bourgeois society is both overwhelmingly conformist and competitive. Agonized by cutthroat competition, we beg for consensus, which triggers fresh competition. Having mostly unidimensional terms, everyone finds his rank ordered by these yardsticks; the very act of agreement produces winners and losers, oppression and humiliation, and endless pleas to "reorder priorities" as if hierarchical ordering was inevitable, and there were no other way to structure the system.

Hence SYNERGY itself includes many facets and there can be no apology for its complexity since the more meanings it has, the more people and wants it organizes. For now, three interdependent definitions, themselves synergistic, will be discussed.

(a) SYNERGY *is the fusion between different human aims and resources to create MORE between the interacting parties than they had prior to the interaction.*

The simplest example is the love relationship—"The more I give you, the more I have," or, in the terms of our principles of development, COMPETENCES which are mutually CONFIRMED are thereby mutually increased. However, synergy also operates at the level of ideas and PERCEPTIONS. Thus the combination of two perspectives may be very much more than the sum of their parts, so that both affective and intellectual surpluses can be created. This dynamic is not lost upon leaders of the poor, for example, Huey Newton.

> The dignity and beauty of man rests in the human spirit which makes him more than simply a physical being. This spirit must never be suppressed for exploitation by others. As long as people recognize the beauty of their human spirits, and move against suppression and exploitation, they will be carrying out one of the most beautiful ideas of all time. Because the human whole is much greater than the sum of its parts.[46]

(b) SYNERGY *is created by the resolution of apparent opposites and social contradictions.*

Consider that the various principles of psycho-social development discussed so far are commonly regarded as opposites. To EX-IST (principle 1) is to stand out from prior understandings, yet to be CONFIRMED, or to CONFIRM others (principle 8), is to give or receive new understandings. To create a unique IDENTITY (principle 3) is to differentiate oneself. Yet to BRIDGE the resulting DISTANCE (principle 7) is to integrate oneself. COMPETENCE (principle 4) is a synthesis of human resources, yet it must be RISKED and SUSPENDED (principle 6), that is, *un*synthesized and held in doubt. *All these opposites are in dialectical relationship.* Different people, groups and organizations can similarly move from dialectical encounter into synergistic relationships, so that upon the quality of fusion among these principles depends the quality of fusion between people.

The time has come to diagram this process. The ten principles of psycho-social development are arranged cyclically. Of these principles, eight have been discussed, number nine is now being discussed, and ten is yet to come.

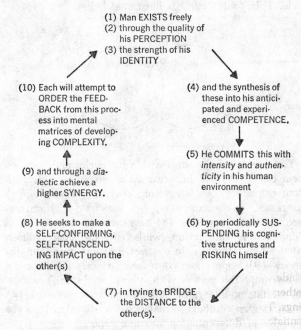

(1) Man EXISTS freely
(2) through the quality of his PERCEPTION
(3) the strength of his IDENTITY

(4) and the synthesis of these into his anticipated and experienced COMPETENCE.

(5) He COMMITS this with *intensity* and *authenticity* in his human environment

(6) by periodically SUSPENDING his cognitive structures and RISKING himself

(7) in trying to BRIDGE the DISTANCE to the other(s).

(8) He seeks to make a SELF-CONFIRMING, SELF-TRANSCENDING IMPACT upon the other(s)

(9) and through a *dialectic* achieve a higher SYNERGY.

(10) Each will attempt to ORDER the FEEDBACK from this process into mental matrices of developing COMPLEXITY.

The cycle illustration above helps to explain the fusion concept of SYNERGY and its interpenetrating definitions.

One cannot define SYNERGY itself without qualifying it with all the other segments of the cycle. The same applies to the other segmental principles. For example, in answer to the question "What is developed PERCEPTION?" one would have to answer, "It is an existential and intentional viewpoint upon the environment of a human IDENTITY whose COMPETENCE is being COMMITTED, *intensely* and *authentically* . . ." etc. The same would apply to definitions of any other of the principles. They are facets of a whole, no more independent than the fingers in a fist.

In fact, there are always at least *two* cycles since one cycle is needed to confirm and to synergize with another cycle. This *double cycle* is illustrated below.

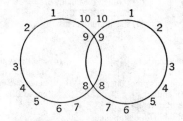

The dialectical opposites within the cycles and between them can be divided into two main categories, *differentiating* principles and *integrating* ones. For example, (1) EXISTENCE, (2) PERCEPTION, (3) IDENTITY, (4) COMPETENCE and the resulting (7) DISTANCE can be viewed as *differentiating* the person, while (6) SUSPENSION differentiates him internally. In contrast, (7) BRIDGING (the distance), (8) being CONFIRMED, and (9) creating SYNERGY, all *integrate* the person with others, while (10) ORDERING FEEDBACK integrates him internally. A personal (5) COMMITMENT to others in dialectical relationship links the opposites of differentiation and integration.

Differentiation and integration are most important ideas in the politics of race and poverty, because they correspond to independence strategies and integration strategies. It makes a great deal of difference if we define these two strategies in terms that are reconcilable or non-reconcilable. If SYNERGY consists of fused polarities, then we must learn to label social reality in reconcilable terminology.

For example, "separatism" and "segregation" refer to voluntary and involuntary forms of differentiation *not* reconcilable with integration. Likewise "assimilation" and "melting pot" are forms of integration, *not* reconcilable with cultural differentiation. Yet "independence" and "integration," as terms, are apparent opposites, yet reconcilable ones. Not only are they reconcilable, they are synergistic in the sense of being more than the sum of their parts and lending each other a surplus of strength. For one can only, as Martin Buber put it, enter into a true relationship with another one set at a distance. Even Black Power cannot grasp new ideas unless it is willing, from a position of sufficient strength, to transact with the wider world. White Power can be little more than a steamroller crushing the Third World until it learns to see through the perspectives of its victims—that is, until it respects the legitimacy and rights of culturally differentiated others.

Because the segments of each cycle do, through SYNERGY, generate and strengthen their resources, they may be conceived as a *double helix* which spirals upward developmentally. This is illustrated below.

The Double Helix

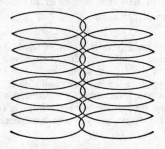

As this helix "spirals upward," existences, perceptions, identities and competences are confirmed, strengthened, qualified, balanced and developed through synergistic relationships with the resources of others. In *Radical Man* I "hung" over one thousand research findings upon this model, in an effort to demonstrate its organizing capacity, a lengthy exercise that I shall not repeat here. The reader is asked to accept the dialectical model as asserted.

The understanding of such dialectical processes is absolutely essential to any ultimate reconciliation between Black and White—apparent opposites if there ever were any! Yet this runs counter to white Anglo-Saxon consciousness, to a whole Puritan, technological, scientific, analytic, dichotomizing, one-dimensional purifying tendency in American thought, obsessed with being No. 1 rather than No. 2, with washing whiter than white, with slicing at every concept with Occam's razor until it is shorn of its synergistic potential. Harold Cruse has doubted that the American mind can really comprehend the fusion of opposites, and because it cannot, Whiteness insists upon subordinating Blackness, as "rationality" oppresses feeling, universalism dominates particularism along with scores of unreconciled polarities. Even within the black movement itself, "separatism" and "assimilationism" have clashed together in futile discord, "Back to Africanism" has fought "Bookerism," civil rights campaigns have clashed with Black Power. Cruse notes that the whole history of the black struggle in America is one of unreconciled oppositions and internal division.

Truthfully, it would have been too much to expect the 1920 Negro radicals . . . to clarify the integrationist vs. nationalist tendencies and mold them theoretically into political fusion. Dialectical processes have never really been understood in America. The two fundamentally basic trends behind Negro racial ideology, though sharply etched out in terms of organizational confrontation, got lost and went unresolved. . . .[47]

This brings us to the third (synergistic) definition of SYNERGY.

(c) SYNERGY *grows out of a dialectical and dialogical process of balance, justice and equality, between persons or groups, and between the ideas and resources they represent; such* SYNERGY *always exists on multiple levels.*

If SYNERGY is the reconciliation of apparent opposites, then clearly the process of reconciliation must include:

a balancing of these opposites

social *justice* to the persons or groups representing the opposites

equality between the opposites, prior to their fusion.

These norms concern processes, not necessarily outcomes. We cannot tell the relative merits of two positions, we cannot even judge their reconcilability until they have been weighed justly. It could be, occasionally, that one of two positions seems totally regressive, like the right of whites to segregate Black Americans. Surely we should just crush this, as one would the devil. Or should we? In fact some legitimate human need can be saved from almost any position, and rendered reconcilable. In the case of segregation, it seems locked against assimilation, as the powers of Darkness are locked against Light. (Notice the racism inherent in all such good v. evil metaphors.) At least that is what we thought, until blacks told us they did not *want* to be assimilated like pledges crawling one by one on hands and knees into an all-white fraternity. So it wasn't good versus evil after all, but a false dichotomy.

Had we understood better some of the needs of segregationists, we would not have been so surprised by the all-black caucuses and the expulsion of men from the room, while women draw up their demands. I am not saying, as many have, that black solidarity is "racism in reverse," or female solidarity is "sexism in reverse." I am saying that both positions contain a reconcilable core, and that is the right to group integrity or cultural independence. It is *not* legitimate, however, for whites to solidify in order to dominate and involuntarily segregate blacks, or for men to do the same to women. Solidarity among the weak and solidarity among the powerful are not equivalent.

Now, two differentiated groups can integrate their resources *if* the encounter is an equal one, just and balanced. Under such circumstances independence is enhanced by integration, it is not compromised. The person who does not think dialectically simply cannot appreciate that you might get more integration eventually by enhancing black independence now; thinking in opposites, he can only believe that one must subtract from the other. Ironically, one does subtract from the other *when and so long as the relationship is an unequal one.* As long as whites hold advocates of black independence in colonial subjection, every increment of "separatism" would reduce "assimilation" and vice versa, which is what independence and integration deteriorate into *when* they are unequal.

It is important to see that SYNERGY exists at multiple levels. If the idea of black nationalism is irreconcilable with the idea of black and white alliances, then nationalists and civil rights advocates cannot reconcile themselves *within* the black community, nor will black and white communities reconcile themselves, nor will America reconcile itself with the Third World.

Where some part of the American mentality dominates over another part of that mentality, for example, "masculine" COMPETENCE over "feminine" SUSPENSION, then men gain power over women, majority whites over minority blacks (with blacks "suspending," i.e., dropping to their knees in demonstrations in order to be integrated), suburbs over ghettos, and the United States over Africa. It remains only to "discover" that many black families are matriarchies and lack Masculinity à la Moynihan. (His definition of professional competence is to treat the poor as clients and dependents.)

Numerous black leaders, Huey Newton and Eldridge Cleaver among others, have recognized that white hostility to blacks, and their unequal relationships of domination and submission, are paralleled by unequal struggles within the white psyche. Huey Newton, interviewed in prison, observed,

> The master (is) the mind, the slave the body. The slave would carry out the orders that the mind demanded him to carry out. By doing this the master took the manhood from the slave because he stripped him of a mind. . . . In the process the slavemaster stripped himself of a body. As Eldridge Cleaver puts it, the slavemaster became the omnipotent administrator and the slave the supermasculine menial. . . . The omnipotent administrator in the process of removing himself from all body functions realizes later that he has emasculated himself. And this is very disturbing to him.[48]

The white man, Baldwin argues, has never come to terms with his own "dark powers," he fears and hates blacks as part of the war within himself, and it is precisely the "gut anxiety" of the black-white encounter that reawakens in the white person all his doubts about impulse control, sexuality, violence, etc.

To say that SYNERGY interpenetrates a number of levels is also to say that the double helix can take as its subject not just a person, but a group, organization, culture, nation, etc. For example, the combination of several person-to-person relationships could form a *group* culture or cycle, so that we could say of that group's relationship to another group,

> Black Group EXISTS freely, through the quality of its PERCEPTION (or information system) the strength of its IDENTITY (or its reputation) and the synthesis of these into its anticipated and experienced COMPETENCE (or potential) . . . etc.

We could illustrate such a group cycle as the joint product of several persons-in-relation, thus:

Alternatively the illustration above could refer to several groups combining to form an *organizational* cycle.

Obviously then, the identity of a black man in the ghetto will interpenetrate with his family's identity, his group's identity, his organization's identity, his cultural identity, his black or other national identity, etc. Unjust, unequal, dichotomized relationships at *any* level will affect the other levels. Relationships between city hall and the ghetto, which make the latter a colony, will foster similar relationships between the pusher and the buyer, which makes the latter a junkie. If the "house nigger" has to crawl to his master, he will likely make the "field nigger" crawl to him. He has been socialized into no other kind of relationship.

If we wish to change relationships to yield more equality, justice and SYNERGY, *then the whole nest of interacting cycles from persons to institutions must be changed at roughly the same time,* and it is essential that poor Americans control their own institutions so that "corporate cycles" are created by, and for the benefit of, the person-to-person relationships, operating within them and through them.

10. *FEEDBACK ORDERED into COMPLEXITY . . . expanded horizons*

There remains to be discussed the final segment of the developmental cycle, or the tenth principle of development. The relationships of SYNERGY established between ideas, people and groups can be incorporated into the experience of each party to the relationship. That is, having established co-operative relationships, having fused their needs and conceptions, each party has access to the "mental map" of the whole, which was greater than his particular part. Thus FEEDBACK from synergistic relationships amounts to an expansion of consciousness and a more effective internal organization of ideas, created by the abstracting of principles from co-operative experience.

Harold Cruse has complained that Black Americans have never been permitted to create social theories out of their *own* native experience, rather they have been squeezed between an American Creed that excludes them and revolutionary Marxist theory that never had them in mind.

> To speak, then, of social revolution in the United States from a Negro point of view, means a reinterpretation of the meaning of social revolution for our times. . . .[49]

Cruse argues that *the* great handicap of the black movement is its "historical discontinuity"—that is, its failure to build up an ordered synthesis of tested ideas and experience over time. He contrasts rebellion, or EXISTENCE (principle 1), as it has been called here, with social theory, or ORDERED FEEDBACK (principle 10).

There have been individualized rebellions aplenty, Cruse complains. The crucial lack, the imbalance within our cycle, is a coherent social theory growing out of rebellions. "Negroes are always marching but never getting anywhere." The March on Washington was in fact a "great impasse."

> There the great Freedom clamor was absorbed in the emptiness of a great void and the protests became like echoes in a canyon that bounce about in mocking repetition. The March led not to victory but to crisis.[50]

A part of the problem lies in the fact that individualistic rebellions and the non-violent "politics of the body" are sanctioned by bourgeois tradition of morality and personal conscience, but their synthesis into an articulated theory of change is not similarly sanctioned. Not only is all dialectical theory regarded as foreign, if not Marxist, but in capitalist philosophy the benefit to the many comes about almost magically after individual choices have been registered in the economic, or the moral, marketplace. Aided by Invisible Hands and placing themselves vaguely Under God, Americans submit the plethora of their subjective wants to a kind of Mystical Sorting Process.

The same tendency is found in the abstracted empiricism of American social science, wherein a veritable deluge of individual bits of data are supposed, someday, to point their own way to a comprehensive science.

It is in the belief that someone, somewhere, had better start theorizing soon, from the point of view of the disadvantaged, that this book is being written.

CHAPTER 2

The Crucifixion Dilemma

It is a peculiar sensation, this double-consciousness, this sense of always looking at oneself through the eyes of others, of measuring one's soul by the tape of a world that looks on in amused contempt and pity. One ever feels his twoness,—an American, a Negro; two souls, two thoughts, two unreconciled strivings; two warring ideals in one dark body, whose dogged strength keeps it from being torn asunder.

W. E. B. Du Bois, *The Souls of Black Folk*

We can summarize the basic dilemma of racism by building upon the principles diagrammed in Chapter 1.

In the beginning, that is, before economic exploitation or racist ideology, there was DISTANCE between the experiences of persons and the need to BRIDGE it (principle 7). Differences in skin color warn of such DISTANCE. They help to create it, and come to correspond with real cultural and class differences. Increased DISTANCE places a strain upon all other segments of the cycle, but especially upon the need to RISK and SUSPEND (principle 6). To strain this segment is to experience anxiety. Attempts to control anxiety involve attempts to control unilaterally the perceived source of anxiety—in this case the DISTANT other, which includes Black and poor Americans. All attempts at such unilateral control cripple the developmental helix, and corrupt the relationship between the parties. However, disproportionate damage is visited upon the controlled as compared with the controllers.

Unilateral control means injustice, inequality and imbalance within and between cycles, which greatly impedes the formation of SYNERGY between parties—that is, the fusion of their perspectives, aims and resources. Such a fusion requires that differences be weighed with tentative equality in order to extract from each viewpoint its reconcilable elements. To treat another as an equal is the greatest compliment one can pay him, or, in other words, it is the most humane PERCEPTION, showing the greatest respect for his IDENTITY and COMPETENCE and the optimal SUSPENSION of one's own conceptions in favor of his, etc.

Now, it might be thought that a greater compliment would be implied in bowing before him and acknowledging his superiority. In fact such praise is counterfeit, because the subordinate thereby devalues the significance of his own CONFIRMATION. He says, in effect, "I, who am not fit to judge you, judge you to be superior." The White Master who evokes this from his Black Mistress might as well masturbate, for all the significance contained within her allegiance. Having reduced her to an erotic stimulus, he has wasted her powers of CONFIRMATION.

Using the principles from the cycle, let us see how inequality between these two actors produces imbalance within each. His COMPETENCE, when not balanced or qualified by equivalent amounts of SUSPENSION, inflates into *dominance*, while his SUSPENSION deteriorates into *prejudice*. Her SUSPENSION, when not balanced by equivalent amounts of COMPETENCE, inflates into *surrender*, while her atrophying COMPETENCE deteriorates into *weakness*. Or again, his concern with his own IDENTITY becomes so exaggerated relative to his PERCEPTION of her humanity, that IDENTITY inflates into *egotism*, and PERCEPTION deteriorates into *callous disregard*. Meanwhile, her PERCEPTION of his demands becomes so exaggerated relative to her own IDENTITY, that PERCEPTION inflates into *hypervigilance* and IDENTITY deteriorates into *self-effacement*.

In effect, the cycle "buckles," with certain segments *inflating* and certain segments *deteriorating*, yet the pattern of inflation and deterioration is *complementary*. When

White Master inflates in one segment, he automatically deteriorates in another segment, and pressures Black Mistress to (1) deteriorate in the segment he has inflated, (2) inflate in the segment he has deteriorated.

Using just the four principles we have mentioned so far, we find the following *complementary imbalances* within each party.

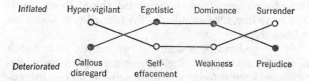

Complementarity takes place because clashing egotisms would produce such hostility, and mutual effacements would produce such estrangement, that in both instances anxiety would increase and become uncontrollable. But when she compensates for his callousness by her watchfulness, and makes room for his ego by effacing herself, a kind of balance is restored and anxiety is reduced. Since he had power to make her suffer greater anxiety than he suffers in any conflict between them, she learns to survive by complementary behaviors. There is a price, of course. They are both "half persons" and neither develops in their "unexercised portions."

The cross-over effects between hyper-vigilance and self-effacement on one axis, and callous disregard and egotism on the other axis, etc., are examples of what I call the *crucifixion dilemma.* The cross is an ancient symbol of conflict. When used to depict the crucifixion of Christ, it represents not only the conflict between Jews and Romans, Jews and Jews, God and the world, but conflict and anguish within, the nailing down of the open hands, the wrenching apart of the limbs, the piercing of the side, the breaking of the heart, the blood and water running out as separated elements.

These elements were isolated just as Christ was isolated, just as inflated and deteriorated principles of growth are isolated from each other and expressed in non-reconcilable terminology. For while PERCEPTION can be reconciled with IDENTITY, and COMPETENCE can be SUSPENDED and RISKED as a means to developing all four principles, egotism is separate from, and opposed to, self-effacement as vigilance is from disregard. Via the enforced inflation and deterioration of their capacities, the poor and the black are crucified every day, torn asunder by the inequality to which we subject them.

So far we have dealt with but two crosses. In fact each of the ten developmental principles can be inflated or deteriorated until it forms a crossed purpose, and an irreconcilable opposite to every other principle. Table 1 takes each principle and illustrates with common evaluative adjectives, the inflation, the equality or the deterioration of that principle in its relationship to the other principles. (NB: The left-hand column in Table 1 is identical to the cyclical model presented on page 33, except that it has been stretched out linearly. In fact, principle 10 would "loop around" to principle 1.)

Reading from Table 1 we can generate a large number of propositions which share this dynamic: that when the oppressor moves into the inflated column, the oppressed is pushed into the deteriorated column, or when the oppressor chooses deterioration, the oppressed must inflate. For example:

Because White is RIGID and PREJUDICED, Black must SURRENDER and VACILLATE if their relationship is to appear flexible.

Because White is *fanatical* and *carried away,* he requires Black to be *passive* and *indecisive,* so that White may appear decisive.

White, who is *ethnocentric* and *parochial,* requires Black to be *"subverted by foreign ideas"* and possibly *traitorous,* so that White may appear tolerant.

White, who is *segregationist* and *authoritarian,* needs Black to be *co-optable* and *coalescent,* if some kind of "co-operation" is to be achieved.

If White is out to *win* like an All-American competitor, he requires Black to *lose*—and from his winning position he forces Black to acknowledge this system as optimal.

If White's racism is elaborately yet falsely *rationalized,* he needs Black to *know nothing* if White's rationalization is to appear intellectual.

And so on.

It is important to see that White's racism makes the center column of Table 1, the balanced and synergistic qualities, uninhabitable for Black. Even were Black to exhibit genuine creativity, perceptiveness, self-awareness and a potent involvement which another black person, or an unprejudiced white, would readily CONFIRM, a racist White might simply refuse to accept any incremental development in Black. In other words, he would define Black's behavior as deteriorated or inflated in accord with his own prejudice. Robert K. Merton has observed

> The very same behavior undergoes a complete change of evaluation in its transition from the in-group Abe Lincoln to the out-group Abe Cohen or Abe Kurakawa. . . . Did Lincoln work far into the night? That testifies that he was industrious, resolute, perseverant, and eager to realize his capacities to the full. Do the out-groups Jews or Japanese keep those same hours? This only bears witness to their sweatshop mentality, their ruthless undercutting of American standards, their unfair competitive practices. Is the in-group frugal, thrifty and sparing? Then the out-group is stingy, miserly and penny-pinching.[1]

The very fact that Black, whatever he does, is defined as inflated or deteriorated by White, spawns another problem. Black may, as a consequence, lose his sense of how much COMPETENCE he *can* safely ask an unprejudiced person to CONFIRM. His PERCEPTION may lose its capacity to distinguish between rejection based upon racism or rejec-

TABLE 1

Principle of Development	Inflation	Balance	Deterioration
1. EXISTENCE ↓	Anarchical Laissez-faire Riotous	Creative Original Radical	Sterile Conventional Bland
2. PERCEPTION ↓	Hyper-vigilant Inquisitorial Voyeuristic	Respectful Perceptive Insightful	Callous Insensitive Blinkered
3. IDENTITY ↓	Egotistic Self-centered Self-conscious	Self-aware Distinctive Personable	Anonymous Self-effacing Depersonalized
4. COMPETENCE ↓	Dominant Brutal Overbearing	Virile Potent Effective	Weak Impotent Ineffective
5. COMMITMENT ↓	Fanatical Carried away Overexposed	Dedicated Involved Decisive	Passive Indecisive Uncommitted
Intensity	romanticized over-emotional	caring concerned	apathetic cold
authenticity	ingenuous artless	sincere credible	tricky disingenuous
6. RISK & SUSPENSION ↓	Reckless Foolhardy Surrendered Vacillating Abdicating	Morally courageous Inner strength Flexible Open-minded Adaptable	Failure of nerve Pusillanimous Rigid Prejudiced Bigoted
7. BRIDGING the DISTANCE ↓	Subverted by foreign ideas Traitorous	Cosmopolitan Worldly Tolerant	Ethnocentric Parochial Factionated
8. SELF-CONFIRMATION & SELF-TRANSCENDENCE ↓	Overwhelming Manipulative Self-gratifying Otherworldly Religiose Mystifying	Impressive Fulfilling Self-actual-izing Immortal Seminal Influential	Ingratiating Frustrated Alienated Mundane Limited Localized
9. *Dialectic* leading to SYNERGY ↓	Winning Assimilated Coalescent Co-opted	Optimizing Mutual Co-operative Participative	Losing Authoritarian Separatist Segregated
10. ORDERED FEEDBACK & COMPLEXITY	Lofted idealism Elaborately rationalized Abstruse	Expanded consciousness Cultured Intellectual	Simplified black/white Dichotomized Know-nothing

tion based upon his own inexperience. In short, he does not know whether to blame others or to blame himself, and when he blames others falsely, he typically *inflates* his COMPETENCE and when he blames himself falsely, he typically *deteriorates* his own COMPETENCE. He is caught, crucified.

The rest of this chapter will deal with issues and examples growing out of the crucifixion dilemma.

Value judgments and relationships

The meaning which is here extracted from value judgments about interpersonal relations flies in the face of the tradition of "scientific" positivism. While social science has many equivalents of PERCEPTION, COMPETENCE, COMMITMENT, etc., the inflated and deteriorated versions of these concepts are often held to lack any testable meaning. They are mere "exclamations of preference," mired in the subjectivity of the speaker.[2] If value judgments are acceptable, then whose is to be preferred in any dispute? This problem can be partly solved by attributing the judgment in the first instance, not to the individual but to the relationship. Hence we can say that a relationship that is demonstrably unequal, with a one-way direction of influence, is pathological from the point of view of development, of learning, of satisfaction, etc. Such a proposition is verifiable, and, in fact, widely verified.[3]

The second question must then be, given the pathology of this relationship, who is the *more responsible* for its continuance? The answer must be that the more powerful of the two has the major responsibility, the one who has more degrees of freedom to alter current patterns, and the one who has coerced the other into compensating for what is lacking in his own style of interaction. We get nowhere in arguing whether America or North Vietnam, Israel or the Arab countries, management or unions, federal agencies or ghettos are more cruel or rude in their style of conflict. We have to ask, What possibilities has each combatant to alter his behavior to yield greater mutual satisfaction? Such possibilities, for the subordinate, are clearly unequal; his responsibility must therefore be accounted as less, although it is still present.

There is a considerable difference between this two-stage value judgment, which looks at total patterns of relationships before attributing responsibility, and the "instant value judgment" of attributing disliked features of the relationship in which one participates to the moral failure of the other party to that relationship. The poor, as of now, are crucified between the traditional culture's habit of reducing all social phenomena to "somebody's fault" and the social scientific habit of finding natural explanations that are "nobody's fault." The poor are alternately exonerated from blame by social scientists, because they are not free to behave otherwise. Or they are thoroughly condemned by politicians because they are free to behave otherwise. In other words, either their EXISTENCE or their moral COMPETENCE is subordinated, and they face the unenviable choice of being freely incompetent or blamelessly determined, of accepting punishment as willful sinners, or avoiding punishment as neutral objects.

Our model avoids this dilemma, for it sees the poor as relatively unfree and less responsible when they are unequals in a relationship, but as potentially free and responsible, and actually so, as soon as the relationship approaches equality. Moreover evaluation does not abort understanding since the relationship must first be studied with care and in its entirety, before the evaluation can be made. This entirety would include, where relevant, cultural and organizational influences, roles, rules, laws and other specifications. The understanding of such influences and constraints is a preparatory step to accepting responsibility for their continuance or change.

What we see in the ghettos are the subordinate *ends* of a number of unequal relationships. We cut human subject from human object, as if the latter was a thing, and then solemnly record the incidence of post-surgical hemorrhage. Remarkable!

The exacerbating opposites

Table 2 lists the inflated and deteriorated symptomology of our ghettos. Typically the situation will seesaw between inflation and deterioration. I have tried to avoid symptoms not verified by black writers themselves, who are typically more condemnatory of each "opposite category" than are white researchers. The Losing End of the Relationship refers not only to relationships between whites and blacks but between blacks more or less influenced by whites and other blacks. I do not claim that these epithets are justified in their application to individuals. By definition these epithets are the products of *"un*justified" relationships. I insist only that these epithets occur, and that they are meaningful symptoms of imbalance. Once caught in a crucifying dilemma, options are very few. It is all too easy to discredit the desperate expedients introduced to lessen the strain. Until we allow black communities enough initiative to achieve their own developmental balance and direction, it may be necessary for them to shout "white devils" if that cry succeeds in halting, to some degree, the escape of Negroes from their blackness. Poor communities cannot presently afford balanced developmental philosophies. They may have to prescribe "full left rudder" in order to avoid a gale force wind generated by white society which is forcing them inexorably to the right. It is foolish under such circumstances to call the helmsman "a left extremist," for his "extreme" course is designed to offset *our* "extreme" influence. The antagonistic balance between such forces may be the very best the poor community can achieve, given the behavior of the dominant system. And, of course, the weaker usually has to make more noise, to appear more extreme, in order to have enough influence to offset the modulated tones, yet crushing influence, of the powerful.

TABLE 2

The Losing End of the Relationship

Principles of Development	Symptoms of Inflation	Symptoms of Deterioration
1. EXISTENCE	Spontaneous rebellion, riot, burning, looting visited upon own community. Vandalism, nihilism, furious inchoate protest.	Sterility, stifling conventionality and "nigger" stereotypes, "opposite Negroes" and "counter contrast conceptions." Black "conduits" for outside funds. *Lumpenproletariat.*
2. PERCEPTION	Police spying, informing. Ever present physical danger leading to a constant preoccupation with defensive watchfulness.	"Hanging out" at street corners, waiting for something to happen.
3. IDENTITY	The "souling" blacks, the "pork chop nationalists," Leadership Cults, religious prophets, i.e., self-consciously, *over-differentiated* blacks.	"Uncle Toms," "Oreo Cookies," "Synthetic Mahatmas," "Black Anglo-Saxon Protestant," "Media Leaders," i.e., *underdifferentiated* Negroes.
4. COMPETENCE	The Hustler, the Pusher, "Superfly," "Blacula," "Shaft," i.e., *machismo,* sexist, hyper-masculine images.	Absent fathers, the "Eunuch Leaders," unskilled laborers, defeated men, the chronically unemployed, the quietly desperate.
5. COMMITMENT	Violence, killings for kicks. "Don't feel, don't think, JUST DO." Aimless activism.	"Always marching— never arriving." Demonstrations that celebrate themselves, and fall in love with own "morality" become rituals.
authentic &	Total, devastating candor.	"We wear the mask that grins and lies." The facing-both-ways Negro.
Intense	Fiery and raging out of control.	"Man—I'm cool."

6. RISK & SUSPENSION	The numbers racket, the *permanent* "turn-on," "dropout," the quick fix, the acid trip, playing "for kicks," prostitution, i.e., *the isolated thrill*, artificially administered. The "praying integrationists" in abject postures.	Chronic distrust, strong prejudice and bigotry, *either* against darker skinned blacks *or* against whites and degrees of whiteness.
7. BRIDGING the DISTANCE	Overly concerned with reaching whites. Madam Walker's straightening comb and skin whiteness. "The Exiles," the "lost in ideological space."	Phobic hatred of "white devils."
8. SELF-CONFIRMATION & SELF-TRANSCENDENCE	Aggressive, exploitive, addicted.	"The Pioneer," e.g., first black to be accepted by whites in a particular field.
	Speaking with Tongues, "Preach it, Brother!" i.e., cathartic and otherworldly religion, isolated from social and political problems.	A deprived, shut-in and constricted existence.
9. *Dialectic* leading to SYNERGY	Winning, conning, exploiting, ripping off.	Losing—"being screwed."
	The assimilated—"a credit to his race." The co-opted "house niggers" and "integration mascots."	The voluntary separatists, the involuntarily segregated and subordinated.
10. ORDERED FEEDBACK & COMPLEXITY	The "Sophisticates," the "Cultured," the "Foreign Revolutionaries."	Chronic educational deficits, widespread illiteracy, dropout culture.

SOURCES:

Bullins, Ed (ed.). *New Plays from the Black Theater.* New York: Bantam, 1969. See esp. *The Death of Malcolm X* by LeRoi Jones, *In New England Winter* by Ed Bullins and *Family Portrait* by Ben Caldwell.

Hannerz, Ulf. *Soulside: Inquiries into Ghetto Culture and Community.* New York: Columbia Univ. Press, 1969.

Hare, Nathan. *The Black Anglo-Saxons.* New York: Collier, 1970. See also the dissenting introduction by Oliver C. Cox.

King, Woodie, and Milner, Ron (eds.). *Black Drama Anthology.* New York: N.A.L. 1972. See esp. *Brotherhood* by Douglas Turner Ward, *The Corner* by Ed Bullins and *Charades on East Fourth Street* by Lonne Elder.

Liebow, Elliot. *Tally's Corner.* Boston: Little, 1967.

Just as development involves a reconciliation of opposites, so underdevelopment is characterized by "seesaw"
phenomena of polarized unreconcilables detailed in Tables
1 and 2. Seething riot *and* stifling boredom; overexposed
leaders *and* faceless multitudes; random, mindless violence
and ritualistic exercises in Mutual Understanding that
change nothing.

These imbalances are set in motion by white power.
Once unbalanced, the inflated and deteriorated opposites
within the ghetto have a tendency to "excite" and exacerbate one another. Nowhere was this better portrayed
than in Lonne Elder's play *Charades on East Fourth
Street*.[4] In a meeting hall the "leaders" of the community
have organized a "civilized" non-violent protest meeting
concerning the brutal treatment by police of local inhabitants. It is abundantly clear that this is a ritual and empty
exercise in the pretense of influence by "responsible citizens." In fact, the community will be brutalized tomorrow
as it was today and yesterday.

In a basement of the same building, directly beneath
the stage, some local black youths have kidnapped and
bound a white policeman believed to have molested one
of their sisters. Periodically the youths switch on a speaker
that relays the empty platitudes and mock democracy from
the meeting above. Each time they do this their rage
against their prisoner seems to increase and they prepare
to torture him.

It is a vivid portrayal of how opposites accelerate one
another's inflation and deterioration. Reading from Table 1
and/or 2 we can see that

1. The *sterility* of the meeting above provokes the furious
   nihilism beneath,
2. The *blinkered* "waiting for things to get better" above
   provokes the *vigilante, inquisitorial* tactics beneath,
3. The "synthetic Mahatmas" above provoke the self-
   obsessed vengeful nationalism beneath,
4. The *passivity* and *impotence* of "Eunuch Leaders" above
   provoke the *fanatical* machismo defense of "black womanhood" beneath.

The symbolism of the public stage above and the private cellar beneath suggests inner frustration building up behind outer calm, the new consciousness growing within the old.

The playwright makes it clear that neither pattern of behavior is really effective. In the cellar beneath, the bound captive is critically wounded before his captors discover their mistake. It was not he who molested the sister, after all. In the heat of vengeance and the excitement of the kidnap, they have seized and tortured the wrong man. And this is no coincidence, for while the meeting above talks and reflects endlessly without real impact, the boys in the cellar beneath act brutally, with little talk and no reflection. The lopsidedness of each group reproaches and infuriates the other group into *more* than making up for that which the other lacks. The struggle between powerless conscience and conscienceless power which characterizes the interface of black and white, is re-enacted within the black community between militants and moderates.

Anxiety and the idea of conspiracy

The idea that anxiety subtly undermines relationships by alternately inflating and deteriorating developmental principles helps to explain the quite extraordinary persistence of racism, despite effulgences about equality and fulfilling human rights. The need to control anxiety is *the* constant in racism and, of course, anxiety is controllable by totally opposite strategies, by the emotional heat of lynch mobs, or by the cold "rationality" of federal bureaucracies, so that segregationists and liberals, South and North, can demonstrate how different and how opposed they are, while controlling their anxieties by the use of "opposite imbalances," and crucifying the poor between them.

The pattern into which anxiety forces black and white, poor and affluent are outwardly so variable, yet inwardly so familiar and destructive that many observers have been forced to allege a conspiracy. We keep encountering "new reforms" that lure poor people into "double arm locks" and

"half nelsons" that would have shamed the grappling powers of an avowed segregationist. Roland L. Warren put it
thus,

> One can approach the "conspiracy" issue by considering the
> proposition. *If it had been the conscious intent of white so-*
> *ciety to produce a subsystem within American society in which*
> *Negroes would be segregated and within which they would*
> *be controlled, exploited, and continually forced into a posi-*
> *tion of second class citizenship, both in their own perception*
> *and in that of whites, such an intention could not have been*
> *fulfilled more effectively than by developing the present sys-*
> *tem of black ghettos.* . . . The aggregate result, in other
> words, appears so purposeful and so coherent, that the as-
> sumption of purposeful, deliberate collective intent seems the
> only logical one. The ghetto configuration works *as if* white
> society were definitely wanting it that way and consciously
> planning it that way.[5]

The problem with conspiracy theories is that they confront us with so much conscious evil, such incredible
hypocrisy, such deliberate oppression extensively organized and elaborately disguised, that there is serious question whether mankind as such is even salvageable. We
must doubt that human beings are capable of choosing
rightly.

My own conviction is that white society is betrayed by
its own body and its visceral anxiety into falsifying again
and again that which mind and directives proclaim to be
true. The conflict within, between feeling and intellect,
being unresolved, we find ourselves betrayed constantly
by a "revolt of feeling," against cerebral control.

This dualism exists at every level. In the bureaucracy,
pure intellectual and rational schemes are devised at the
high-status, "mental" levels of the organization, but must
be carried through by lower-middle-class and working-
class functionaries. Social science researchers seldom fail
to detect racist feeling within "the body" of such organizations. Pristine strategies, computer simulated, are betrayed
by fallible "Middle Americans" who distort the master
plan by racist styles of delivery. The Top Planners believe

themselves free of anti-black impulses, and in a sense they are freer, because they very seldom come into contact with their clients. Their racism consists precisely in avoiding such contact and in cutting mind from feeling, abstract thought from experience. It remains for them only to lament the "irrational" influence of George Wallace and his followers upon their own immaculate perceptions, and to fail to see that they too control their anxiety, not by barefaced domination, but by icy detachment.

Dominative and aversive racism

Actually we have a "two-directional" style of attack

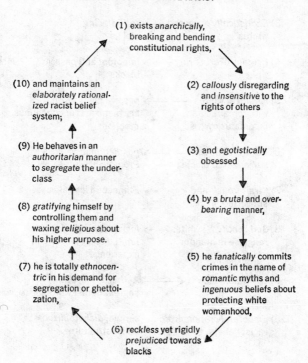

THE DOMINATIVE RACIST

(1) exists *anarchically*, breaking and bending constitutional rights,

(2) *callously* disregarding and *insensitive* to the rights of others

(3) and *egotistically* obsessed

(4) by a *brutal* and *overbearing* manner,

(5) he *fanatically* commits crimes in the name of *romantic* myths and *ingenuous* beliefs about protecting white womanhood,

(6) *reckless* yet rigidly *prejudiced* towards blacks

(7) he is totally *ethnocentric* in his demand for segregation or ghettoization,

(8) *gratifying* himself by controlling them and waxing *religious* about his higher purpose.

(9) He behaves in an *authoritarian* manner to *segregate* the underclass

(10) and maintains an *elaborately rationalized* racist belief system;

upon poor people with top level bureaucrats and respectables setting up the victim and low level functionaries coming in with a "double whammy."

In order to understand this, we must first diagram two preponderant styles of racism, the dominative and the aversive.[6] To do so I shall use the cycle model, the italicized words being from Table 1.

Dominative racism is clearly recognizable as "southern

1) *Anarchical* whites ⟶ *conventional, stereotypical* blacks

2) *hyper-vigilant* blacks ⟵ *Callously disregarding* and *insensitive* whites

3) *Egotistically* obsessed ⟶ *self-effacing* whites blacks

4) *Brutally overbearing* ⟶ *impotent* and *passive* whites blacks

5) *Fanatical* whites ⟶ *passive* blacks with with *romantic* and *apathetic* and *disingenuous* *ingenuous* myths reactions

6) *Reckless* whites ⟶ *pusillanimous* blacks *surrendered* blacks ⟵ *Prejudiced* whites

7) *"traitorous"* and ⟵ *Ethnocentric* whites *subverted* blacks

8) *Self-gratifying* whites ⟶ *ingratiating* blacks, *religiose* in manner *limited* and *mundane* in experience

9) *co-optable* blacks ⟵ *Authoritarian* and *segregationist* whites

10) *Elaborately rationalized* simple, *dichotomized* racist beliefs ⟶ belief structure

style," but also as "police style" in northern ghettos. The weakness of such racism is its tendency to discredit itself by its own lawlessness. As predicated earlier, each inflated or deteriorated principle produces its own opposite within the oppressed group.

The plight of the southern Negro clearly emerges from this pattern. Yet there are variations. Oppressors know better than to let the oppressed get used to invariable patterns. Thus whites may be alternately anarchical *and* superconventional, ingenuous *and* tricky, manipulative *and* ingratiating, etc. Real terror is caused by the flip-flop, the paternal smile that shades into a punitive leer, and the pious intonations of the night rider. The victim must be ready to hop smartly into the opposite category as the switch takes place, smiling gratefully and cringing fearfully by turns.

Another form of racism has been called *aversive*. It involves either avoiding black people altogether, or—and this is the form that concerns us here—relating to them in the most distant and inhuman manner possible. The complex industrial society of the North with its vast bureaus and machines, elaborate credentialism, standards, designations, etc., practices aversive racism par excellence.

The cycle on p. 61 uses an institution, a federal agency, as its subject and a grantee ghetto organization as the object of discrimination. Once again the italicized words are from Table 1.

Once again each inflation or deterioration has the tendency to produce its opposite as the ghetto organization desperately tries to inject some life into the relationship on which it depends, and seeks to exercise initiative. The characteristics enclosed within the rectangles are those of the agency. The arrows are the direction of its preponderant influence over the client.

The pattern on p. 62 should be familiar to those who followed the stormy progress of the Community Action Programs, the disorderly White House conference following the Moynihan report, the tactics of Mothers for Adequate Welfare, and the more recent $2 million destruction at the Bureau of Indian Affairs, to cite but a few instances.

Although the federal agency depicted in the diagram utters no racial slur and boasts hundreds of college graduates, a dozen Ph.D.'s and scores of certified liberals, its behavior is remarkably similar in effect, while opposite in style, to the southern "cracker." We can profile dominative v. aversive racism as follows:

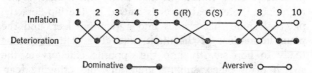

Just as dominative racism could flip-flop to include aversive features, aversive racism flip-flops to include dominative features. Federal agencies are quite capable of switching from facelessness to publicity seeking, from abdication to rigid insistence, from ineffectiveness to overbearing presence. In fact, since agencies are both civil service bureaucracies and political patronage systems, they can employ by turns the alienated unresponsiveness of bureaucracy and the lightning power play of politics. Hence neither dominative nor aversive racism is a "pure type." Much of the purpose of dominating blacks is so that one can avoid them most of the time. Of course, one cannot avoid them continuously without losing control of their services and good behavior, so that some domination has to be used.

The problem with the "mostly aversive" type of mechanical relationship between federal agencies and ghetto organizations is that the poor are goaded into angry and desperate reactions so that *they,* not southern deputies, break the customary norms of civility. Civil rights demonstrations failed so dismally in the North because a bureaucracy can out-wait demonstrators with icy calm and total lassitude.

(1) The aversively racist Agency remains, *bland, sterile* and *conformist* in demanding that it is black grantee does not deviate from allegedly "value free," "universalistic" and "neutral" requirements.

(10) The Agency thus entangles the grantee in an *elaborately rationalized* and *abstruse* system of rules and regulations that scarcely make room for its existence, and comprise an ex post facto defense of its own righteousness.

(2) It maintains an "objective" *inquisitorial* scrutiny of its client

(3) while itself remaining *faceless* and *anonymous*

(4) largely *ineffective* in its support and

(5) *indecisive* with *apathetic* rituals and *disingenuousness* in its day-to-day operations.

(9) and obliging the grantee to become little more than an appendage to the Agency *coalescing* with its nether regions.

(8) resulting in endless *frustration* to the grantee and gross *limits* upon its function

(6) It periodically comes close to *abdicating* all responsibility with chronic *failure of nerve*

(7) while requiring the assent of so many groups who are so widely differentiated that the possibility of agreement is largely *subverted*

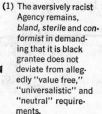

1) provokes *anarchical*, even *riotous* protests, or, at best, a host of minor infringements of rules with attempts at political pressure on Agency to make exception ← Bland, *sterile*, *conventional* following of "neutral" procedures and criteria

2) Maintains an "objective" *inquisitorial* scrutiny of its client → *blinkered* vision, narrowly concerned with the bureaucratic minutiae necessary for survival

3) postures and parades *self-consciously* to attract attention ← Remains *faceless* and *anonymous*

4) becomes shrill, *overbearing* in its concern with communicating its need for survival ← Is largely *ineffective* in its support

5) *overexposed* leadership carried away in *emotional* denunciations and *artless* indignation ← *Indecisive*, with *apathetic* rituals and *disingenuousness*

6) pushes client into *recklessly* gambling with future as time runs out ← Chronic *failure* of nerve in making decisions

Abdication of responsibility → leads grantee to stake all on beliefs *rigidly* grasped

7) *Subverts* possibility of agreement by requiring assent of numerous highly differentiated groups → so that the client often lays siege to the Agency or forms *factions* in order to close ranks and decrease differentiation and divisions in his own ranks

8) the latter attempts to cover its tracks by internal *manipulations* and maneuvers ← *Irritating* the grantee by incessant requirements and imposing gross *limits* upon its function

9) Obliges the grantee to become little more than an appendage, *coalescent* with the Agency → thereby provoking furious *separatist* rhetoric and/or enabling grantee's "contact man" with Agency to assume *authoritarian* rule via his control of funds and access to Washington

10) Agency entangles grantee in *elaborately rationalized* and *abstruse* system of rules and regulations, which comprise an ex post facto defense of its own righteousness → the client is reduced to reacting to *simple, dichotomized* Do's and Dont's, meaningless to him, and irrelevant to his organization, which rapidly loses all sense of continuity and direction

"How do you fight a huge self-righteous marshmallow?"[7] Give it a furious punch and your fist sinks in, sprinkling you gently with confectioners' sugar. One is confronted by a vast, intricate, rationalized system which waxes righteous upon the very tears of rage that the poor shed against it. It stiffens with disdain before human impulse, like a Pharisee affronted by publicans and sinners, and its machinery mutters out through interdepartmental memos, "I thank thee, Lord, that I am not as other men are . . . profane, uncivil . . ." This is how you cripple poor Americans with the "double whammy." Aversive racism sets them up, gets them boiling mad, and just at the moment when their indignation reaches the point of a public exhibition, you call the police—POW!

In 1970 I attended a meeting called by the National Institutes for Mental Health on the possibility of citizen participation in the administration of programs. At an obscenely luxurious resort in Virginia I encountered the phenomenon just described. The embryo citizens' board, led by spokesmen of the poorest and darkest minorities, gave passionate and grandiloquent speeches, so word-perfect as to hint of extensive practice. Racism, they averred, was America's number one mental health problem. Would NIMH immediately, as a sign of good faith, pledge $1 million for fighting it, so that present discussions could be based on reality? NIMH would not. The elder bureaucrats said that it was "not possible at this time . . . we have no such department . . . racism is not an incapacitating mental disturbance for which patients offer themselves for treatment . . ." In contrast, the younger members of the agency frantically abdicated their barely existent authority. "We are all guilty—steeped in racism." And they seemed to believe that the poor were somehow being benefited "therapeutically" by their every word of denunciation. "I do want all of you to feel free—quite free, to *express basic needs* and underlying antagonisms." (They had not shown much reluctance!) "And may I say, I think NIMH must *listen*, because that's so important . . ."

As for the Black, Chicano and other poor Americans, they were given the dubious privilege of verbally flaying white bureaucrats for two days by the swimming pool, before the latter returned to their well-upholstered bureaus, and the former returned, empty-handed, to their tenements. Probably the leaders of the poor were less credible to their followers after this episode, and the lower level functionaries in NIMH were less credible to their bosses. The poor were damaged in their leadership structure, the affluent in their "followship" structure; it was an unequal contest, with unequal damage, which insured not only the continued domination of the poor, but the subordination of "effeminate" lower elements at NIMH. I began the introduction of this book by asking how a "rhetorical democracy" managed to overlay structural domination. We are beginning to see how.

The seesaw of IDENTITY and CONFIRMATION

We saw in Chapter 1 that the rooted past of the black identity, its intrinsic, permanent blackness, could not be stripped from the changeable part of the identity without serious damage to development. "Color-blind" acceptance by whites had the characteristic of co-opting the idiosyncratic achievements of a person, while stripping him of those characteristics that joined him to a collective black consciousness.

The dilemma in this instance takes the form of a seesaw. One's CONFIRMATION can go *up*, if one's genuine IDENTITY disintegrates and goes down. Or one's IDENTITY can remain black and proud, but then CONFIRMATION by, and rewards from, white society will go down. In either event, learning, that is, FEEDBACK ORDERED into COMPLEXITY will suffer, in the first instance because identity is the organizing principle of learning, in the second instance because rebuff causes one to doubt the validity of *any* ideas about life and oneself.

The students in 98 per cent black George Washington Junior High were clearly suffering from dismembered identities. They were several grades behind their white counterparts in other schools. This account illustrates why:

> Every common derisive word, all the abusive nicknames, nouns and adjectives, all the big-lip, liver-lips, burr-heads, fuzzy-heads, kinky-haired, nappy-headed, big-leg, high-ass, apes, monkeys and too-blacks were dragged out daily and heaped on each other casually, or furiously continually and fanatically. . . . The blacker a kid was, the kinkier his hair, the wider and flatter his nose, the larger and more everted his lips, the uglier he was and the more crap he had to take. . . . "When it dark outside nobody can't even see Fletcher! Watch out somebody don't steal your head for a watermelon!" . . . It never stopped. It was a characteristic of the tribe. They agreed that the qualities which they all shared to some degree from birth were to add up to *bad*. It was crucial that they join the people most hostile to them all to establish relative degrees of ugliness, so that some might be less ugly.[8]

However, those who choose the strategy of relative paleness to garner scraps of white CONFIRMATION now have to face the rage of the advocates of positive black IDENTITY, who are themselves deprived of white rewards, and are in no mood to forgive their "opposites" in the black community.

> Man, we were getting ready to go to lil' Joe's party. Rose had dolled herself up with Miss White Woman's cosmetics and all. She was primping away like Miss Ann. She was saying, "Mirror, mirror, on the wall, who's the fairest of them all?" (Breaking up) Man, I screamed! Ha, ha, ha, ha . . . I cracked up! I told her, "SNOW WHITE, YOU BLACK BITCH, AND DON'T YOU EVER FORGET IT."[9]

To be black, at this moment of time, is to catch it from one side or the other. There is no impunity.

The sterile capacitated v. the creative incapacitated

If one's purposes are blocked by oppressive definitions, one has to break out—that is EX-IST. The rising bourgeoisie, especially religious non-conformists, were blocked from attributed status by their lack of nobility and their lack of religious conformity. They did two things. They first redefined excellence as something achieved, and then they achieved it.

However, the very act of redefinition makes one suspect. Consider this encounter between Richard Wright and a white housewife appraising him for housework.

> *Woman:* Do you steal?
> *Richard:* Ma'm, if I stole—I sure as hell wouldn't tell you!
> *Woman (furious):* ARE YOU BEIN' SASSY?[10]

Like many of those oppressively defined, Wright tries to break out, using the wit and skill that later made him a writer. The woman, however, first humiliated him within her racist stereotype, then punished him for trying to break out of her mold.

In ghettos and poor rural communities, sources of funding have skillfully sliced COMPETENCE from EXISTENCE, to produce two feuding factions, "the sterile capacitated" and the "creative incapacitated." For the most part, blacks who receive federal and other monies and are thereby "capacitated" are conduits, that is, they are not the origins of anything, neither protests, ideas, wealth nor culture. Their reliability consists precisely in the fact that they pass on the instructions of the agency without resynthesizing them.

For example, there are "approved ways" of running mental health clinics, job referral agencies, etc. The approved way may require middle-class professionals in a number of posts, but especially will it isolate that organization's function from other functions, just as each federal agency is demarcated and the approved professionals are specialized. Suppose a mental health clinic got together with a job referral agency to study the jobs most readily available to blacks. If it showed that these jobs evoked *four times* the amount of anxiety symptoms compared to jobs reserved for whites,[11] such a demonstration would surely get both centers into trouble. It is an "illegitimate synthesis" because it troubles the relationship between HEW and the Department of Labor.

Forced into the position of powerless loudmouths, the rhetoric of the creative incapacitated typically escalates. They press home their verbal and imaginative advantages, ripping into the sterile capacitated with many of the epithets listed in Table 2, including and along with "Oreo Cookie, Black Anglo-Saxon Protestant, National Association for the Advancement of *Certain* People, and blacks living in Never-Negro Land." In fact the accusation that the sterile capacitated are "fronting for the Man" may be enough to deny federally funded ghetto organizations anything more than opportunistic support within the community, so that even those who receive their salaries from the project may damn it rhetorically and refer to "ripping off" the government. In the meantime "the Dignitaries" and "Eunuch Leaders" will issue official condemnation against the "extremism," "nationist yearnings" and "unfortunate references to bovine excreta made by our divisive brothers." It is *only* necessary to channel funds selectively to the safely sterile, and the poor community will obligingly tear one another to pieces. That is neo-colonialism for you. Look, no hands!

The epitome of federally sponsored arrangements for self-disparagement among the poor was achieved in the Model Cities programs, especially in the provision for citizen participation. A huge amount of controversy and hope has centered upon the idea of citizen participation in federal projects. In the terms of our developmental model, participation is COMMITMENT (principle 5), but one must

ask *of* what and *to* what? For if such participation is cut off
from EXISTENCE and IDENTITY, if it fails to contribute to
the SYNERGY of a community, it may signify no more than
a mechanical or compulsive act. Such isolated behaviors
are common in ghettos. A character in the black theater
expresses it as follows:

> I relate to everything and at the same time to NOTHING.
> Like a beast when he's doing the Twist . . . the Jerk . . . the
> Monkey . . . the Fly, and all that crap. Relate to NOTHING.
> DON'T TOUCH! DON'T FEEL . . . NO MEANING. JUST DO! PRE-
> TEND! MAKE LIKE REAL, BUT DON'T BE! DON'T BE![12]

If federally mandated "participation" were only isolated
from creative meaning like twisting and jerking, that would
be serious enough, but in fact it is worse. A study of federal projects in some twenty Model Neighborhood areas
found that all of them had adopted the "diagnostic paradigm" or the official PERCEPTION of the Welfare Establishment, that social problems resulted from the *individual
deficiencies* of poor people.[13] Hence the definition of the
problem in which representatives of the poor participated
asked, "How can the system of service delivery be better
organized to compensate for, and to rectify, the personal
failings of poor people?" Such a PERCEPTION asks for a
COMMITMENT by the ghetto resident to the *in*COMPETENCE
of his friends, neighbors, family, etc. He can "join" but
only in an evaluation that degrades his sisters and brothers,
separates him from his "pathological" community, and co-
opts him into the "rescue apparatus"—so that he has the
same kind of vested interest in the "sickness" and "moral
failing" of his own community as a plumber has in blocked
drains.

Nor is he likely to refuse to serve, for the great corruption of the affluent interacting with the poor is that in
so unequal a relationship some poor persons will always
accept jobs to which desperately needed funds are at-

tached. The project could be sheer idiocy from the point of view of poor people. They still could not afford to turn down paid positions in their own communities, and for every person who did object, there would be a hungrier person who assented.

In none of the Model Cities areas studied was there any significant innovation. Although the guidelines asked for co-ordinated projects drawn from many different state, federal and private agencies, what emerged were "laundry lists" of projects funded by different sources, defined in isolation as those sources had defined them, and quite unorganized and unsynthesized by the perspectives of the poor.[14]

The image is still of rope ladders hanging down over the ghetto from bureaucratic scaffolding erected above. The poor are invited to climb *as individuals,* away from poor companions, towards the bureaucracy above. The climbers are occasionally assisted by the "steadying hands" of social workers and other officials who train them carefully to plant a judicious foot upon the fingers of those climbing behind and beneath.

Religions of the poor—the isolation of the integrative functions

Nothing better illustrates the dismemberment of poor communities and their minds than the pattern of their religious practices. Consider the problem of religion in a culture of overwhelming physical and psychic scarcity. How can one express undying love for a nieghbor when there is only one job for the two of you, and you intend to have it? And yet you want to commune with others— all the more because you have grabbed scarce things away from them—but you still have to commune in a way that permits you to keep on grabbing.

The "solution" is to create an oasis of camaraderie apart from the miseries of daily life and to partake jointly of something *not* in scarce supply. The "Love of God" not only has these advantages, it also descends upon you at particular prearranged times, filling you with "light" and permitting an intense, ecstatic and temporary solidarity that does not bind you beyond the time and place of worship. Competitors, alienated by struggle, require an *external* force to mediate their solidarity. They need a shoulder-to-shoulder, rather than a face-to-face relationship, with all eyes upon the Object which evokes their emotion on cue. The emotion, the longing for reconciliation, has had to be inhibited throughout many suspicious days. Those who dared to express genuine feelings of trust or concern would attract exploiters thick as flies, and so they must find a safe place to express feeling. And they must not admit that they themselves are the origins of love, for might this not cause debts to be called, and claims to be made on desperately scarce resources?

This pattern isolates *authenticity, intensity,* SUSPENSION, CONFIRMATION and SYNERGY—the *integrating* functions of the cycle—from day-to-day EXISTENCE, PERCEPTION, IDENTITY and COMPETENCE, the *differentiating* functions. James Baldwin remembers his own time as a minister:

> There was no music like that music, no drama like the drama of the saints rejoicing, the sinners moaning, the tambourines racing, and all those voices coming together and crying holy unto the Lord. There is still for me no pathos quite like the pathos of those multi-colored, worn, somehow triumphant and transfigured faces, speaking from the depth of a visible, tangible continuing despair of the goodness of the Lord.[15]

The poor and the black are faced with the problem of being *over*-differentiated, *under*-integrated, both among and within themselves, and in their relationships to the dominant culture. They attempt to solve this dilemma by integrating themselves in a different place, at a different time, on a different dimension, and in another world from that in which they are so differentiated. Doubtless they achieve some solace, but at a price. Reading from Table 1, we could say, they are *carried away* in *over-emotional, ingenuous* forms of surrender to impulse, in the course of *parochial, overwhelming, otherworldly* exercises in *coalescence* and *lofty idealism.* Yet much of the rest of their lives remains unchanged, that is, *anarchical, hypervigilant, depersonalized, brutal, impotent* and *passive,* together or by turns. The integrative functions, severed from the differentiating ones, seesaw in desperate attempts to maintain an antagonistic balance.

The principles were Blindness, Loneliness and Terror, and the first principle necessarily and actively cultivated in order to deny the second and the third.[16]

Escape from religion: the isolation of the self-differentiating capacities

In James Baldwin's account of his adolescent years in Harlem, we can see clearly what brought him into the Church, what eventually drove him from it, and the predicament he now faces. It is the story of a zigzag, from isolation to suffocating coalescence and back to a new isolation again. It teaches us much of what even a talented black person faces in American society.

Growing in adolescence in Harlem made the young Baldwin terribly conscious of the personal dangers he encountered in an alienated world. "Whose little boy are you?" asked the pimps, the hustlers, the numbers men and the junkies leering at him from doorways and alleys. Everyone, it seemed, wanted to recruit him into a fraternity of sin. He shrank from them, alone and terrified. One day he visited a female pastor.

There she sat in her robes, smiling, an extremely proud and handsome woman, with Africa, Europe and the America of the American Indian blended in her face . . . in our world she was a very celebrated woman. My friend was about to introduce me when she looked at me and smiled and said, "Whose little boy are you?" . . . I unquestionably wanted to be *somebody's* little boy. I was so frightened, and at the mercy of so many conundrums, that inevitably, that summer, *someone* would have taken me over; one doesn't in Harlem, long remain standing on any auction block. . . . When the pastor asked with that marvelous smile . . . my heart replied at once, "Why, yours."[17]

This marks the beginning of the period in Baldwin's life when the Church enveloped him. Now he is insulated from the dangers of the street but the price is self-deception.

I rushed home from school to the church, to the altar, to be alone, to commune with Jesus, my dearest friend, who would never fail me, who knew all the secrets of my heart. Perhaps He did, but I didn't, and the bargain we struck, actually, down there at the foot of the cross, was that He would never let me find out.[18]

So Baldwin chooses. It is to be self-knowledge and self-differentiation. Cohesion and fraternity are dangerous achings of the heart that betray the reason, so he is alone in a world where culture is white. All his yearnings to belong come flooding back when he visits the Black Muslims. He is shown into a room where sit "half a dozen women, all in white . . . much occupied by a beautiful baby." There were seven or so young men "very imposing."

The sunlight came into the room with a peacefulness one remembers from rooms in one's early childhood—a sunlight encountered later only in one's dreams.

Then Elijah Muhammad came into the room:

Something came into the room with him—his disciples' joy at seeing him—his joy at seeing them. It was the kind of encounter one watches with a smile simply because it is so rare that people enjoy one another. . . . Now he turned toward me, to welcome me, with that marvelous smile, and carried me back nearly twenty-four years, to that moment when the pastor had smiled at me and said, "Whose little boy are you?"[19]

Yet Baldwin sees a trap in this smile, in the serene companionship around him. "Take your burdens to the Lord, leave them there," is what the smile says to him. And so he remains alone—and crucified.

> I knew the tension in me between love and power, between pain and rage and the curious, the grinding way I remained extended between these poles—perpetually attempting to choose the better rather than the worse. But this choice was a choice in terms of a personal, a private better (I was after all a writer): what was the relevance in terms of a social worse?[20]

And Baldwin looks out over Chicago's South Side, where few can even read the books he writes, where his words feed no one, and those who do consume his works do so less to learn than to "learn new attitudes." Even his passion becomes a commodity on the white market, rather than a gift of love for his people.

The War Game

A major avenue of upward mobility for the poor and black has traditionally been the Armed Forces. In America's Asian wars it has been the poor and the black who fought disproportionately and died in still greater disproportion.

Historically, Black Americans have achieved some economic and civil rights during time of war. The expansion of war industry and national conscription have often swelled the demand for cheap labor. The need for national solidarity, the escalation of ideals noble enough to command sacrifice, all have given poor minorities some slight leverage. This was true in the time of Lincoln's Emancipation Proclamation, which gained him 186,000 black soldiers, and of Roosevelt's executive order No. 8802, which forestalled a March on Washington during World War II.[21]

Others have seen the military as a paragon of race relations. Blacks are employed in the Army in a greater proportion than their share of the population—but not among commissioned officers. In the tight framework of military discipline, dedicated to God and country, who could reasonably fear black advancement? If white soldiers can be drilled to obey, even unto death, why not to obey the edicts of integration?

It has not worked out that way. "Fragging" incidents abound. Warships have had to be pulled out of action duty because of race riots and sabotage, and, most serious of all, the aftermaths of wars have witnessed serious backlashes against black advances.[22]

The reason is to be found in the nature of war itself—a regressive phenomenon either racist in itself or with racist implications. All war is directed at a hated outgroup. Ideological conflict is usually cast in terms that destroy the development cycle. For example, America's Cold War ideology pits "freedom" (the *differentiating* principles of the cycle) against "socialism" (the *integrating* principles of the cycle). Not unsurprisingly differentiation inflates into avariciousness, and integration inflates into a communality, coercive upon the individual. Each bloc threatens the other and its own citizens with lopsided half-truths, so that dissenters are silenced in the Soviet Union, and co-operators condemned in the United States.

The specific dilemma for blacks recruited into the Armed Forces is that they are urged to fight against a co-operative ethic which, however flawed in particular instances, is quite essential for their own emancipation. Having strenuously exaggerated the evil of Them, who are so DISTANT from Us, the military must simultaneously proclaim that the DISTANCE between blacks and whites *is* to be BRIDGED. "Gooks" represent an unbridgeable gulf; blacks, a bridgeable one. Concern and empathy is to be felt in the second case—but not in the first. The obvious dilemma is that any genuine sensibility that feels for the fate of "remote persons" would generalize from blacks to the Asian enemy. Since the overall strategy of war is *not* to solve problems by mutual understanding of SYNERGISTIC resolution, but by *winning, dominating* and *overwhelming* (among other inflated principles), it is curious to expect soldiers to solve problems in other ways among each other.

In effect, war and the emergencies it creates are lethal to the *moral* courage needed to RISK and SUSPEND (principle 6). You meet a "gook" on the roadway who is fiddling inside his clothes. It could be a grenade—perhaps one chance in ten. What do you do? You kill him, of course. It is the only way to survive in a world where you may encounter two "fiddling gooks" a month, in a twelve-month tour of duty. The "unprejudiced" soldier would have less than an even chance of surviving. It is simply absurd to regret the lapse of "individual morality." The situation, not the man, cripples the developmental process. To expect veterans to emerge from such a situation fit for interracial living is naïve.

The sham practiced on Black Americans who see the military as their opportunity was succinctly portrayed in *A Medal for Willie*, a play by the black playwright William Branch. Willie, a black southern youth, joined the Army after lengthy unemployment and has died heroically defending a mountain pass in Korea, thereby saving most of his company. His small southern town and segregated school become targets for patriotic ceremony and the post-humous award of a medal.

The play opens with the black community abuzz with excitement and gratitude that the seats at the ceremony will be unsegregated. Willie's mother and sister prepare to receive the congratulations of a Dixiecrat general from the Pentagon, an obsequious white mayor and superintendent, and a distinctly "colored" school principal. The mother's speech is even written for her. The local newspaper editor is arranging to "build up" the story:

> How this teenage little colored boy from the darkey town slums went over there and fought and died for his country, his native land, to preserve the American way of life . . .[23]

The speeches begin. The superintendent looks heavenward and vows to Willie "to preserve those sacred principles—you laid down your sweet life defending." The mayor cannot quite get his tongue around "posthumous" and so speaks of a "post-humorous award." The general thanks Willie for "battling alien ideologies that threaten our homes and children."

All this is too much for Willie's mother. The dam finally bursts as she throws away the prepared speech.

> What has your fine talk ever meant to Willie? He walked around this town nearly all his young life and nobody cared. You jim-crowed him and shunned him and you shoved him off in the corner. You gave him third-rate schooling and when he wasn't quiet like a mouse, you put him out on the street. You looked down on him and you kept him down 'cause he was black and poor and didn't know no better than to believe that was the way things were supposed to be! . . .

> That's why this is all such a big lie. You-all here ain't really honorin' Willie. You here tryin' to tell yourself that you been right all along . . . 'cause you can get boys like Willie to go out and fight and die for you and never know the difference. . . . I can't help thinking Willie died fighting in the wrong place. *Willie shoulda had that machine gun over here!* . . .[24]

And she hurls the medal at the general and the principal has a fit.

Notice how the crucifixion dynamic works in this case. First Willie's COMPETENCE is systematically DISCONFIRMED, so that it inflates into an *aggressive* fury, which is skillfully channeled towards another underdeveloped group, Koreans, and so becomes "heroic." There would still be difficulties in celebrating this feat were Willie not dead. As it is, a "reconciliation" can now take place without RISK or SUSPENSION since it concerns an abstraction and not a real person. There follows a hideously inauthentic celebration wherein SYNERGY customarily deteriorated into *segregation* now inflates into *co-optation*. Willie's family, *surrendered* to grief, are considered easy prey for *manipulation*. Finally, his family's memory of Willie, the ORDERED FEEDBACK, is wrested from the grasp of his community, severed from his own intentions, to become a saga of southern racism.

To conclude this abbreviated discussion of just a few of many dilemmas, let me add that crucifixions, like their synergistic opposites, interpenetrate every level of functioning. The splitting at the level of communities cuts through to the very core of human beings to show up as schizo-phrenia, literally "split-soul." For what are *elaborately rationalized*, extreme states of *hyper-vigilance* and concern with *traitorous, subversive* activity, except paranoia? When language and action become ultimately *anarchical*, bizarre and inappropriate, when *impotence* and *passivity* freeze into catatonia, then can we derive the many symptoms of "mental illness." Could the fact that the poor, the black and the female are disproportionately incarcerated in mental institutions be one more episode in the history of oppression? The "diseases" from which they suffer are curiously similar to the shadows cast on prone victims by those who loom over them. All of which is another subject, which I am pursuing elsewhere.

CHAPTER 3

Social Science Against
the Poor

*Much of the sociological apparatus functions, I suggest, to sup-
port a ritual of decontamination between the scientist and his
subject. It is essential that the sociologist view his subject only
with professional eyes and that he resist the look in the eyes of
the sick, the poor, and the aimless who turn his questions back
upon him. In this way the erotic symbiosis of talk is reduced
to the interview schedule or attitude survey in which the client
comes clean before the professional voyeur.*
John O'Neil, *Sociology as a Skin Trade*

As the center cities decay, as patterns of racial discrimination stubbornly persist, as unemployment afflicts
particular minority groups, much as the Great Depression
once afflicted the whole, it is to the social scientists that
the nation has turned in desperation, and it is these professions that consume a large proportion of the funds ap-
propriated and spent in the name of the poor.

No one who has watched Mobilization for Youth, the
War on Poverty, sixty years of mental health and mental
hygiene campaigns, and the rise and fall of the concept of
juvenile delinquency can claim success for the "profes-
sionalization of reform." Poverty, crime and (so-called)
"mental disease" have washed over the experts like the
rising tide that soaked the dignity of King Canute. If
social scientists are still deferred to, it is out of desperation,
not on the basis of our confidence or their success. The
unfulfilled yearnings for a secular faith, and for a scientific
substitute for saving grace, testify to the triumph of hope

over experience. Yet it is a peculiarly corrupting position in which to find oneself—where either success or failure assures one's expansion.

In the broadest sense, psychology, sociology and psychiatry have, like the poor, always been with us. Men of affairs have seldom been without deep-rooted assumptions concerning the motives of others, the creation and maintenance of social systems, and the healing of the soul. The social sciences have not been invented as much as organized, professionalized and bureaucratized.[1] As this process has accelerated there have grown orthodox bodies of assumptions and outlooks about the styles of investigation, pressures for conformity deriving from hierarchies of differential status and reward, and recognizable "game plans" whereby the professions engage political authorities, educators and the general public. These overall strategies will be called *paradigms*.[2]

Part of the tragedy of the social sciences is that they have become bureaucratized before they have ever become useful, and before they have found their Kepler, much less their Newton.[3] Even the division into sociology, psychology and psychiatry is quite arbitrary and may be impeding the flexibility of thought necessary for a new synthesis. In the meantime, knowledge of man and society that was once the province of all has become the special province of professing elites.

A certain tension arises when specialists deal not with subjects remote from laymen's understanding, like nuclear physics, but with the everyday reality of our experienced world. Commonsense understandings vie with the understanding of those who profess their superiority. We will understand nothing about the paradigms of various social sciences unless we grasp that they all share a rival—the common man and his commonsense understandings of the world. So long as these hold sway the professional has not yet "made it." He has justified neither his specialization, nor the indispensable nature of his contribution. Common sense must either then be reformed, or, pending this, ignored and bypassed. Even more important to its ultimate "put-down" is the belief that common sense is the mere end product, or the epiphenomenon of natural laws that control it.

Consider the epithets directed by various paradigms at common understandings. The Marxists have their lumpenproletariat, false consciousness and bourgeois morality. Behaviorists lambaste anthropomorphic subjectivism, private mental events (mentalism) and introspection. The functionalists of sociology dismiss utilitarianism, "psychologism" and "do-goodism," as motives of inquiry. Anthropologists warn us against the false consciousness of the Informant's Model.

In this chapter there is only room to discuss three main currents of thought that dominate sociology and psychology and impinge upon the life of the poor. In experimental psychology the dominant creed is Behaviorism; in sociology it is Structural Functionalism; and there is a loose assemblage of experts under the banner of Mental Health, who draw their inspiration mostly from psychiatry and clinical psychology. Although each of the three groups disagrees fundamentally with the other two, changing the poor has periodically become the object of their rivalry. For the poor, this is an experience somewhat akin to being preached to death by three wild curates of opposing faiths.

All three disciplines model themselves upon an ideal of science—which means the spectacularly successful physical sciences. The methods, the mathematics, the parsimony, detachment and precision of physics is immensely influential and admired. For example, the influence of Freudian psychiatry can hardly be accounted for by the rate, speed or scope of cure, which is, at best, modest. Rather, the imitation of physical science and of intrepid explorers in the "discovery of the unconscious," and its model of man's mind in the form of a Victorian steam engine, gave it that "scientific look" and aura of authority necessary to impress the public and further its influence.

The bourgeois strain

Social scientists have the same envious relationship to the physical sciences that the petite bourgeoisie have to the haute bourgeoisie, with the same tendency to apply with exaggerated strictness, norms long ago abandoned by their successful counterparts.[4] Thus B. F. Skinner—the arch apostle of behaviorism—combines the dour verities of small-town America[5] with turn-of-the-century Logical Positivism, calling this viewpoint "scientific" to the near exclusion of other social inquiry.[6]

The loss of freedom

Man is free, and the scientist makes a choice when he directs his gaze, and adopts a paradigm that interprets and filters his vision. In the same way, poor people *must be* enabled to choose, must experience themselves as sources of value, as "paradigm makers" in their own right. Only thus can they come to experience themselves as human, potent, effective, co-operative and whole.

Virtually all these tenets are flatly denied by behaviorism, which defines "science" as the capacity to predict and control the response of the experimental subject by various contingencies of stimuli and reinforcement. It stands behind the subject, so to speak, in order to investigate what caused him to behave. Various manipulations of the "independent variables" (stimuli and reinforcement) shape the subject's drives, so as to elicit the "dependent variables" (the subject's responses).

The arbitrary choice of the investigator to place himself in the environment and from there goad the subject into predictable behaviors, makes any exercise of freedom by the subject a direct threat to the experimenter's ambition to create a science. It is equally arbitrary to define science as prediction and control—when, for example, the Theory of Evolution can do neither. B. F. Skinner explains:

> In the traditional view, a person is free. He is autonomous in the sense that his behavior is uncaused . . . to the extent that he is autonomous he is by definition not changeable at all . . . Unable to understand how or why the person we see behaves as he does, we attribute his behavior to a person we cannot see. . . . [he] initiates, originates, creates, and in doing so he remains, as he was for the Greeks, divine. We say he is autonomous—and so far as a science of behavior is concerned, that means miraculous.[7]

Behaviorists certainly have a problem, even if it is one of their own making. Merely because a free or creative act is in some respects unique, does not mean that all free acts are not lawful and identical in other respects, nor that they lack pre-conditions, an underlying structure, and have partly predictable consequences. To say that a person's response must be capable of prediction, in its entirety, by someone standing in his environment is quite preposterous—or else miraculous. The real believer in miracles is Skinner himself, who has come to believe that what is important about humanity corresponds with what is revealed by outward behavior of the most verifiable kind, as if Mother Nature were a stripper.

Where an investigator stands not outside the subject looking at him, but beside the subject looking out with him, then both subject and investigator can regard their perspectives as freely chosen, but, once chosen, as having probable consequences. The freedom versus determinism dilemma in behaviorism and in functionalism is a self-imposed dilemma consequent upon the investigator's choice of taking his stand alongside contingencies or social norms in the environment, and defining "science" as the study of their control over man. Such arbitrary definitions of science lead directly to attempts to control the poor through "reinforcement tokens" in ghetto schools[8] and to such Office of Manpower studies as one entitled *The Role of Social Reinforcement Parameters in Improving Trainee Task Performance and Self-Image.*[9]

Sociology, particularly the school of structural functionalism that has dominated it for more than a generation, exercises similar constraints upon individual freedom. Consider these "first principles" enunciated by Émile Durkheim. "The first and fundamental rule is: *Consider social facts as things.*"[10] Talcott Parsons, who is to functionalism what Skinner is to behaviorism, has held that "exteriority to and constraint of the actor" are the implications of Durkheim's principle. Robert Murphy has summarized the situation.

Social facts, according to this well-known view are embodied within the individual but emanate from the domain of the social. Durkheim wrote, "Indeed, the most important characteristic of a 'thing' is the impossibility of its modification by a simple effort of will, they [social facts] determine it from without: They are like molds in which our actions are inevitably shaped. These 'things' are both external and coercive . . ."[11]

The implications of this definition cannot be overstressed. Since "social facts" are not readily visible and since the doctrine of positivism demands observable entities, it is the constraining, shaping and molding effects upon the individual that become evidence for the very existence of "social facts," the raw material of functionalist sociology. If such "things" stopped coercing us, the philosophical bottom would fall out of the functionalist enterprise.

But at least Durkheim knew what his followers appear to have forgotten. "Social life consists," he wrote, "of free currents perpetually in the process of transformation and incapable of being mentally fixed by the observer and the scholar cannot approach the study of social reality from this angle."[12] Instead, "he must endeavor to consider them from an aspect that is independent of their individual manifestations." There were two major tactical reasons for laying down this doctrine. Both were really demarcation issues. First, it was essential to attack utilitarian economics and laissez-faire individualism, which Durkheim saw as rival explanations, wrecking religious faith and spreading anomie. Secondly, sociology had to carve out a province, separate from psychology. "Every time that a social phenomenon is directly explained by a psychological phenomenon we may be sure that the explanation is false,"[13] Durkheim assured the faithful.

Sociology's belief in what Alvin Gouldner has called "the potency of society and the subordination of men" amounts to connivance at the widespread powerlessness of an increasing number of Americans.[14]

Unlike behaviorists, functionalist sociologists had a major influence in shaping two of the biggest anti-poverty campaigns, Mobilization for Youth in New York, and the Community Action Program under the Economic Opportunity Act.[15] In strict accordance with functionalist doctrine, juvenile delinquency and urban decay were viewed as being caused by dysfunctions within the system. Poor people *wanted* to conform to the social norms governing their lives. Indeed they did their best to do so. But while the American Creed orders them to "succeed!" there is a lack of "opportunity structure" to channel this obedience. The orders "win," come through louder and clearer than the qualification "within the rules."[16] Moreover, "illegitimate structures" have sprung up in poor communities in the absence of legitimate ones, to which criminals and delinquents have higher "differential access."[17]

The remedy was to build a structure of rules and opportunities around neighborhood youth groups, Community Action agencies and Model Cities programs. In this way the poor would realize their only true freedom, which "lies in the interstices of authority," and numerous federal programs could be co-ordinated at the bottom, with the poor safely locked into roles, statuses and otherwise constrained by "social facts."[18]

Of course, it failed to work out that way. Many community programs discovered that they did not wish to conform at all. All manner of rude words and protesting acts were loosed against the very norms assumed to command universal affection and assure our equilibrium.

The crucial weakness of poverty theory was its failure to question the validity of the American creed of success. This "social fact" and the people alleged to be in its thrall were essential parts of the functionalist credo. For a "scientist" may not react personally towards the values of society, rather he must treat values as facts, which function or fail to function in commanding allegiance. Unless he can discover "commanding facts" his whole investigation is imperiled, and a revolt against such facts puts him to the great inconvenience of having to find other "deviant, subcultural" facts to explain the revolt. Hence the most obvious flaw in the success ethic, namely that it has always required and has always created losers, and that the losers, given a chance, will revolt against "The Game," seems to have been missed altogether. Rather it was assumed that there is an intrinsic pleasure in playing the success game, even for those in the bottom 30 per cent.[19] If we were to let them "participate," they would have themselves a ball!

Alone among the three paradigms that afflict the poor, the Mental Health perspectives include the potentiality for human freedom. Unfortunately, mental illness is, by definition, "unfreedom," so it is only necessary to spot a symptom or two, in order to regard the victim as being helpless, yet blameless, in the grip of some disease.

Ironically, personality theorists and psychiatrists regard as largely pathological the reactions which behaviorists and functionalists require of the individual in order to create a science. Hence, conformity, approval motive, other-directedness, acquiescence, powerlessness, submission, conventionality, religiosity and being "stimulus-bound" are all scales which correlate with, or even constitute "poor mental health."[20] If behaviorists and functionalists have their way with you, the mental healthers will certify you sick. It is difficult to know which is more unfair, to have one's particular subordination to the social system elevated to a Universal Condition, or to have the cruel fate of being structurally subordinated attributed entirely to failings within one's own personality so that one "suffers from *feelings* of fatalism and inferiority." In contrast, a middle-class person like myself would have all the feelings of importance, traceable to the fact that Doubleday distributes my work, attributed to "strengths" in *my* personality—a most egregious form of self-conceit.

Evading the contradictions

In earlier chapters, it has been emphasized that poor people as well as social scientists must be allowed to focus upon the contradictions between image and reality and between their own values and the status quo. It is the right of oppressed people to help define such contradictions so that they can help resolve them. If they are to grasp these contradictions fully it is necessary for social scientists to understand how poor people construe social reality and how they perceive their dilemmas.

Behaviorism is totally incapable of fulfilling any of these requirements, since it denies scientific meaningfulness to the "mentalism" of what people see and experience. There can be no contradiction between motive or ideal on the one hand, and behavior on the other, since the former are merely "explanatory fictions" for the latter. Functionalism denies the contradiction in precisely the opposite way; human behaviors are but specific examples of the reality of norms which constrain and guide them. The assumed homology between norm and action in functionalism, and the allegedly unverifiable nature of mental states in behaviorism, remove one side of the potential contradiction and then the other. This is done in the name of Positivism, since to be "positive" of what you see, to enunciate the doctrine of immaculate perception, it is necessary to subordinate and subsume rival perceptions.

At the roots of functionalism is a nineteenth-century belief in moral absolutism. The meanings of rules are assumed to be the same for all normal persons—to be unproblematic, external and timeless.[21] Believing this enables the sociologist to evade both the potential contradiction of rival interpretations and any judgment of the content of the values. If values bind a society, then they "function," and the absurdity, superstition or mystification involved in believing them is not for him to judge.

In a collection of essays entitled *American Sociology,* published in the midst of the Vietnam War, during the greatest campus upheavals, and with ghettos burning, Talcott Parsons reflected a "dominant mood . . . of self-congratulatory celebration." He is "that rare creature, the contented moralist."[22] This is achieved by overlapping definitions. To the extent that subjective views converge upon social facts, the consensus, but not the disagreement, becomes "objectively real." The focus on norm-directed actions avoids the contradiction between norm and action, morality and reality, or where such contradictions are unavoidable, facilitates the view that dissent is normless, unrealistic or immoral. Because Parsons defines political power as a "generalized capacity to secure the performance of binding obligations," he can ignore the system's use of illegitimate power, its unfulfilled obligations, or its power to impose obligations in the first place. Since authority is assumed to evoke willing obedience or "voluntarism," the very words "power" and "authority" vanish from the functionalist vocabulary when force is used to maintain them! The "integrated" meanings of such concepts are always benign, and there is a near-total lack of oppressive or "dysfunctional" equivalents.

This fusion of authority, legitimacy, power, morality, allegiance, obligation and "voluntaristic" compliance, all functionally intertwined, is made possible by the view from the top down. Any view from the bottom up would all too rapidly discover illegitimate force and involuntary obedience.[23]

The same could be said for all the other dualities and potential contradictions. Thomas Kuhn, an historian of science, has argued that "normal science" proceeds within professional paradigms in the form of "puzzle solving" and "mopping-up operations" by "paradigm workers"; that is, groups of relatively docile and uncreative technicians who accept the methodological norms of their guild and who attempt "to force nature into conceptual boxes." Sooner or later, Kuhn argues, anomalies appear within the professional purview, stubborn contradictions leading to crises which the conventional paradigms cannot solve. Crises bring on a conceptual revolution in which new paradigms replace the old, and the incremental advance of "normal science" starts again.[24]

The tragedy of behaviorism, functionalism and mental health perspectives is that they are so heavily blinkered against the contradictions that signal their obsolescence. The very existence of the poor is *the* great anomaly, threatening not only conceptual revolutions in social science, but a reconstitution of the very meanings by which Americans live.

The politics of positivism

The problem lies not only in systematic biases, but in the huge latitude that the norms of social science give for political maneuvering of the more conservative kind. Let us consider in some detail how two social scientists deeply involved in the appraisal and/or implementation of the poverty wars use social science as a kind of priestcraft to screen out or screen in whatever they wish to see. Since Walter B. Miller and Daniel Patrick Moynihan miss few opportunities to congratulate each other and to present each other's insights, I have taken them together.

In his appraisal of the "Poverty Ideology" and "the Movement,"[25] blanket terms referring to all those connected in some way with federally sponsored anti-poverty work, Miller first objects to the biased overtones in the word "poverty," which imply that it is a readily identifiable condition and that it is pitifully rather than reprehensibly bad. The term thus effectively serves the public relations purposes of the Movement, but at a formidable cost. The cost is "massive confusion."

Miller himself recently headed the Roxbury Delinquency Research Program. Delinquency implies a readily identifiable condition, associated with Roxbury, and denotes reprehensible rather than pitiful badness, which presumably serves the public relations purposes of the punitive-minded. Yet Miller exempts himself from any ensuing confusion.

By dint of placing a metaphorical telescope to a blind eye, he fails to "see" any real poverty at all! "In America," he assures us, "poverty in the absolute sense is virtually non-existent. When from time to time some diligent investigator discovers a family on the edge of starvation . . . the event is sufficiently noteworthy to make national headlines."[26]

The absence of poverty which Miller has no trouble in verifying is guaranteed "by an extensive network of public health and welfare organizations . . . [which] make it virtually impossible for any substantial proportion of our population to be denied necessary food, shelter, clothing or health care." This is an interesting example of the functionalist fallacy, by which the promulgation of general rules assumes their exemplification in specific situations. Notice that while public health legislation convinces Miller about the universality of a healthy public, anti-poverty legislation does not convince him of the presence of poverty.

What "Poverty Ideologists" are really talking about, Miller insists, is *"relative* poverty," the existence of which must be doubted since its measurement is "beyond the scope of our most advanced investigative techniques." It consists of "subjective experience" and "expressions of discontent are quite easy to elicit from most people under the proper circumstances." It amounts to little more than the old adage "Envy breeds discontent." So-called poverty, then, is *"deduced* by ideologists on the basis of considerations other than the findings of reliable empirical investigations." (Miller has himself deduced the absence of poverty from the existence of welfare legislation. He may even have "elicited" the reassurance of officials on this point— but that is different!)

It is, of course, perfectly possible to see poverty, relative or otherwise, by the use of the "hardest" and most physical statistics on such conditions as infant mortality, maternal deaths, lead paint poisonings, decreased longevity, growth retardation, nutrient deficiency, anemia and deaths from preventable diseases. The absolute or relative neglect of poor minority groups can easily be pinpointed. *Relative* poverty need not be defined by the opinions of the poor, but by comparing, say, the salaries of white high school graduates with black college graduates and noticing that they are almost the same! Physical deficits, due to hunger, are, on the basis of samples, estimated to afflict ten million Americans.[27] Such facts are available to anyone whose head is not buried in a methodological wastebasket.

But when Miller turns his gaze from those alleged to be poor to those "ideologists" making this designation, his vision improves markedly. He now sees that poverty is a code word for a "Movement objective," hidden from the rest of us, which is "the elimination of the lower class life style." Having doubted the subjectivity of the envious poor, Miller is yet able to plumb the very depth of the Movement's subjective state. This insight is presumably quite free of the "ambiguities" which make relative deprivation and relative poverty into "a perfect jungle of the most intricate, abstruse, and thoroughly speculative philosophical issues."

Among other observations that strike Miller with fearful clarity is the fact that "the Movement" helped precipitate the ghetto riots, that the alleged unhappiness of the poor is a myth projected upon them by middle-class ideologists and that "deprivation in the objective sense is too rare to justify the scope of the Movement."

Then Miller reaches the apex of his "objectivity." Having accused the poor of "obsessive masculinity," the desire to "take" and "con" one another—subjective judgments all—and having accused unspecified ideologists of everything from humbug to secret plots to fomenting riots, he abjures us all to be "as free *as possible* from unexamined values." We must avoid at all costs:

> The blaming-the-blamers tactic along with that [tactic] of Negro leaders—"You say *we're* to blame, but we say *you're* to blame—" [which] assumes the form of a classic dialogue between eight-year-olds. "It's your fault"—"No, it's your fault," with about as much profit.[28]

Here we see a typical outcome of mixing positivism with politics, the detailed denunciation of one's own mirror image. Daniel Moynihan adopts the similar stance of warrior priest, thrusting home his sword, then swiftly reversing it to form a cross and making ex cathedra pronouncements upon the skirmish. His famous judgment upon "Negro family pathology"[29] was a masterful exercise in the art of political put-down and "savage discovery,"[30] to which social science so readily lends itself.

Why did Moynihan write his famous report on black "pathology," which found its way into President Johnson's address at Howard University? Lee Rainwater and William Yancey, both supportive of Moynihan, interviewed government officials about the political context of the report:

Having reacted to the [civil rights] movement's demands for a decade, the government learned that it was impossible to satiate [sic] the new Negro American. Something had to be done . . . so that the government would not continue to be a "reacting" force. To quote one government source, "We could never catch those guys—the only thing to do is to get ahead of them." Another government source said that much of the Howard speech was designed to "leap-frog the movement."[31]

Hence the purpose of the report was *to wrest initiative away from the disadvantaged* and restore it to President Johnson. Reportedly, high government officials read the report, exclaiming, "Pat, I think you've got it!"

The report argued that because of past slavery, the Negro family was now "pathological." Evidence for this came from government statistics on fatherless households, illegitimacy, etc. Official statistics are, of course, part of the overwhelming bias against poor minorities; but social scientists, starting with Durkheim, have always regarded a statistic as a purer form than the minor official from which it emanates. Thus Durkheim, in his classic treatise on suicide, first redefined the term as an officially reported fact free of "subjective bias," and then collected all the statistics based on what the coroner believed, the relatives believed, that the deceased intended to do! Thus are the viewpoints of authority smuggled into thousands of "scientific" reports.[32]

Moynihan's accusation of "pathology" based on these statistics is an excellent illustration of the mental health paradigm in political use. Where is the pathology located? one might ask. Inside Black Americans? Inside their families? Between blacks and whites? Or in the oppressive behavior of white people? If we regard the social oppression of blacks by whites as a total dynamic, why is the black end of this dynamic more pathological than the white end, or than the total phenomenon? And how does one distinguish a "pathology" from an "heroic adaptation to overwhelming pressure"? Suppose that a mother-centered household is the best possible response to a society that discriminates in employment more against black males than against black females. If you broke a black man's arm so that his wife had to do the heavy work, would it not (literally!) add insult to injury to diagnose him publicly as effeminate? Yet this is the implication of the mental health perspective wielded like a club by Moynihan. He arbitrarily separates the mental state of individuals or families from the context in which they struggle to survive and attributes to the family the full responsibility for being different. This difference he then labels pathological.

But even if it could be demonstrated that black matriarchy was maladaptive to oppressive conditions, and that even the poor need the Texas-style masculinity that gave us Vietnam, it would still not justify the use of medical terminology in the political arena. Senator Goldwater successfully sued for libel when this was done to him by a small magazine. Doctors do not broadcast diagnoses over the public address system.[33] The road to hell is paved with research "findings" communicated in ways that increase their salience.

The one consistent theme running through this affair is Moynihan's curious concern with masculinity. It was he who recommended that poor blacks attempt to find their manhood through induction into the Armed Services, which, in the context of the times, meant killing Vietnamese in a war not without racist overtones. And if the admissions of government officials are true, the Moynihan report was inspired *not* by concern for black "matriarchy" but by the government's *own* history of "effeminate" response to "virile" civil rights agitation. It was an example of what Rainwater and Yancey called "the benign Machiavellianism of the Johnson Administration." In short, the incident bears the marks of the prototypical racist encounter, wherein white believes a source of anxiety inside himself to be an attribute of black and the "pathological cause" of their mutual tension.

In fact, the War on Poverty *did* succeed in wresting from the civil rights movement its initiative and momentum, which it has never recovered. Moynihan recounts the fact.

> The War on Poverty was not declared at the behest of the poor: it was declared in their interest by persons confident of their judgment in such matters. . . .
> The principal source of political power in a capitalist democracy being votes and money, and the poor having an insufficiency of either, it was more or less ordained that they should become in some degree clients of the persons interested in their plight . . . Inevitably the content and the effort of the kind of program that resulted was influenced by professional judgments . . . the poor had nothing whatever to do with it.[34]

Except that it was not "ordained" or "inevitable." It was managed, in part, by Moynihan himself.

The denial of relationships between knowers and known

When attempting to relate to poor people and/or to persons of different background and ethnicity, it is more than usually necessary to put one's hypotheses about them "at risk"; that is, to SUSPEND one's cognitive structures, including such designations as "poor," in a manner sufficient to have one's way of thinking altered. There is almost no principle that is more important in fighting poverty than this one. No formerly poor person could possibly have escaped poverty, were there not sufficient numbers of persons willing to think about him in perspectives other than "hard-core," "disadvantaged," "dependent variable" or "product of poverty subculture." By definition, a person can only develop by fostering changes in the way other people regard him. When such perceptions are fixed and unchangeable, like objective categories, he rightly complains of prejudice.

It is on the principle of disciplined open-mindedness that traditional science takes its stand. The rationale for the hypothetico-deductive method is that the investigator puts his general hypothesis "at risk" in specific situations, giving nature the opportunity to say "no" each time. It is believed that if the investigator is as detached and objective as possible, he will avoid eliciting the verdict he seeks and will more readily accept the disconfirmation of his hypothesis when it comes. The great advantage of the laboratory type experiment is that it permits the investigator to follow the progressive logic of his own calculations, filling in his theory like a tapestry instead of waiting, sometimes for years, for a natural combination of events.

This seems so eminently reasonable that social scientists have been unable to resist it. But the very same norms that permit a degree of openness when studying lifeless objects become overwhelmingly dogmatic and prejudicial when applied to relationships between human beings. Let us see why.

First, the openness of the hypothetico-deductive method operates only *within* the scientific paradigm, after the experimenter has controlled every variable but the one his "progressive logic" wishes to deal with next. He does not SUSPEND his assumption as to who is the dependent variable, or who is culturally determined.

Similar, if not greater, degrees of flexibility might be found among southern segregationists, who may patronize, avoid, lynch, blacklist, fire, warn, co-opt, domesticate or seduce a black person, depending on the situation. Within his paradigm the segregationist shows a degree of nuance and imagination that puts "reinforcement" to shame. Yet all concerned refuse to change their overall style of conception, and must therefore be regarded as prejudiced. There can be no absolute right to follow "the progressive logic of one's own calculations" where that logic runs roughshod over the progressive logic of the person being studied. What social scientists have illegitimately claimed for themselves is the unilateral right to label social reality.[35]

We may conclude that no paradigm that fails to suspend its structures so as to accommodate the consciously wrought and conflicting perspectives of persons being studied, or which fails to regard such perspectives as potentially novel sources of enlightenment and change, can conceivably claim to be open or unprejudiced in human terms.

It is absurd to claim that one is "at risk" in any social sense, while controlling 95 per cent of experimental variables. A substantial proportion of animal experiments, for example, turn the contours of the experimenter's paradigm into the bars of cages, the pain of electric shocks, or the necessary conditions for continuing to eat and drink. Bertrand Russell once compared the animal experiments done by American behaviorists with those done by German Gestalt psychologists. He wryly observed:

> One may say broadly that all the animals that have been carefully observed have behaved so as to confirm the philosophy in which the observer believed before his observations began. Nay, more, they have all displayed the national characteristics of the observer. Animals studied by Americans rush about frantically, with an incredible display of bustle and pep, and at last achieve the desired result by chance. Animals observed by Germans sit still and think, and at last evolve the solution out of their inner consciousness. . . .[36]

It is no different in the case of poor people who react according to the particular bind in which social scientists force them. Recently Lee Rainwater enumerated five perspectives in which social scientists have seen the poor; (1) the medicalizing, (2) the apotheosizing, (3) the moralizing, (4) the normalizing, and (5) the naturalizing. These perspectives regard the poor as (1) weak and defective, (2) strong and heroic, (3) dangerous and defective, (4) no different from anyone else, and (5) the products of social laws. Each perspective, Rainwater contends, is a defense against the anxiety of perceiving a humanity so different from one's own. Each investigator is saying to himself, "I couldn't live like that!" Anxiety is controlled by (1) looking down and pitying, (2) looking up and worshiping, (3) looking down and condemning, (4) denying the difference, and (5) depersonalizing the issue.[37]

It is a weighty concession for Rainwater to make: that years of detachment, objectivity and professional discipline have turned the poor into mere reflections of professional, middle-class anxiety.

Social scientists have to face the fact that SUSPENSION of their assumptions in the presence of threatening subjects has nothing to do with scholarly detachment, objective calm or puritanical discipline—quite the opposite. SUSPENSION is part of a dialectical process, full of anger, excitement, joy and woe, wherein the linchpins of one's deepest beliefs become dislodged to be assembled anew. We can never enter into an understanding of how others see the world without dissolving our own paradigms, at least temporarily, to bumble around awkwardly and inexpertly among their personal constructions. To understand these constructions we have to feel them, as well as know them, to despair, rage or love with the person we know, and still be able to think intelligently. This is much harder "discipline" than objectivity, involving the alternate loosening and tightening of discipline itself, for to relinquish your paradigm even for a moment is to risk that you will never be the same again, or, worse, that much of your life has been wasted.[38] To hold two or more opposed conceptions in your mind at the same time and still retain your capacity to function is a kind of mental crucifixion, and I defy the one-dimensional man not to let in the second dimension without wincing.

Hence, while the astronomer sees the stars more "openly" when he is detached (since they are, in fact, quite separate from him and his desires), the social investigator can only see the poor "openly" when SUSPEND-ING himself in the process of becoming attached (since they are, in fact, related to him and his desires and need better relations with him and others if poverty is to be overcome). Nor is there any escape from eliciting *some* kind of reaction. Human beings do not remain unaffected by scrutiny. Since scrutiny inevitably evokes, it should be such as to evoke from the poor useful insights and a maximum of initiative. This is no irrational belief in the nobility of the poor, but merely a belief that potentiality of any kind must first be evoked in order to be discovered, and that the realization of potentiality is one aspect of emancipation itself.

To try, somehow, to unfreeze with anger or pleading the unsuspended paradigms of academics, to explain that the rigidities of detachment dovetail with the rigidities of conscious racism, is for Moynihan "a nudge towards paranoia."[39] He even regrets "the quite unprecedented display of mourning and self-indictment" following the murder of Martin Luther King. The answer to our failure in fighting poverty, according to him, is to be more, rather than less detached, to separate the functions of understanding poverty and fighting it, lest the anger and compassion generated by the latter corrupt the scholarship of the former.[40] How can you breach a mind locked in such tight compartments? Remain "scholarly" and you are merely ruled out of order, if not out of science. Become furious and you are self-condemned.

> The critical test for the authenticity of a cult movement lies in the intensity of anger evinced by the faithful when a basic tenet of the ideology is called into question by someone who cannot easily be ignored. The bitterness and virulence of Movement attacks on the Moynihan report leave no doubt as to the genuineness of the Poverty movement.[41]

You cannot win, can you? Especially by expressing your "inauthentic" anger at Miller's "authentic" contempt and disdain.

To argue that the poor, the black or women might see a different reality due to their different economic and ethnic identities is to loose an explosive charge at the very foundations of positivism.[42] For positivists, "objective truth" is a bridge of reason over a quicksand. To undermine it is to drown singly in a bog of relativism. Hence there is a natural hostility to black or feminist studies, based on the "metaphysics of identity." It is a different matter to investigate women or black people as objects of study. The objection is to a "segregated" perspective upon social life. Although many positivists are quick to admit that private agendas have often become entangled with objective truth, they see this only as a call for greater discipline and the tighter subjugation of personality.

It is a constant tendency of social scientists to mistake the working out of their own purposes, to regard the functional equilibrium they impose on social systems and the alienated domination they achieve over experimental subjects as properties of the people they observe. This involves a massive confusion between mind and environment that was supposedly taken care of by the discipline of detachment, but which, like Victorian sexual taboos, seems only to escalate both the impulse and the repression. It involves a denial of the relationship between the knower and the known and denial that what the detached observer sees in the other is in part the sour reflection of this denied relationship. No wonder America has come to the verge of genocide in Southeast Asia, while insisting that it was only responding to "aggression from North Vietnam." We have a total mind-set that sees the locus of hostile emotion as outside ourselves.

For some extraordinary reason it is thought that the detachment towards, and pessimism about, experimental subjects is less biasing and evocative than warmth and respect, with the result that we decline all responsibility for the human costs of our niggardly spirit. It is axiomatic that controlled indifference will evoke angry and emotional outbursts, yet when this happens we speak in hushed and shocked tones about the insurgent poor.

> . . . the power of the weak: the power to disrupt, to embarrass, to provoke, to goad to punitive rage, but banking (usually) on the inhibitions of those goaded. A gentleman does not strike a lady.[43]

One can detect in Moynihan's description the genteel shudder of the superior intellect. His reaction is similar to Nisbet's: "With every fresh assault on the traditional authorities of the social order, the day of what Burkhardt called the 'terrible simplifiers' . . . comes nearer."[44]

Perhaps the terrible simplifiers have been with us for some time. How else can we account for the behaviorists, who remind each other to understand "the sentimentality which ordains the frantic assertion, 'I'm a person, not a thing!' . . . however absurd, pathetic and in error it may seem to be"?[45] What can you say to the "scientist" who tells you, "There is no choice. Only by dehumanizing man can we learn where his humanity lies, and only with that knowledge can it be preserved"?[46]

The dominant paradigms also protect themselves from self-awareness by prohibiting *ad hominem* attacks. This doctrine holds that a communication should be judged independently of its source, since a flawed man can still contribute valuably. This argument militates against a phenomenological perspective, which holds that our values and preferences organize what we see, so that to break the connection between man and concept cuts the former off from self-knowledge. After all, social science is about *hominem*, the observing and the observed. To hold that the cathedral of learning should be some kind of sanctuary against those violated by the conceptions of "social science politicos" is to claim a dubious immunity.

There is ample evidence that scientific paradigms are, in fact, adopted for reasons of personal background and predilection. American behaviorists have a strong tendency to come from small, rural towns.[47] Perhaps they seek to recreate within the university the sparsely simplified world of their childhoods. Gouldner found that nearly 30 per cent of functionalists, but not other sociologists, had "seriously thought of becoming clergymen." Approval of functionalism correlated strongly with approval of religion. In a correlation analysis by far the best predictors of a variety of attitudes were the underlying a priori assumptions about human nature.[48]

It might be thought that social scientists shrink their own identities as impartially as they shrink the identities of those they study. Alas, no such justice prevails. The investigator tries to leave his selfhood outside the laboratory door, which places it in the rest of the university. There his identity dwells in the land of academic freedom, professional status, seekers after truth and the entire liberal philosophy that undergirds the university. The academic receives high levels of respect, freedom and tolerance outside the framework of his professional paradigm. The assumption of a plastic identity is for others—the poor in spirit, if not in possessions.

In short, we have groups of professionals who, while receiving freedom and respect, *do not pass it on* to those in desperate need. Just as academics catch the money that might otherwise go to the direct relief of poverty, they also claim "academic freedom"—a supposedly superior freedom, which includes the right to cast ordinary citizens in the role of hollow men.

It only needs experts in community psychiatry to persuade these hollowed containers that they are at least partly full—of mental disease symptoms.

A typical study was reported in *Psychological Factors in Poverty*. Children in adjoining poor and moderate income neighborhoods were variously treated to psychiatric interviews and symptom checklists were read out to their parents and the answers coded by computers. *Ninety-one per cent* of the children were found to be "impaired"; 9 per cent were well. Moreover, of those investigated by the computerized checklist and the interview, 96 per cent were "impaired," only 4 per cent were well, and many more were "seriously" and "moderately" impaired than among those merely interviewed. The researchers blithely explain:

The more data one sees the more pathological the individual looks. This is an old saw of psychological testing. A recent study also showed that direct methods [interviews] uncover less pathology than indirect methods [computer coded checklists].[49]

Since "ghetto psychiatry" is the most indirect of all, with psychiatrists placing an administrative ladder between themselves and the poor, and since selected poor people get desperately needed salaries so long as they find symptoms among their neighbors, it will only take one more checklist and one more computer for the "well" individuals to become totally extinct! Over half the parents of the poorer respondents being studied believed that mental health care conferred little benefit on their children. Luckily the researchers were able to explain this anomaly:

Our data shows that it is typically the lower income families who are forced to bring their children into therapy through the schools or courts. Their reaction, therefore, is unlikely to be positive.[50]

The decline of equality and concern for justice

An obvious and early casualty of the ambition of the professing positivist is the ideal of equality and social justice. You cannot dream that "your" independent variable, be it reinforcement, social structure or therapeutic intervention, is explaining, predicting or controlling a host of other variables, without countenancing the subordination and dependence of much of the world beyond your profession. "Fairness and justice," B. F. Skinner informs us, "means only that we are making wise use of reinforcers."[51] According to a disciple:

> The idea of justice is a mere fiction until expressed in law, its ostensible instrument of control . . . In this sense power is real and justice is not.[52]

Another father of behaviorism in *Can Science Save Us?* reproves his readers for the "luxury of indignation" that accompanied the struggle against fascism in World War II.

> This country, for example, has recently enjoyed a great emotional vapor-bath directed at certain European movements and leaders. Such indignation ministers to deep-seated jungle-fed sentiments of justice, virtue, and a general feeling of the fitness of things, as compared with what scientific diagnosis of the situation evokes.[53]

One reason why the ideas of justice, equality and democracy have been so seriously undermined by social science is that the original justification for these norms made its appeal to the nature of man. Thus McV. Hunt, a psychologist writing for the Institute for Research on Poverty, explains:

> When our forefathers declared it to be a self-evident truth "that all men are created equal" they uttered biological and psychological nonsense. But they were not thinking in terms either biological or psychological. Their concerns were ethical and political.[54]

It is clear that for Hunt, though not for Lincoln, psychology must be dichotomized from ethics and politics. Notice how this fragmentation has already subordinated "Hunt the ethicist" to "Hunt the psychologist." The evaluating *in*expert citizen gives deference to the norms of his society, while the detached, expert scientist sees inferiority and superiority all around him. The poor, of course, will encounter the scientist in his professional capacity.

Functionalists have ingenious ways of evading values, such as social justice. I was weaned sociologically at the Harvard Business School on Alexander Leighton's oft reprinted essay "The Functional Point of View" (as were many of today's business leaders).[55] Leighton asks the student to imagine a mountainside where wolves are devouring sheep or a hive where damaged worker bees are stung to death. It is totally unscientific to regard the wolves as *causing* the death of sheep, as it is to call the destruction of tired workers "wicked." Were more facts known—for example, that there was insufficient food for the sheep—the investigator "may find that the balance of nature is such that the wolves aid the sheep more than harming them," or that "the destruction of bees functions to perpetuate the hive." In the functional point of view . . . the investigator

> Does not take sides with the sheep, wolves or other animals in such a way as to blind his understanding of how they are interdependent. . . . One's own hopes and fears, and ideas of what *should be* are set aside in favor of discovery of what *is* . . . If war is threatened, if economic depression descends, if unemployment appears . . . we always give far more attention to discussing the rights and wrongs of the situation, in deciding who is to blame and in taking sides, than to understanding the forces that have brought it about. . . .[56]

Although this doctrine spreads over and smothers the pain of conscience and compassion, like a large dose of Pepto-Bismol, it contains an important half-truth. It is essential to postpone value judgments, until as much as possible of the information contained within a system has been taken into account. The slogan our professor used to write on the board, EVALUATION STOPS THOUGHT, did apply to some students who became fixated upon a particular "immoral act," usually by workers, and were unable to see the context. The fallacy lies in setting aside the value judgment *permanently* rather than temporarily, and in forgetting that value judgments will be reconstituted by *someone*, typically top management, as soon as the description ends. Moreover, the description itself will evoke certain judgments in preference to others.

Since the functional point of view presupposes that some particular massacre of sheep, bees or people is "balanced out" somewhere else, the inherent bias is to continue looking, dry-eyed, tough-minded and unprotesting until the equilibrating factor (or the excuse) is found, and *then* stop. Just as imbalance (or injustice) can evoke the intervention of a witness to set things right, so the assumption of balance (or justice), despite appearances, evokes a smug conservatism and a wait-and-see attitude.

So while behaviorists and mental health researchers break down the human frame into fragments too small for the adherence of rights, and so purge their "science" of ethics and politics, the functionalist builds up society into a Mysterious Equilibrium that subsumes all ethical and moral questions about the bits and pieces that are man, and refers them to some Ultimate Function yet to be revealed. Let us see how the values of equality and social justice might be retained in a social psychology of development.

It is self-evident (and verifiable) that relationships of justice and equality between men (that is, relationships that all parties agree are just and equal) constitute the most accurate, sensitive, pleasurable and enlightening way to exchanging information and support. It is also self-evident that man makes the greatest use of his several capacities and endowments when none of these are subordinated or sacrificed to others, and when none of the persons who variously personify these capacities are subordinated. In fact, we are created in a way that makes justice, equality and ecological balance essential to our psychological, social and biological development.

Notice that this formulation does not require a Noble Savage spoiled by the Sin of Socialization. Equality and justice are not paradisical states from which Man is fallen, nor are they just norms that glue—but *essential aspects of the methodology of knowing.* Like all paradigms in social science, "the assumption of equality" prior to investigation tends to be self-fulfilling, as are the technology of behaviorism and the functional hypothesis. But it is *less* self-fulfilling, less intrusive upon the other, to assume his equality than to designate him as a dependent variable. Detachment of the knower from the known is also strongly self-fulfilling, leading to mutual withdrawal and destroying the relationship, which has been our unit of study. Hence equality is less intrusive upon the other's desire to relate as he wishes, than either domination, subordination or detachment. It is the method least likely to impose the knower's own preferences upon the known. Justice, equality and SYNERGY are vital parts of a developmental and humanistic epistemology.

It seems to me, therefore, entirely proper that a humanistic social scientist should be "partisan" in the sense of insisting that many political and social problems are unsolvable until the subordinate party is given an opportunity to bring his views and influence to bear. There is no reason for impartiality as between ghetto residents and their jailers, as between Asian victims and American bombardiers. There are periods in our current affairs in which all would-be knowers *must* protest that they are totally cut off from saving knowledge by the subordination and the brutalization of one party to a conflict. Instead of the shrillness and "irrationality" of victims being used as an excuse for further impugning their humanity, it should warn us that we are in grave danger of losing the "justifying" perspective, without which a developmental solution is impossible.

Ultimately we cannot say that any person is *un*equal to us, unless we specify certain criteria along which that person falls short in some degree. But why insist on one criterion? And how can a stranger whose purpose we do not know be treated as higher or lower, until such a time as his purpose becomes plain? Even those we know well have the right to periodic reassessment. Equality is a promise by men and women to all their fellows that the definition of excellence will never be closed. We should treat others as equals, especially DISTANT others, because they may be discovered to have a value, undreamed of in our philosophies, which qualifies our existing values in a way that transforms our symbolic universe.

Equality does not mean structured equality, which holds that one man should not risk rising or falling in the other's estimation as a result of what he says or does. Equality does not mean homogeneity. We must also reject Daniel Bell's false dichotomy between equality of opportunity v. equality of result with the first dominating the second. The resolution is equality of social process. The problem with one man having twenty times the wealth of another is not so much that it offends some sacred principle of economic parity, but that the rich employ their wealth so that they need no longer relate to the poor. They do not meet in debate or confront the other's humanity—a secret call to the White House or a sizable campaign contribution, and the issue at conflict is not even stated, much less resolved synergistically. "Tyrants engage in monologues over a multitude of solitudes . . ."[57] Dominating wealth bribes and browbeats a thousand unjust solutions every day.

The miniature working crucifix

Whenever social science attempts to model "real" events "out there," it runs the danger of reproducing in its laboratory and conceptual language the existing social contradictions that are impeding resolution and progress. If anything, these reproductions and simulations are *more* resistant to transformation and change than their originals. This is because models usually simplify events, purifying them of "irregular" and "unpredictable" variables, and because simulation destroys the emotional commitment to genuine events. It is through such emotion-arousing irregularities and anomalies that real changes occur in politics.

Take, for example, Robert Merton's influential essay on the sources of *anomie* in American society, with its synthesis of behaviorism and functionalism, and its later strong influence on Mobilization for Youth and Community Action. It is a paragon of elegance and simplicity.

Thus the culture enjoins the acceptance of three cultural axioms: First, all should strive for the same lofty goals since these are open to all; second, present seeming failure is but a way station to ultimate success; and third, genuine failure consists only in a lessening and withdrawal of ambition.

In rough psychological paraphrase, these axioms represent, first, a symbolic secondary reinforcement of incentive; second, curbing the threatened extinction of a response through an associated stimulus; third, increasing the motive-strength to evoke continued responses despite the continued absence of reward.

In sociological paraphrase, these axioms represent, first, the deflection of criticism of the social structure onto oneself among those so situated in the society that they do not have full and equal access to opportunity; second, the preservation of a structure of social power by having individuals in the lower social strata identify themselves, not with their compeers, but with those at the top (whom they will ultimately join); and third, providing pressure for conformity with the cultural dictates of unslackened ambition by the threat of less than full membership in the society for those who fail to conform.[58]

Like so much of Merton's work it contains brilliant insights. Here we see the crucifying contradictions in which the poor are caught and the cruel hoax that is played upon them. But there is one insight lacking, *that the language*

and conceptualization of his versions of psychology and so-
ciology are themselves part of that crucifixion.

It is no coincidence, surely, that psychological and sociological concepts reveal so clearly what is wrong, yet failed
miserably when the "solution" tried was to reprogram
the poor, only with fewer conflicts within the schedule of
reinforcements. Empiricism has in one sense "triumphed"—
by reproducing, concept by concept, a perfect working
model of repression and suggesting only that its orders to
the masses be purged of unrealizable and unbalancing directives.

Typical of such reproduced contradictions is the Prisoner's Dilemma Game, billed as a "co-operative" answer to
pure competition and a liberal alternative to win-lose sav-
agery. The very title of the game suggests a jaundiced
view of human co-operation, which is seen as driven by
fear of something worse. It concerns two prisoners accused
of a joint crime. If neither talks, the attorney general cannot indict either of them. If both talk, each will get five
years. But if either *one* decides to talk while the other remains silent, the stoolie gets a reward and the silent one
gets ten years for his refusal to co-operate.[59] It isn't such
an inaccurate model of the ghetto, where agreements between black people are broken up by white bribery and
co-optation. The notion of social scientists playing attorney
general while experimental subjects play prisoner is just
about "where it's at."

To show how severely alienated are the game's assumptions, let us illustrate it with heterosexual human relationships, and call it "The Rapist's Dilemma." The supreme
thrill for the male game player is to penetrate the body of
a screaming, struggling female, but he may be prosecuted
and made to pay heavy damages, or her family might
have him castrated. Hence the compromise solution,
which "bifurcates self-interest" and lets each gain a little,
is to join in sexual intercourse, or "love" if one insists on
being fuzzy conceptually. While intercourse is a modest

pleasure, without the exhilarating payoff that comes with the mastery and subjugation of female flesh (or the righteous maiming of the lusting male), it is clearly the wisest course, one calling for the control of lust, and the subordination of impulse to rationality. The desire to love others, rather than castrate/rape them, is only maintained by fear of punishment.

The grotesque nature of this example has been achieved simply by using as an illustration a kind of relationship in which SYNERGY is often attained, whereas in the more alienated spheres of economics and politics, it is rarer, and win-lose or compromise solutions are admittedly common. My complaint is not that the Prisoner's Dilemma Game is a poor model of some spheres of life, but that the model precludes synergistic solutions. Ghetto prisoners are modeled by "laboratory prisoners"—but this includes the entrapment of the original, with Science (and Mathematics) now the jailer. Further, the whole suspense is *about* the possibility of conquest/subjugation; but for these contrasting outcomes, we would be stuck with boring-old-love-and-mutuality.

The "findings" from such research reproduce exactly the dilemma of its original premises. The "co-operators" among student populations include the mystic, those hip on oriental religion, needful of abasement, succorance and counseling. There are also independent, activist and protesting types. The "exploiters" were defensive, intolerant, dominant, achievement-oriented and confident.[60] In short, we have *another* false dichotomy, Appeasers v. Aggressors. The pendulum swings from Munich to Southeast Asia and perhaps back again. Yet in this research there was a shadow of a solution. During a rest period in The Games students tried informally to negotiate a pact, to break out of The Game itself and achieve SYNERGY. It says much about the methods of social science that solutions are created the moment the Cage of Rationality is momentarily suspended, and dialectical logic rather than formal strategy is employed.

The purification of existence

Were I to choose one tendency in these social science paradigms above all, for its lethal impact upon developmental processes, it would be their attempts to purify the concepts of experience, by reduction, isolation, cloture and

TABLE 3

ISOLATION, REDUCTION AND UNBALANCING OF
CONCEPTUAL IDEAS

Principles of Development		
1. EXISTENCE (in the sense of freedom)	is isolated and reduced to	Free Will, that is, an unreliable link in the chain of cause and effect.
(in the sense of out-thrust values)	is isolated and reduced to	Value Relativism and Value Objectification, so that values are seen from the outside in terms of function, not as claims upon the investigator.
2. PERCEPTION	is isolated and reduced to	A Stimulus or "thing seen," or to Cognition —a term shorn of its opposite, Conation, or Explaining—a term shorn of its opposite, Understanding.
3. IDENTITY	is isolated and reduced to	Subjectivity, or to Introspection, or to some in-dwelling homunculus.
4. COMPETENCE	is isolated and reduced to	Motive Strength, or IQ, or n Power or n Achievement, among many such narrow aptitudes.
5. COMMITMENT	is isolated and reduced to	Behavior, or Response, or Action.
authentic	is isolated and reduced to	Naïve subjects, unconsciously projected information or the minimizing of observer bias.
intense	is isolated and reduced to	Affect, mere exclamations of preference with no testable meaning.

6. RISK	Is isolated and reduced to	Hypothesis Testing, or wagering, or testing one's game-playing skill.
&		
SUSPENSION	Is isolated and reduced to	Detachment from "thing" observed.
7. BRIDGING the DISTANCE	Is isolated and reduced to	Social Distance, *not* bridged.
8. SELF-CONFIRMATION	Is isolated and reduced to	Positive Reinforcement or rewards for approximating pre-defined behaviors as distinguished from personal fulfillment.
9. *Dialectic*	Is isolated and reduced to	Games and Strategies that compete for scarce resources.
leading to		
SYNERGY	Is unbalanced by reduction so that ...	Stimulus, Cognition, Explaining, Narrow Aptitudes, Behavior, Detachment, Social Distance, Reinforcements and Games, etc.,*rule over and subordinate* Free Will, Values, Conation, Understanding, Subjectivity, Naïveté, Affect and Personal Fulfillment.
	Is isolated and reduced to	Co-operative Strategies and compromise solutions, or Adhesive objects and norms commanding consensus.
10. ORDERED FEEDBACK & COMPLEXITY	Is isolated and reduced to	Behavior control technologies, and a rationality of means, as opposed to ends. Linear orderings full of subordination and invidious distinctions, so purified that their lateral connections are lost.

purgation—very much the habit of a chronically over-individuated culture. In Table 3 the left-hand column restates the ten principles of development, presented in Chapter 1 in cyclical form, with principle 10 feeding around to principle 1. These concepts, let us recall, were synergistic, that is, comprehensible only in toto, like the fingers of a hand. Yet see what happens to them in the right-hand column, where they are defined atomistically and "scientifically." EXISTENCE deteriorates into "free will," human IDENTITY shrinks to subjectivity or even solipsism, being CONFIRMED in one's wholeness is reduced to reinforcement, etc. The entire social process disintegrates in a manner that *permanently* defeats resynthesis, and leads to the subordination of the unreliable "inner man" to the stereotypical and measurable "outer man" and his physical manifestations.

What has gone wrong?

The problem lies in the fact that translating value-free, scientific neutrality and detachment into human relationships has resulted in a very close approximation to Puritanism, probably the deepest and most persistent religious bias in the American character. There is the desire for purification by creating "ideal types," along with balance, symmetry, simplicity, control and parsimony.[61] The principle of Occam's razor is reminiscent of the shaven heads of penitents and the shrunken identities of marine recruits. The demand for precision, invariability and replication are sparse copies of ritual virtues. The stern dispassion, hard discipline, the public demonstration of rectitude through pristine experimentation, the perpetual inner struggle to repress one's personal biases, with the inevitable fallings into sin, all are surely familiar. The conviction, when this happens, that man's weakness, rather than God's Good Method, is at fault, provides endless opportunities for minor mutual criticism of outward form, without the heresy of basic doubt. The Puritan desire to succeed *through* some Superior Agency is perfectly met by subordination to method. Man alone is weak and in error, but, armored in methodological righteousness, he prevails. There is the same division into the Elect and others with the same grim struggle about where to draw the line.

There is the same underlying contradiction between belief and behavior; just as the Puritans did not regard their predestined state of grace as providing an excuse for relaxation, social scientists do not regard their own theoretical determination by outside variables as excusing them from publishing lest they perish. Rather, all must labor prodigiously *to establish the truth of their initial assump-*

tions. Life becomes a battle against inner doubt, an un-smiling solidarity against the heathen, and an energetic exercise in mental and social exclusion, sewn in scarlet letters on the poor. There is the same Devil, now in the form of sinful subjectivity, the abyss of relativism and the clamor of passions. And, saddest of all, there is the same age-old cruelty and indifference to suffering and poverty.

CHAPTER 4

Community Development:
The Counter-Institutional Strategy

The bright ideals of the past—physical freedom, political power, the training of brains and the training of hands—all these in turn have waxed and waned, until even the last grows dim and overcast. Are they all wrong, all false? No, not that, but each was oversimple and incomplete—the dreams of a credulous race-childhood, or the fond imaginings of the other world which does not know or does not want to know our power. To be really true, all these ideals must be melted and welded into one.

W. E. B. Du Bois, *The Souls of Black Folk*

The answer must be . . . a Negro Economic Cooperative Commonwealth . . .

W. E. B. Du Bois, *Dusk of Dawn*

In Chapter 1, we examined developmental processes among the poor on the level of psychology and interpersonal dynamics. While these are major elements in the growth process, they are emphatically not enough. There is a delusional quality about all those humanistic and developmental schema that individualize a "naked spirit" in man, assumed to grow without social, economic or other structural supports. In fact, people are fed, fueled, protected, employed, empowered, informed and variously rewarded by institutions. Anti-heroism and man-alone-against-the-system are middle-class ideals, which have more to do with the personal predilections of creative writers to remain at their desks than empowering their ideas through action.

Some time ago, the giant institutions of this land discovered that they could "tolerate" free-floating spirits and empassioned pens, if not actually profit from distributing dissent.[1] In such circumstances, we may have to reconsider some favorite postures. The Outsider, the Metaphysical Rebel, the Man of La Mancha are all becoming separated from their authentic origins and the social conditions to which they were appropriate. Radical Chic has relegated such postures to the fashion parade; they are Lone Rangers on astro-turf. We cannot go *on* "raising consciousness." It is raised by now and tens of thousands of us have been hawking our consciences on the streets since the mid-sixties.

The failures of middle-class dissent and of poverty wars are traceable to a reluctance to institutionalize and incorporate alternative structures. Perhaps middle-class dissenters confuse their own needs with those of the poor. Defying the bureaucracy, leaking its secrets, resigning in protest, denouncing its ideology, we treat organizations much as the pole-vaulter treats his pole, thrusting it away from him as he reaches the apex of his spectacular jump. As we float through ideological space, apparently unsupported, we forget that what the poor need more than anything else is some version of what we so "freely" discarded and without which we could never have taken off.

The Welfare Establishment is especially notable for making a fetish of the client's individuality. Regarding poverty as an exceptionalistic failure of individuals, it extends personal services to the ailing indigent, until he can "make it on his own." That is the ideal. The reality pits an institutionalized professional, preaching individuality, against an uninstitutionalized client, experiencing bureaucratization.[2] Milton Kotler has asked:

> What ordinary man, or for that matter exceptional man, wants an individual relationship with government and its might? Such a relationship would be a suicidal compact.

What balance is there between the force of government and one man's might, let alone his defenceless reason? Granted, man seeks a responsive and comfortable government, but not through his individual relation to the State. Instead he seeks a closer relationship to government through his group, where there is enough collective human strength to further his interest and defend him from State power. It is the group which relates man to the State for self-defence and the good life.[3]

The belief that white professionals can "develop" single black clients of a submerged class has its basis in the expansionist aims of the professions concerned. Historically *no* poor migrant groups in any country, at any time, have climbed out of poverty on therapeutic ladders proffered by an elite. Urban ethnic groups in America have emerged from poverty, *as groups,* by creating and manning their own institutions. Without dominating certain institutions such as the needle trades (Jews) and laundries (Chinese), without a high, expanding demand for low-skilled labor which made unionization and collective bargaining possible, without ethnic grocers, suppliers and other small businessmen that made capital accumulation possible out of rising wages of ethnic workers, without bossism, the urban machines and patronage jobs, millions of immigrants could not have made it.

For various reasons these institutional opportunities have all decayed. The demand for unskilled or low-skilled labor has declined. No longer can rising immigrants contract out through labor gangs the muscle of their own ethnic newcomers. Union membership is shrinking and union policies are exclusionary. Bossism is "reformed" and replaced by an entrenched civil service that uses an impenetrable maze of tests and credentials to exclude outsiders. Even where city hall can be captured, it is broke. The era of small business is over. It seems that every earlier wave of upward mobility left some exploited residue— those on whom someone else had clambered a bit too hard to make good his own escape. So now we have segregated minorities and mixed residues—all bereft of effective institutions.

To understand the necessity for institutions, it is necessary to supplement the model of *human processes* introduced in Chapter 1 with their equivalent *organizational structures*. These are compared below.

This chapter will deal with processes and structures 1 to 5 and I to V. Chapter 5 will deal with the others.

The fact that each of the ten processes of our development model has its own structural-cum-organizational equivalent is hardly surprising. It illustrates the fact that a person models organizations upon ideal images of the self. They are intended as large-scale replications of human functioning, into which persons fit according to particular divisions of labor. Just as a handle fits a hand, a pedal a foot, so do the various social structures contain means and instruments designed to guide, protect and enhance various aspects of the development process.

There are important reciprocal influences between the human processes in the left-hand column and the social structures into which they supposedly fit. Understanding these mutual influences is made no easier by the fact that the processes are often claimed by psychologists as their specialty, and the structures are claimed by sociologists as theirs, and each uses his own variables to explain the other's.

For every "left-hand" explanation there is dialectically opposite a "right-hand" one. For example, ghetto laborers are often "found" by psychologists to be lacking in motivation, in regular work habits, requisite job attitudes, etc.[4] But the structural explanation is that they behave in precisely the way the casual labor market uses them. Corporations require casual laborers, who are hired and fired at a moment's notice, and will be fired regardless of how well they work to avoid social security payments and other benefits, which have to be paid immediately following anything more than a few days' continuous employment.[5]

In Chapter 2 I proposed "a law of the stronger" in assigning responsibility for debilitating relationships. In this case, the casual laboring structure is clearly stronger and more determining than whatever human process the laborer can muster against it. A similar situation pertains to the poor client's relationship to the Welfare System. The system requires for its smoothest operation and maximum justifiability a "certified slob." Any hint of initiative from the client, the smallest sign of a social bond, raises the Awful Possibility that welfare services were never required in the first place and the bureaucratic noose immediately tightens to squeeze the life out of this possibility.

Hence the absence of ghetto institutions does *not* mean the absence of institutional forces pressing upon the poor. It means that the poor bear the impress of external structures which they had no hand in designing and over which they exercise no effective control.

An important innovation of the War on Poverty was the concept of reinstitutionalizing the ghettos and rural areas. Unfortunately, the plans were influenced by sociological believers in the determining nature of imposed social structures—of the right-hand column of Table 4. It was thought that Community Action agencies and Model Cities legislation, conceived in Washington by "absentee thinkers," could honeycomb the ghettos with opportunity structures, so that the poor could emancipate themselves within the interstices of federal guidelines.[6]

The basic conception was seriously flawed, not, as Moynihan argued, by heady idealism, but by *lack* of realizable ideals. What was attempted was an extension of the "empirical reality" of sociologically shaped persons. What was needed was the ideal possibility, and occasional reality, of persons creating, controlling and using institutional structures for their own development. For part of the process of psycho-social development is to learn how your structural and institutional tools feed back to influence your human processes. Certainly structure shapes process, but how and to what extent is best discovered when human processes can also control and experiment with different structures.

A group with the right and capacity to create its own structures will usually do so out of the experience of its own human processes. Hence there is a "developmental fit" between newly created structures and their human creators. The easiest way to insure law and order with authority and legitimacy is for persons to experience social structures as their own, genuine crystallizations and extensions of shared experience. Once rules, authorities and requirements are experienced as pointing in developmental directions, such rules are trusted, even if in the short run they appear to limit and circumscribe. The use of extensive violence by police against ghetto residents should not be confused with legitimate authority. Those who must constantly resort to force lack authority in the eyes of those so abused.[7] Social structures that truly guide development are willingly respected until such a time as the human processes outgrow them.

The problem for ghetto residents is that externally imposed structures, reinforced by police violence, are just about as destructive as the lawbreaking they are designed to combat. For white law and order not only upholds the absentee landlords, the usurious creditors and all manner of legal exploitation, it reaches a modus vivendi with organized crime and illegal exploiters.

For example, it has been estimated that $223 million was siphoned out of Central Harlem, the South Bronx and the Bedford-Stuyvesant areas by dope rings and the numbers syndicate during 1968. The gross income of one New York syndicate was equivalent to more than 80 per cent of all federal, state and city welfare funds poured into these poverty areas.[8] This is a massive hemorrhage of lifeblood out of a community.

The prime concern of a white-controlled police force is not to stem this bleeding, but to minimize outward disturbances which endanger the policemen personally and which publicize disorder.[9] Such a definition of their function requires at least tacit agreement with the siphoners, and often explicit corruption, for the "bleeders" would certainly shoot it out on a grand scale with anyone seriously threatening their multimillion-dollar operation.

Such examples can be multiplied indefinitely, and the result is to make the system of authoritative expectation in a ghetto at best confusing and at worst destructive. You see a black brother struggling with a policeman. Is he a small-time hoodlum, or a citizen humiliated beyond endurance? You think you see a break-in next door, so you call the police, and watch them rough up or even shoot another neighbor's teen-age sons. Are you a public-spirited resident, or a "pig caller," a friend or traitor to black people? It is really an unanswerable question, for the dilemma is a crucifying one. There is no solution for the unorganized citizen in such a situation, and homilies about individual morality are absurd. The only hope is to change the situation so that the dilemma is not imposed, and that requires the organized power to restructure.

In this particular case only a black-manned, black-controlled police force, truly representative of the neighborhood, could care enough about the millions of dollars sucked out of the neighborhood in exchange for addictive poisons, and about the thousands of predatory junkies thus produced. Organized depredations on this scale can only be fought by better-organized communities, with brothers and sisters willing to risk death in the attempt to cut the giant leeches off the face and body of their community. Who else except an organization of victims could conceivably command the necessary effort and sacrifice?

It is axiomatic that no police force can really be successful without the co-operation of the community and the information supplied by citizens, and such co-operation is only forthcoming where citizens respect the system of structures that police uphold. A structure illegitimate in the eyes of poor residents will twist social experience into ambivalent shapes. Those with money and influence in the community get it by collaboration with the leech-handlers.

It is not enough to require that a community "make plans" (structure II); it is also necessary to be sensitive to what a community PERCEIVES to be the problem (process 2). The instruction to "build consensus" (structure IX) has to take into account SYNERGISTIC desires (process 9), etc. If you order a community to arrive at a particular consensus with a stronger organization, then freedom, integrity and other human processes may have to be sacrificed to attain this, and the whole developmental cycle will become inflated and deteriorated into pathological and crucified fragments.

It should be the purpose of ghetto institutions to brace poor individuals against the forces inflating and deteriorating their human processes. The crucifixion dilemma can be avoided where the government's power is blunted, not by one man's COMPETENCE alone (process 4) but by the organizational status and position (structure 4) that braces this COMPETENCE. Yet if he is not to be a prisoner of the armor used to protect him, there has to be control by poor people themselves of their own structures.

The type of institutions and social structures which are best suited to ghetto and rural development are Community Development Corporations (CDC's). A group of their directors meeting in Albuquerque, New Mexico, defined CDC's as follows:

CDCs are permanent local institutions, owned and controlled by the local community, in and through which, the local community decides and determines its own destiny, which generates power for that community to control its own development utilizing economic power as the foundation and stepping stone from which to deal with a wider range of community concerns and needs including, but not limited to economic, social and political resources, power and stability.[10]

A more elaborate description is offered by the Center for Community Economic Development:

> A community corporation, or local community development corporation (CDC), is essentially a cooperative, set up in a neighborhood to run economic and social service programs for the community. Its main activity at the moment is operating business or profit-making ventures for the community. Some have set up factories or shopping centers. Others run maintenance services, gasoline stations or stores. Other community development corporations operate local services, as well as perform municipal services under contract from local government. The community development corporation can be set up by civic groups and churches, by a Model Cities Board or poverty program Community Action Agency, or by any group of individual residents of that community. It really merits the title of community development corporation, however, if any community member may join.
>
> Once it is established by law, it has the legal rights of any corporation, including the right of limited liability. Depending on the manner in which it is set up, and on its activities, a community development corporation may or may not be exempt from some taxes.[11]

Appendix A contains a necessarily incomplete list of CDC's by state—some of which are so small that they may no longer be with us by the time this is read. Appendix B takes selected CDC's and illustrates the range of their social and economic functions. The selection is a product of my knowledge and circle of friends and in no way represents a judgment on worthiness and relative significance. With the attempted destruction of the Office of Economic Opportunity, up-to-date knowledge is increasingly difficult to obtain. CDC's are lying so low that even their friends are unsure what they are doing.

The origin of the CDC movement is an instructive example of the capacity of the leaders of the poor to create their own models of development. Agencies like the Ford Foundation and the late Office of Economic Opportunity accepted the organizational and structural innovation created by poor communities themselves. The idea of CDC's arose in a reaction to the successes and failures of the civil rights movement.

> The successes of the movement in bringing about improvements in the legal status and privileges of blacks only put into high relief the basic economic deprivation that this group suffered. . . . The vast majority of black people, despite all the civil rights victories, still face an economic future that raises basic questions about the means and the processes (of struggle) that have cost blacks so much.[12]

The CDC, as an institution, "evolved as a reaction to the promise, the accomplishments and the disappointments of the central institution of the anti-poverty program, the Community Action Agency."[13] It was these agencies that were charged with the sociological mission of creating an infrastructure of opportunities and roles for community building at the neighborhood level, and of thus achieving the co-ordination at the grass roots, which various state and federal agencies had never achieved at the top. In fact, CAA's never represented poverty areas as such, but assumed the working out of a tripartite consensus between representatives of social agencies in the area, local government appointees and representatives of the poor community. At best, then, the poor had only a minority voice, and when they raised that voice to a pitch that distressed federal and local representatives, they quickly learned that he who pays the piper can muscle him into piping down. The glaring weakness in this situation was the absence of any independent source of funds. The poor were in the ironic situation of laying siege to their own paymasters.[14]

With Congress also breathing down the necks of foundations, wondering aloud whether their tax-free status had not already been jeopardized by support of civil rights activity, poor communities were everywhere reminded of their chronic financial dependence upon outside sources. The burgeoning Black Power philosophy required that black communities redefine themselves as an independent force, but where was an equally independent economic source to be found? At least one model was already available. In 1965 the East Central Citizens Organization of Columbus, Ohio, had set itself up on a "neighborhood government" model advocated by Milton Kotler.

So it was that the notions of community-generated economic activity seemed to occur almost simultaneously to at least half a dozen poor communities across the land. In 1967 the Hough Area Development Corporation in Cleveland officially incorporated itself and unveiled plans for the Martin Luther King Shopping Plaza. The following year Zion Investment Associates, a self-help group centered on Philadelphia's Zion Baptist Church, which had been growing since 1962, sprouted Progress Enterprises, Inc., and extended rights of ownership from church members into the entire neighborhood. The same year Shindana Toys sprang fully armed from the head of Operation Bootstrap in the Watts district of Los Angeles. About the same time Project Action in Venice, California, unveiled Action Industries, and Harlem Commonwealth Council, originally a research group, purchased Acme Foundry. In January 1968, the FIGHT organization of Rochester, New York, a veteran of bitter confrontations with Eastman Kodak, begat Fighton.[15]

Mention should also be made of the Bedford-Stuyvesant Restoration Corporation, the product of extensive negotiations between that Brooklyn community and the late Senator Robert F. Kennedy, and founded in 1967. This institution is unusual among CDC's, in that it owes much of its program to the initiative of outside persons. However, Kennedy's experience proved crucial, since it was he and his fellow New York senator, Jacob Javits, who co-sponsored the Special Impact Program, an amendment to OEO legislation, later that same year. It was this program that helped to fund some forty CDC's in the next few years, and inspired many more.[16]

A good idea of the community development "lobby" can be gained by looking at the aborted attempt to pass the Community Self-Determination act, introduced in the Senate in July 1968. Among the brains trust were Roy Innis and Floyd McKissick of CORE; Gar Alperowitz, a former staff aide to Senator Gaylord Nelson; and John Mc-Claughry, a Washington consultant. The bill was supported by a bipartisan coalition of thirty-three senators and thirty-six Republican members of the House. The support mirrored the fact that the CDC philosophy was borrowed from Left and Right, public and private sectors, and included Charles Percy, Gaylord Nelson, John Tower, Fred Harris, Charles Goodell, Jacob Javits and others.[17]

CDC leaders appear to have had, from the first, the clearest idea of the need for social structures and institutional roles in their communities. Franklin Florence, then president of FIGHT, explained this necessity to a group of senators at a Community Self-Determination Symposium in 1968:

> What we have to give our kids is an example of manhood. That is what we are giving them. . . . If they can say that black adults have stood up, fought racism, brought in self-determination, then we will have won . . . In the past that is what young kids roaming the streets have not had. They have always had to look for white heroes, and Uncle Tom blacks and Aunt Jemima blacks, because they have been without organization, but not in Rochester, a young guy can come up through the ranks and be Chairman of the Board. . . . He couldn't be that in any of your top businesses in this country, but now he can because he has black heroes that are standing up fighting for black power community organization and giving him an example of manhood. That is how you motivate them. That is the way you train them.[18]

And a few moments later Roy Innis of CORE and founder of the Harlem Commonwealth Council, extended the same argument.[19]

But it was almost as if the CDC had been discovered

after the War on Poverty had been declared lost. Actually Daniel Moynihan had sounded its doom over two years earlier; in his book, *Maximum Feasible Misunderstanding*, he wrote off as a failure the entire attempt to structure the ghetto, without even mentioning community economic development.[20] The media, scolded by Spiro Agnew for abetting dissent, had focused their attentions elsewhere. The Vietnam War had become an obsession, and students appeared to have decided that "the racism bag" was "last year's thing," and were off to fresh fields and postures new. One of the most promising and innovative institutional experiments in America's history unfolded in virtual silence, subsisting annually on an OEO budget of $35-40 million, about the cost of one day's bombing by B-52's of the Hanoi-Haiphong area of North Vietnam.

Ironically, the resilient infrastructure of the Vietcong and North Vietnamese was probably the prime cause of our frustration in Southeast Asia, while the lack of effective infrastructure in America's ghettos was the prime cause of failure in repeated efforts to war against poverty. In any event, the first important steps taken by America's poor in building such structures for themselves went virtually unnoticed.

Before we consider structure building in detail, a word needs to be said about the relationship of economic development to psycho-social development, for up to now I have dealt only with the latter. In *Radical Man* I showed that the productivity, creativity and morale of at least a dozen business organizations and work groups which had been researched,[21] were a part function of social learning and development upon the cycle model. Psycho-social development is a necessary but not a sufficient condition for economic development, because the latter requires specialized skills and techniques, in addition to communicative and social structuring capacities. Different technologies also call for different levels of social learning, which can vary from industry to industry and from level to level of the hierarchy. For example, the relative success of several different plastics companies operating in uncertain, innovative environments was found highly correlated with the degree of psycho-social development among their top and middle level managements. On the other hand, the financial and technical "success" of a Detroit automobile factory was found to require so *little* psycho-social development of low level factory workers as to be a danger to their mental health and stability.[22]

Complex though these relations are, we can safely say that most impoverished and oppressed groups do require intensive mutual interaction and "all-round" psycho-social development in order to build effective economic institutions, and, conversely, that such building is a process that develops its participants psycho-socially as well as economically. Running such economies, as opposed to creating them, could be less beneficial but would certainly involve many more "developmental opportunities" at far higher levels of organizing ability than the poor now enjoy, and the political and social goals of a CDC could prevent or reduce the "moronizing" influence of lower level factory work. Yet this problem is *not* solved merely by declaring popular sovereignty and community ownership. The problem is solved by a kind of psycho-social-cum-technological learning, which even the affluent part of this nation has not yet mastered. We have to learn what it is that technological "imperatives" do to social structure, and what such mandated structures then do to human relationships. When we know, we can choose or design technologies according to their known humanizing impacts. Yet this feedback loop, from technique, to structure, to human relationships, and back to altered technique is only possible when human relationships collectively control the other two variables. The CDC that legitimizes decentralized social ownership of economic means could be an invaluable "learning structure."

We shall now take a closer look at how each of the ten

cyclical human processes can be integrated with each of the ten organizational structures, and how CDC's are attempting to do this—and substantially succeeding in a number of cases.

PROCESS 1   *Free EXISTENCE*
STRUCTURE 1   *Generation of surplus value*

The dilemma for any underdeveloped community or nation which is being "developed" by a powerful neighbor is how to protect its capacity to EX-IST and originate values. Routinely the dominant "helper" will attempt to transfer technological power, without requisite social or political power. He will give nothing that endangers the client status of the recipient. But even where technology is transferred "without strings," the tools themselves will still alter, as if by fiat, the social sinews onto which they are grafted. There will still be "white ghosts" in the machinery.[23]

Often the dominant "helper" will see "traditional" values as impediments to the modernization process, rather than vital yet fragile skeins of social continuity. Take an "obviously" anti-developmental norm—the idea that persons should not desire too much wealth or too many worldly possessions, since these are foredoomed to frustration. In fact, such a value may be a thread by which the sanity of a poor community hangs. Given the danger of expectation outrunning productivity, only a preference for human bonds over material gain may stand between a community and an epidemic of corruption[24] or a Gadarene rush to sell out one's own community to the Man.

It is absurd to think that any poor community, surrounded by affluence, can be developed through the desire of its members for "outside" money and techniques. Such desires could only disintegrate the community through centrifugal forces, ensuring that any member at any time could be auctioned off to the highest foreign bidder. The desire to "get to the top," regarded by Americans as a sine qua non of development, is of dubious value to the poor, when the "top" is alien. It may be true that "achievement motivation" is a universal norm of development, but it begs the question, for who defines what achievement shall be?[25] Without a strong social base that (a) defines achievement in native terms, and (b) makes sure that achievements accrue to the benefit of the poor community/nation, there may be only those "achievements" that benefit Swiss bankers. The Saigon street urchins who would follow American GI's shouting, "You want my sister, soldier? She number one fuck," were presumably "achievers," and exponents of a very private enterprise, but their activities serviced Americans and did not accrue to the benefit of Vietnamese social life and cultural standards.

What makes a Community Development Corporation a useful vehicle for development is that it combines a community-wide value base with an economic structure of advancement and mobility, grounded in that community's power of definition. Bernard Gifford, until recently the executive director of the National Congress for Community Economic Development, expressed this idea:

> It is incredible that anyone, today, would suggest to a group such as ours that we approach the white man on grounds that we're going to be just like them and make our world more perfect by fitting into their mould. If that's all it's about, then forget it . . .[26]

Gifford went on to warn his fellow directors against being even temporarily false to their own values and "bowing to the system until you get what you want."[27]

The kind of structure created through CDC's—lacking in virtually every other kind of poverty-fighting organization —is one that creates surplus value. The original meaning of surplus value comes from Adam Smith and was later used by Marx. It refers to that proportion of economic value, generated by productive activity, which is over and above the proportion necessary to maintain human and technical organization. The implication of generating surplus value is that the neighborhood organization and its members experience themselves as the origins of wealth and value.

But a CDC greatly expands the definition of value beyond the economic realm to include social, political and institutional innovation, of which the CDC is itself an example. In a country glutted with products, it is necessary to represent and originate more than a deluge of plastic bottle caps and eyelash combs. Just as Andrew Carnegie's steel mills were a social as well as economic innovation, so in a city reeking with pollution and decay, a kind of human innovation is needed that does not merely add to the debris.

It is within reach of CDC's to be an origin of wealth and products imbedded in the context of innovative social ideas and political solutions. For so long as the poor receive only redistributed tax dollars, these mean amounts will be relinquished with ill grace and condescension by persons convinced that what they generate is "theirs" and that everyone else, from professor to garbage man, is a "burden" upon the bottle cappers and hard-working eyelash combers of this land.

There is, then, a chance for CDC's to be *radical,* in the best and existential meaning of that word; that is, they can go to the *roots* of value creation and alter the basic reason for productive work. To build enterprises for the collective emancipation of poor people could return to work the meaning and value it once had. Production that has a social purpose beyond itself, and beyond mere consumption, could do much to transform America's social and cultural climate. In origination lies emancipation—and a shortcut to power. For all the victims of our society have at least one potentially valuable piece of expertise—they know the system's failures, from underneath, where the fissures are obvious and the oppressions crude and undisguised by gentility. In motivation and awareness they have a head start in devising remedies.

It will be "A Long Revolution" in the view of Gar Alperowitz, yet with internally generated funds, collectively owned and controlled, a large number of valuable experiments in human living could be conducted through neighborhood corporations across the land.[28]

The beginning of such a process has been made, for example, by the Southwest Virginia Community Development Fund in Roanoke, Virginia. With the help of a consultant, Stuart Lichtman, extensive surveys and interviews have been conducted with citizens, together with public meetings, in order to discover their preferences as to the kind of jobs, distance traveled, optimal size, location and general significance of various productive enterprises.[29] The idea is to help productivity grow out of shared neighborhood values. There have been CDC experiments in the common ownership of productive tools, and with enterprises specifically aimed at integrating the community. For example, several CDC's have placed retail facilities strategically near the center of the community, to draw people together. Three are pursuing cable TV franchises, on the grounds that they have something vital to say and wish to own a powerful and revenue-producing means of saying it.[30]

PROCESS 2   *The quality of PERCEPTION*
STRUCTURE II   *Plans and Objectives designed by and for the community*

In Chapter 3 we encountered the notion of paradigm—the basic perceptual and conceptual assumptions that lie behind a profession's world view, and which it translates into "game plans" for engaging the government, schools and private sources of influence and funds. We saw that the poor become fixed like objects in the gaze of professionals, that they are less talked *to*, than argued *about* between different parties.

Strategically the poor serve as the most easily manipulable "no-fail" element in the paradigm of "Helpers." If they respond as predicted to the inputs of professional reformers, they are science fodder and empirical "building blocks" for a new theory. If they do not respond as predicted, an Appalling Crisis is announced, with Pathologies-and-Deficiencies-far-more-Severe-than-Previously-Known —all of which is assiduously publicized.

The presence of anomalies and contradictions within professional paradigms, so far from leading to their abandonment, will, in the short run anyway, merely escalate the fury and scope of "mopping up operations."[31] Soon the ghetto Target Area will bristle with the arrows of outrageous fortune, computer-guided, data-banked, linear-programmed, factor-analyzed in the same whiz-kid pentagonese that has mystified the public about defense spending.

If it puzzles congressional watchdogs, one can but guess what it does to the poor upon whom such "concentrations" are loosed. Increasingly the poor will encounter those drawn into the fray by the maxim "There's money in poverty," a state of mind not unconnected with the existence of poverty and exploitation in the first place. The failing paradigms will attempt to make up with hustle and scientism what they lack in humanity and realism, with the result that the poor are pushed off balance, seen rather than seeing, planned *for*, rather than planning, and acted *upon*, rather than acting. The purported remedy intensifies the alleged pathology.

The answer is for the organized poor to have paradigms of their own—that is, consistent and coherent ways of perceiving contradictions and articulating plans to resolve them. The role of helpers, if any, is to empower these plans. The poor must have institutions, and a CDC with its multiple objectives or a neighborhood conglomerate, are two possibilities.

Take, for example, the $223 million leeched out of New York's poverty areas by gambling and drug syndicates. The traditional approach is to label this "a medical problem" (if you are liberal), "a police problem" (if you are conservative), or a moral/social/economic problem depending upon what technique you happen to be touting.

The typical response of federal and state governments is a methadone clinic here, a sponsored black capitalist there, and a neighborhood counseling center to discuss them both. Such are mere palliatives. The only real chance is for the community to marshal and deploy a synthesis of forces designed to out-organize and defeat the leech-handlers. For example, a community-controlled police force is necessary, but *not* sufficient. Since effective police depend upon the co-operation of citizens, there must be political and social organizations to achieve this. As long as people want to gamble, the community must have a lottery, or the Syndicate will have the support of all those craving a little excitement in their lives. Unless the community also controls a methadone maintenance program, its own addicted pushers cannot break the puppet strings. Since local collaborators with the Syndicate are hirelings, the community must have the resources to hire them back or somehow sustain them. If addiction and compulsive gambling are the products of alienation and anomie, the CDC must create a new solidarity around more meaningful activities. It must create symbols of community respect other than money alone, because those who exploit the community can, for the foreseeable future, outbid those who struggle to sustain it. We have come a long way from the crude polarization of the liberal's medical problem v. the conservative's police problem, or other variations upon "they're sick v. they're sinning."

I argued in Chapter 2 that a ghetto mental health clinic would seldom join with a job referral storefront to expose the mentally debilitating nature of available job openings, partly because HEW would not wish to entangle itself with the Department of Labor. But even in the unlikely event that the respective agencies did not object, the two grantees have reasons for being reluctant to co-operate with each other. Poor communities are typically dotted with small groups, each representing the isolated function of their grantor, rather than any real community concern. CDC leaders have called such groups and their leaders, the "ad hoc hustlers" and the "racial racketeers."[32]

As long as these functional groups continue to disseminate "drug information" and "job counseling," no one can hold them responsible for mounting addiction and chronic unemployment. They have distributed x pieces of literature and have made y number of referrals, and if problems deepen, it makes a better case for refunding. Who can deny liberal Compassion when there is such desperate Need? The danger for *functional* groups in joining in a planned community *project* group with realizable goals, is that they and it *could* be held responsible, as could their federal sponsors, and that upsets the entire "no-fail" strategy and the dream of General Sickness requiring Ever Expanding Function.

For what CDC's can do—and the various ganglia of federal agencies reaching into the ghetto cannot do—is set up project and venture groups with specific co-ordinated strategies for tackling interlocking problems. Project teams made up of those with the expertise relevant to the particular problem could discover, for example, what methods are needed to keep down absenteeism and turnover in community-owned plants. Such a group is even free to discover that absenteeism, in this instance, is unconnected to the monotony of the job, but is a problem of inadequate day care facilities and poor transportation. A group funded specifically by the National Institutes for Mental Health would never make such a discovery but would proceed to spread its universal unguent on frustrated mothers and commuters all.

The advantage for communities of defining for themselves the goals to which they will drive is that this process generates the motivation, which is often missing in the task of measuring up to someone else's yardstick. The desire to complete high school, to take job training, etc., only assumes importance in the presence of at least one of two conditions. Either the technique to be learned must be clearly envisaged as a means towards an end desired by the learner, or, and this is the usual case, the learner must trust in those authorities who teach him, that if he struggles to master some seemingly abstract scheme, far from his daily experience, then the benefit to him and those close to him will subsequently become clear.

In a powerless, planless community, without rights of definition, the relevance is not clear, nor can trust in authorities be justified by later rewards.[33] It is interesting to note that "Negro IQ" has been found to lag behind white IQ in just this area of abstract reasoning. The various apostles of black inferiority have seized upon this in triumph as illustrating that "culture-free" tests show more inferiority than "culture-full."[34] But abstract thinking is exactly the kind requiring sufficient trust in one's mentors to climb the abstraction ladder away from familiar sounds and signs. The alienated and the exploited would obviously find this harder, and justifiably so, for what are the chances that a black computer programmer in an IBM training school will be working on a program that accrues to the benefit of his race? Those who study abstract systems place themselves in the power of those policy organizations that utilize the techniques. Without a CDC prepared to do sophisticated planning, why should a poor resident master abstractions?

Consider this verse written and sung among poor whites in Appalachia:

> I don't mind failing in this world . . .
>> Don't mind wearing ragged britches,
>> 'cause those who succeed are the sons of bitches.
> I don't mind failing in this world . . .
>> I'll stay down here with the raggety crew,
>> 'cause getting up there means stepping on you.

> I don't mind failing in this world . . .
>> Somebody else's definition
>> Isn't going to measure my soul's condition.
> I don't mind failing in this world . . .
>> Some people ride in a car so fine,
>> While others walk on a picket line . . .[35]

Conventional analyses of this state of mind might include "the culture of poverty thesis"[36] or "the stereotype of soul"[37] or "affiliation motivation overcoming achievement motivation"[38] or "the presence of work restriction norms"[39] or the "lower class life style,"[40] each of which treats the co-operative ideals expressed as some kind of individual misfortune. Alternatively, we can say that the singer redefines achievement and virtue as a collective emancipation from poverty, rather than an individual and opportunistic escape. Unable to institutionalize her definition, she despairs of matching her "soul's condition" to any existing, institutional yardsticks. Her problem would be resolved by collective planning that synthesizes affiliation with achievement and ensures that abstract learnings lead directly back to a community's warmth and support.

PROCESS 3   *The strength of IDENTITY*
STRUCTURE III   *A high quality role structure, with rootedness and mobility*

When Alvin Poussaint, the well-known black psychiatrist, tangled with a Mississippi policeman ("Hey, boy! Come here!"), he identified himself *as a physician*, while protesting that he was no boy. But the policeman persisted:

> "Alvin, the next time I call you, you come right away, you hear? You hear?" I hesitated. "You hear me, boy?" My voice trembling with helplessness, but following my instincts of self-preservation, I murmured, "Yes, sir."[41]

The role of physician is clearly not enough to stave off such rabid bigotry without an institution to back him up and uphold the dignity of his role. The Black Panthers gained early recruits by following arrestees to the station house and bailing them out. The Citizens Committee of East San Jose has a community patrol car that monitors and films police patrols. If occupational roles like doctor or psychiatrist are not enough to stave off verbal and physical assault, then each role must be protected by a network of legal, political and investigatory roles that provide mutual protection. Once again a CDC is uniquely designed to make this possible, with legal service branches and other resources to back them up.

But CDC role structures are far more than protective in function. They permit poor people to fill positions of skill, variety, mobility and importance, roles which stand in marked contrast to those of "welfare recipient," "dependent child," "problem family," "hard-core jobless," and "high-risk, target area resident." Psychiatrists sometimes refer to "negative identity,"[42] which is a learned version of the old adage "Give a dog a bad name and you might as well hang him." The evidence, from witch trials to the modern day, is that many oppressed people prefer a distinctive pathology to the alternatives of invisibility and non-existence. A modern welfare state is an avalanche of such opprobrious labels.

Although the War on Poverty tried hard to create new roles for the poor, the positions were considerably less imposing than a first glance might suggest. The vast majority of jobs were deadend ones. Worse, there was not even lateral mobility between programs, so that, for example, a Headstart citizen co-ordinator was stuck in one program in one city.[43] Since the roles were created by extra-community fiat and the composition of boards was federally regulated, the role occupants became helpless dependents upon federal guidelines and largesse, owing their continued existence to absentee and inscrutable authorities. Their neighbors generally saw them as "having joined the Establishment" and they were not infrequently observed to "become harsh, punitive and authoritarian in their treatment of poor people."[44] As minor officials without security or mobility, such symptoms are hardly surprising.

A CDC can offer an "industrial model" with highly flexible structures depending on the situation. In contrast, the "professional model" weighs you down with sickness paradigms, with certified, registered ways of being dead wrong, and with prohibitions against "amateurs" and cross-professional syntheses.[45] The industrial model combined with an organized cultural and political base provides roles for president, directors, board members, staff, helpers, brothers, organizers, block leaders, workers and a host of social functions. All such roles could be attained by poor persons in a relatively short time, and there is considerable lateral and upward mobility within and between CDC's and their co-ordinating center, the National Congress for Community Economic Development, in Washington.

In Chapter 1, two aspects of IDENTITY were distinguished, the rooted part connecting ethnicity to self-acceptance, and the changeable parts which dare to experiment with new selves, without losing the thread of continuity. Like many other polarized concepts in our schizoid culture, ethnic identification has come to be regarded as no better than an ethnocentricity resisting all change and suspicions of outsiders.

A *living* ethnicity with cultural distinctiveness is described in *Urban Blues* by black anthropologist Charles Keil.[46] The book revolves around the black concept of "Soul." This connotes:

> Strong emotions and feelings especially when shared with others; something pure, non-machined; staying power and wisdom through suffering; telling it like it is, being what you are, and believing in what you do. The concept denotes further a tight intermingling of sex, love, and reciprocal responsiveness which constitute the pattern of Negro Dionysianism, manifest in the swing of the blues-jazz-gospel musical

milieu and in the brilliant, moving linguistic innovations which spring from it. The pattern emphasizes the erotic, the frenetic and the ecstatic—a pattern which when made ideological constitutes a claim to emotional depth and authenticity.[47]

Not inconsiderable virtues one might think—and a potential powerhouse for cultural development. A soul of this quality maintained in the face of centuries-old oppression should be prized; roles should be found for its expressions and dissemination. Yet Bennett Berger, a white sociologist, has no sooner quoted the earthy passage above than he seems seized with concern lest its erotic penumbra and seductive intimacy lead him to some fresh conception, so he hastily reaches for the douche bag. The idea of soul, he insists, "is a stereotype" and "as an attribute of race, it is nonsense." Whatever its flavor of Africa, the rural South and evangelical Christianity, "it is mostly lower class."

> The soul ideology does not suit that probably enormous number of Negroes that would gladly trade a piece of their abundant emotionality for a piece of American affluence and who care less about having an "authentic" and "worthwhile" culture than about having a good job and a house in the suburbs. . . .[48]

The idea of soul is thus shrunk by the Reductionist Fallacy to "lower class." In addition, the physicalism of research combines with the materialism of the dominant society to give substance to "a house in the suburbs" and to deny substance to authenticity and abundant emotionality. The author of *Urban Blues*, Berger insists, "is misled . . . by . . . a need to affirm his solidarity with black people."[49]

It is hard to see why blacks must swap their souls for suburbia, when blues, jazz and other derivatives of black culture are so profitable to the corporations that record and distribute black music and other arts. The expressions of black soul can be regarded as a major American contribution to world cultural forms (Harold Cruse would say, America's only original contribution). Nor, according to available research, is soul ideology strong among mainly lower-class blacks. Rather it is the cutting edge of a newly mobile and assertive black leadership and finds its expression in Black Studies programs.[50]

Insofar as the urban blues idioms *are* a response to oppression, with compensatory features, white society provokes the wailing, and then records and sells the wails. If the Sounds of Racism are best sellers, at least the profits should accrue to the victims, and it is the CDC, with its cultural, community and business components, that can help to assure this. Should black collective advancement ever become contingent upon the popularity of erotic and exotic forms of communality—and there are certainly trends in this direction—then what they have to give WASP "culture" could be nectar to thirsty nomads in a desert.

Where a profession or industry is strongly linked to ethnic consciousness, as psychiatry is to the Jewish experience, and as blues are to black experience, then such professions become avenues for the collective upward mobility of ethnic recruits. The chief hope of society's victims is to turn their experience of victimization into a redefinition of the socially desirable. If you feel blue, organize blues singers and sing for all blue people everywhere. If you have been a drug addict for ten years, do not expect this society's institutional categories to make an individual exception for you—that would undermine the function of categories. Rather, organize your own categories of ex-drug addicts who can help addicts because they have been through the experience and come out of it.

More than a few CDC's are organized to give cultural self-expression to their communities via films, arts, murals, publications and educational materials, as well as healing services.[51] Origination, art, community building and striking at America's weak spots to supply the missing elements —all are parts of the CDC strategy. For when we look at what America does magnificently and what she does badly, there is a consistent theme. America represents the triumph and failure of bureaucratic technique as an instrument of policy. The production and distribution of material goods, space flights, precision bombing, etc.—in all this the capacity of bureaucratic means is unlimited. Yet bureaucracy is counter-productive in solving many other problems: criminality, addiction, prejudice, war, imperialism, mental "illness," poverty and discrimination. Bureaucratic techniques have failed entirely to solve them, whether applied directly or used as a delivery system. Even worse is the fact that the problems are themselves seen as the *products* of technocratic structure. And there is a failure of human love, companionship and cooperation. In the relatively rare exceptions, significant human relationships have always been salient—often accidentally.[52]

What detached technique only exacerbates, a cohesive, co-operative community can accomplish. None of this is to decry technique in its proper context, and that context is as a tool of communal purpose, as a conduit for the expression of soul.

PROCESS 4   *The experience of COMPETENCE*
STRUCTURE IV   *The ascription of status, and the signaling of recognition*
There are three ways in which CDC's contribute towards the building of COMPETENCE. They organize "inside" viewpoints. They make possible a synthesis of competences, and they permit compensatory strengths wherever a community may be particularly vulnerable.

It is essential for any group that has been left behind in the scramble for power and wealth to view its progress and achievements from "inside" the community, relative to earlier conditions, and compared with dire alternatives. Dunkirk was a "victory" for the British from this angle, whereas detached observers might have regarded it as a bare-assed and ignominious exit. Who are more heroic, a group of residents who have battled with rats, garbage and oppressive authorities, or a group of affluent speculators who have turned some extra millions? Most national indices would favor the latter. Only a community that knew siege conditions at first hand and the human costs of resistance could adequately appreciate and rank the courage needed to survive.

But COMPETENCE viewed from the community's own standpoint must still register upon external environments and to do this it must be a synthesis. . . .

> Work, culture, liberty—all these we need, not singly but together, not successively but together, each growing and aiding each, all struggling towards that vaster ideal . . . the ideal of human brotherhood.[53]

Such limited gains as have been made by Black Americans derive from movements that have synthesized different COMPETENCES and provided climates of recognition for these abilities. Thus Martin Luther King joined his own persuasive and moral COMPETENCE to the power of the mass media, to the legal COMPETENCE of the NAACP, to the legislative power of an unusually liberal Congress (following the Goldwater debacle), to the social cohesion and infrastructure of black southern church members, and to the economic power of boycotts. He was especially brilliant in the way he took the familiar language of evangelical Christianity and transformed it into socio-political implications, giving his followers rootedness, continuity and change simultaneously.

King's movement began to flounder only when the synthesis broke up. Congress moved to the right after the 1966 midterm elections. Demonstrations palled as media entertainment. As civil rights campaigns moved away from their disciplined social base in southern churches, coherence was lost. But above all, the non-violent "witness" style of protest was suited to *dominative* racism, southern style, but not to the more hypocritical *aversive* racism of the North. In the North non-relationship posed as relationship; blacks had to grapple not with hot-blooded sheriff's deputies, but with the cold, clinical detachment of organizational machinery deliberately used to impede its "clients." Now *blacks* lost their tempers with their remote controllers—and the latter responded with Pained Expressions and Cerebral Calm. The game of One-Upmanship had been reversed.

But even at the height of its effectiveness, the civil rights movement lacked substantial economic components and hence the ability to turn the symbolic triumphs of the movement into solid, lasting economic gains. Nor were there the necessary institutions to assemble and hold fast the components of a developmental synthesis. It was closer to a one-man balancing act, and it suffered grievously through the assassination of that one man.

It is arguable that CDC's do more than provide the "missing" economic ingredient to the black movement; they give to black culture a compensatory economic emphasis. For among the problems faced by blacks in striving for economic development is the relatively low status of the businessman in black culture, as compared with the preacher, entertainer, sportsman or politician. While black preaching and playing equals that of whites in skill, black business has been relatively puny. From Booker T. Washington's accommodationism, to Madam Walker's straightening combs and whitening creams (for years the mainstay of black retailers), to the black Chicago numbers syndicate of the thirties (to which much black business was in debt), black business has singularly failed to inspire the loyalty of black customers.[54]

Whatever hope there is for an ethnic market depends

on the social and moral authority that CDC's or an equivalent local agency can wield in the communities concerned. There are recent reports that the Federation of Southern Cooperatives in Georgia is seeking to supply thirty thousand families in Newark and Harlem that have formed into consumer clubs.[55] The success of such ventures must depend heavily upon the quality of social trust and community organizing, without which black business is scorned by its own customers.

There are many additional reasons why in a CDC conglomerate, synthesizing competences is crucial. Ghetto districts receive nothing like their share of state and municipal tax dollars. Any enterprise locating there must fight a dozen civic battles against poor services, bad roads, unjust tax assessment, poor transportation, urban renewal and the "ghost ownership" of ghetto real estate. (Finding the person responsible for a crumbling, dangerous building is like groping into an infinite recess.)

Several CDC's have bid successfully for municipal contracts. The greatest advantage of collecting one's own garbage, for example, is that one receives a share of the total city service budget, based on population, which ends the gross discrimination against poor districts in the discharge of various services. Large parts of San Francisco are immaculately clean, due in large part to "the Scavengers," a member-owned and communally run garbage disposal service.[56]

Political muscle is required for poor communities even to hold their own. The very geographical integrity of poor neighborhoods is interrupted by highways into small slivers separated by bands of noise and fumes. A case history of one successful effort by the "Highwaymen's Lobby" to abort a law which would have given neighborhoods the right to appeal to Washington against the bulldozers, listed the following lineup against the neighborhoods: civil engineers, construction companies, road machinery manufacturers, oil and gas companies, auto industries, the steel industry, tire manufacturers, trucking groups, wrecking companies, motel and hotel operators, departments of public works and chambers of commerce.[57] Several CDC's owe their origins to sit-downs before bulldozers—notable among these are FIGHT, the Lower Roxbury Community Corporation and the New Area Association in Newark, New Jersey.[58]

Another area in which the residents of poor communities suffer major handicaps is in their status as consumers. There is evidence that the poor pay more, that prices rise on the day that welfare checks are received, that loan sharking is rife, sales techniques ruthless, credit terms usurious and methods of collection draconian.[59]

Although white legal advocates have sprung to the defense of many isolated and more shocking cases of poor persons victimized by shyster tactics, such ad hoc battles are won in the context of a losing war. For ghetto merchants are all that the poor have and an end to usurious credit and loan sharking means an end to all credit and loans. Ghetto merchants will merely leave. I have visited ghetto agencies where the staff had to drive two miles for a sandwich and three miles for an aspirin. Dueling with individual merchants will only substitute aversive racism for dominative racism. For there *is* a measure of social exchange between the poor and their suppliers. The poor offer their docility and gullibility as a substitute for what they lack in buying power. Punishing the exploiter is not going to create a non-exploitive relationship, but no relationship at all. If the merchant is prepared to argue with middle-class legal advocates, then he will want to sell to that class as well; if not, he'll just go out of business.

What, then, *could* poor people offer, except exploitability, that would make a relationship with them worthwhile? One answer is organization and cohesion. Poor residents need to replace the reliability inherent in subordination with the reliability inherent in organization. A supplier relating to a consumer club of, say, two hundred families, confronts an equal in power, a legal entity and a regular, efficient contractual arrangement on which he can rely and which will keep him up to the mark. Poor families still have to pay their bills, but the urging of friends and neighbors, the need to remain in an association that provides substantial economies, and the felt obligation to those one meets daily—all of these replace the slashed tires, mashed toes, garnished welfare checks and similar crudities.

Very important also is the creation of an internal price structure, made possible by organized purchase, some reduction in variety and better buying intelligence. One oppressive feature of mass society is the nationwide pricing policies aimed at what "the market can bear," but what the poor cannot. Time was when poor districts in major cities had price structures of their own, responsive to the means of their residents. But with modern marketing, the "aggregate consumer" is the target and those below this ever rising mark are in very serious trouble.

Consider automobile purchase and maintenance. Spare parts distributed by local monopoly dealers are marked up some 100 per cent, partly because those whose cars are broken down are in a weak and often desperate bargaining position, partly because the high expense of maintaining an aging car drives people into buying new ones. What the middle-class car owner experiences as annoying cross-pressures is quite catastrophic and crucifying for the poor, who are literally forced off the road and out of jobs by mounting repair costs. Since public transportation is especially bad in poor neighborhoods, the loss of one's car can cut mobility more than 90 per cent. One's job record is then as reliable as an eight-year-old car.

The West Side Planning Organization, a rural CDC near Fresno, California, canvassed its Chicano residents and found that, above all, they needed an automobile center. Until it began operation almost no Chicano farm workers had been able to maintain a car. With group insurance and their own garage, most are now mobile and there is an internal price structure maintained by collective dealings with the outside (one does not *have* to mark up spare parts 100 per cent).[60]

Compare the CDC's capacity to strengthen the individual's status in several salient aspects of his life, and in proportion to local preference, with the teaching of unilinear skills by many different federal programs (now mostly cut back). Examples of the latter include a "Headstart" for your child, which fades with her return to ghetto schools; Job Corps training for your son at a camp a thousand miles away, where he is trained for a job he cannot practice in his own community; on-the-job training for you, *if* you had the transportation to get there, *if* you didn't have to take the baby to the hospital for an all-day wait, and if the collection agency's goon was not waiting for you outside, demanding the fifth installment on the car you had to scrap last year.

A good example of the strategic deployment by a CDC of institutions, for the purpose of raising the all-round status and competence of residents comes from the Watts Labor Community Action Committee, in Los Angeles. After an extensive analysis of existing needs and skills in its area, WLCAC created a vegetable, fruit and flower farm in vacant lots beneath the city's high-tension power lines, a poultry and egg packing farm, two auto service stations, one auto repair center with training facilities and a chain of supermarkets with local price structures. They run a Community Conservation Corps which has started a tutorial center, ceramic plant and showrooms and numerous vocational, recreational, and educational activities. Twenty vest-pocket parks have been opened and maintained, a federal credit union, a consumer action project and a community bus service.[61] During the recent panic over the rising price of beef, WLCAC community market was selling cuts from its own herd at 20 per cent below market price.

PROCESS 5   *COMMITMENT, authentic and intense*
STRUCTURE v   *Emotionally significant opportunity structures and required interactions*

A poster during the 1968 student worker rebellion in
Paris read:

> *Je participe*
> *Tu participes*
> *Il participe*
> *Nous participons*
> *Vous participez*
> *Ils profitent*[62]

This raises the serious question as to whether forms
of participation short of a share in economic ownership
and the creation of surplus value is much more than a
shell game. What the owner of capital says to the worker,
in effect, is, "Here is some money, my ownership, all I
want in exchange is your working life." The worker is
not only structurally subordinate to the owner of capital,
but his *presence* or "participation" is subordinate to the
owner's *absence*. The fact that a manager, the owner's
agent, has read *On Becoming a Person,* has attended the
National Training Laboratories, and has learned "how to
understand the worker from his own point of view" and
"respond warmly" to his suggestions, may only be cushion-
ing an exploitive relationship.

This is not because the principle of CONFIRMATION of
another's COMMITMENT is unimportant, but because until
such processes are given legal and structural form, their
expression may only disguise the true purpose of the structure. Where a structurally dominant person "listens sin-
cerely and allows participation" beyond any legal obligation or structural necessity to do so, he may be substituting
his "volunteerism" for what poor people should receive as
a right. He comes over as a "democratic manager" de-
serving gratitude and loyalty in exchange for what he has
"given." But a change in structure and ownership alters

the entire psychological context so that any equality characterizing relationships is not a gift descending from above (to be rescinded if it fails to contribute to morale and productivity) but a mutual obligation to commit oneself to a common enterprise.

The difference between "participation" in an opportunity structure controlled by someone else and controlling the structure in which one participates was illustrated in the famous confrontation between FIGHT and the Eastman Kodak Company in Rochester, New York. A conference of CDC's was told how it happened:

> We had signed an agreement on December 20th, 1966, wherein FIGHT and Kodak agreed that FIGHT would recruit between 500 and 600 hard-core unemployed people [for on-the-job training and employment by Kodak]. On December 21st, the presidents of Proctor and Gamble, duPont, Lever Bros., and a number of others flew into Rochester and met that night. On December 22nd, two days after the agreement was signed, Kodak hanged one of its own vice presidents, saying he had no authority to sign such an agreement. They had opened Pandora's Box in dealing with the community. We had bypassed the Community Chest and Urban League and all those other institutional forms where we have to deal with these companies on our stomachs instead of our feet. All of a sudden they recognized that we had established a "dangerous precedent . . ."[63]

What had happened, of course, is that FIGHT had nearly gained control of a piece of Kodak's structure, its hiring and employment functions. Kodak was willing and had already pledged to hire 600 hard-core community residents. The "participation" of individual black workers in Kodak's structure, on Kodak's terms, in Kodak's good time, was perfectly acceptable. But FIGHT's control of even a part of Kodak's structure was not to be tolerated. The idea that a profit-making corporation had any legal obligation and should undergo structural modification to make it responsive to poor people was indeed a precedent.

Such an arrangement would have permitted the employed workers to thank their *own* leaders and their *own* organization for their employment opportunity. They would have ceased to be the aggregate individuals which Kodak wanted and might have become a cohesive group. Kodak explained that it could not "discriminate" in favor of certain groups of poor people at the expense of the unorganized—an interesting example of how organized power keeps individuals "fairly" and "equally" powerless.[64]

The story illustrates how futile is COMMITMENT in an opportunity structure not controlled by the participants. It shows how campaigns to enroll the poor in factory jobs or to fill vacancies on poverty boards whose structures are mandated elsewhere have little practical meaning for the "fillers."

Sherry Arnstein has constructed a "participation ladder" to try to distinguish between different meanings of the word, and has arranged these meanings in a rough order of the degrees of genuine COMMITMENT within a structure controllable by the actor. The ladder (see Table 5) leads from Manipulation at level 1 to Citizen Control at level 8. We can see from Ms. Arnstein's own examples that the kind of participation allowed under Urban Renewal and Model Cities legislation falls considerably below that which is possible with CDC's.

For example, below level 3 the citizen is regarded as not remotely COMPETENT—in fact, he is being exercised like a cripple for therapeutic purposes. Below level 5 he has no rights of issue definition or EXISTENCE-PERCEPTION. Below level 6 he has no control over whose IDENTITY will represent his own and his community's viewpoint. Only at level 7 does he begin to get a grip on some part of the structure (the point at which Kodak kicked), and even then the powers ceded to citizens can be withdrawn (a day later!). Only at level 8 do citizens participate in *creating the opportunity structure itself,* and hence gain some control over the social reality of their neighborhoods.

An important feature of CDC's is that they teach the arts of democracy at the grass-roots level. One model permits all resident shareholders of a designated area to *one* vote upon the purchase of their first share. Subsequent shares may be purchased but do not confer additional voting rights. However, there have been legal difficulties with this arrangement, and the failure of the Community Self-Determination bill to be reported out of committee has not helped matters.[65] Essentially the CDC's greatest potential strength, that it is partly a corporation and partly a political and social organization, has mired it in the conflicting regulations applying to the different areas.

A more common arrangement is to give all existing voluntary organizations within the CDC's designated area the right to appoint delegates either directly to a board of directors, or to a voting body which then elects the board. For example, FIGHT delegates power from the total cross section of Rochester's black community, from the Black Panthers to black fraternity groups. Delegates constitute 5 per cent of all the area's residents, and represent some 50 per cent, that is, virtually all local residents who are also members of voluntary associations.[66]

In this way CDC's join together ghetto organizations of whatever original purpose, and invite them to deal with the economic, social and political realities facing the community. While the CDC is enabled to draw upon an entire range of organized talent, the various groups have participatory rights in the CDC.

Such networks sometimes use money like impulses in neural pathways. The Woodlawn Organization in Chicago is one instance. TWO acts as the hub to dozens of black clubs and voluntary organizations, which pay it fees in exchange for the programs it initiates and the co-ordination and information services it provides. Stopped or reduced payments denote dissatisfaction and act as a signaling system for the decentralized social network that links the community.[67]

CHAPTER 5

Community Development Corporations:
Their Promise and Insufficiencies

The major innovations in the economy tend to come, as was demonstrated by Schumpeter long ago, through emergence of entirely new businesses based on some new invention, new technology, or new market. But this points to a far more general pattern: In any social situation nonincremental innovation tends to come from outside the established system or pattern of relationships. . . . The alienated observer must turn to some reality and some theoretical model other than the (existing) group process, if he is to have a prayer of finding a way out of the very bondage of that group process.

Theodore J. Lowi, *The Politics of Disorder*

In this chapter we shall deal with the remaining human processes, 6 to 10, and their corresponding organizational structures. These are:

Human Processes Development of men's capacities for . . .	Organizational Structures Require organizations that . . .	
6. SUSPENSION and RISK	VI	Give control over degrees of uncertainty and vulnerability in daily life.
7. BRIDGING the DISTANCE	VII	Build formal alliances and balance the ratio of differentiation to integration.
8. SELF-CONFIRMATION & SELF-TRANSCENDENCE	VIII	Confer social benefits, fuse social and material rewards into a symbolic system, and become a repository of meanings.

9. Dialectic leading to SYNERGY	IX Provide arena for conflict resolution, between laterally structured, interdependent groups requiring a multiple synthesis of ends.
10. FEEDBACK ORDERED INTO COMPLEXITY	X A system of authoritative and legitimate expectations based upon neighborhood sovereignty. A marshalling and deployment of community resources.

PROCESS 6 *SUSPENSION & RISK*

STRUCTURE VI *Controls degrees of uncertainty and vulnerability in daily life*

We saw in Chapters 1 and 2 that racist behavior was in part a "tension contest," a struggle by White to control his level of RISK and SUSPENSION, so that his resulting tension did not shade over into unbearable anxiety. He typically controls his own tension either by controlling Black unilaterally (dominative racism) or by avoiding Black in various degrees (aversive racism).

An encounter between White and Black when White is organized into, say, a welfare department and Black is *un*organized, is just no contest. The organization always has the strength to impose its own requirements upon the applicant. No matter how "sensitive" and "enlightened" the social worker may be, she has the check which the client needs to survive, so that her "friendly suggestion" offered in a "non-directive" manner only leads the client to search her face more vigilantly to discover what he must do and say in order to survive.

The welfare agency rarely SUSPENDS or RISKS, for it has no positive outcome to justify the hazards which include political investigation. In theory, improvement of the client is the positive outcome sought, but in practice the client's visible capacity to help himself is fraught with the suspicion that he never needed help initially. A client moving from chronic dependence to relative affluence in the course of a few months might actually provoke scandal for the department rather than paeans of praise for the regenerative services it provided him.

In practice, then, the only measurable criterion of welfare "success" is the absence of suspicion and a slavish adherence to legal procedure, a RISK*less* and SUSPENSE*less* process.[1] Yet because the client needs the relationship if he is to survive, he is forced into compensating for the Agency's refusal to hazard. He must SUSPEND himself utterly, divulging everything, and RISKING that some detail in his full and abject confession of need will trigger a mysterious ineligibility rule.

In the terms of our crucifixion dilemma (see Table 1), the Agency's refusal to COMMIT itself to him represents a deterioration into *passivity*, while the client's confession inflates into a pathetic *overexposure*. The Agency's SUSPENSION deteriorates into *rigidity*, while the client's inflates into *surrender*. The Agency's RISK-taking deteriorates into *pusillanimity*, while the client's total prostration would be considered *foolhardy*, were there any other alternative open to him.

We have seen that almost every government agency, if it can, will devise a "no-fail" strategy so that it is justified in either or all events. This minimizes RISK and SUSPENSION but only by transferring the vulnerability to the client. Just like the "double-binded" schizophrenic who is labeled opprobriously whatever he does, the poor individual is "chronically needful" if he falls within the Agency's categories, or a "welfare chiseler" and "drain upon the public purse" if he does not. Who, after all, can fault an organization that deals only with the pitiable and/or the reprehensible?

The trick is achieved by Welfare's dual identity and the three-cornered relationship in which the poor are constantly trapped. If the department decides to help the victim it wears its Mask of Compassion. If it decides not to, like a quick-change artist, it appears in the guise of Guardian of the Public Purse. It alternately defines itself as in relation to the Public and the Poor, depending upon convenience. Since "the Public" is an abstraction, the human consequence is an on/off relationship with flesh-and-blood victims, upon which the client can never really rely even in the face of death.

Thus the Providence *Journal* reported that a commissioner of social services had refused the purchase of a special food under Medicaid for a four-month-old infant who doctors had certified needed the diet *in order to survive*. The commissioner said:

> I can underwrite the expense without filing for federal or state aid reimbursement in an isolated incident. I chose not to because I think it would be whimsical and arbitrary of me to spend the money of the taxpayers of Jefferson County this way.[2]

The child was saved only by press publicity which gave Mead Johnson a public relations opportunity to "give" $150 worth of food to the family. Two cheers for the private sector!

An organization like a CDC holds the RISK and SUSPENSION of its members within tolerable limits, thereby contributing to optimal excitement, instead of anxiety/boredom. And it does so by obliging other organizations to share the RISKS of interaction. Because there are an assortment of roles within the CDC with varying risk-potentials, these can be matched to the occupant's capacity. Since black/white DISTANCES contribute substantially to RISK, only the more capable within a CDC need tackle these "boundary relationships," acting on behalf of the less capable, who are weaned in "the bosom of the community" until ready for greater tensions.

The CDC also risks itself *corporately*, for a positive outcome, which welfare systems lack, and members of the CDC can agree together upon the level of collective hazard. A genuinely cohesive organization can also make it possible to SUSPEND more, for relatively less RISK, within its own boundaries. If members know that criticism is fraternal and motivated by concern for common welfare, they can open themselves up (SUSPEND) to wider and deeper ranges of qualifying perspectives than if they suspect that criticism is aimed at destroying them. By prescribing member co-operation and punishing exploitive tactics, the CDC can take some of the uncontrollable tension out of efforts at brotherly love.

Where the CDC negotiates on behalf of the poor, organization confronts organization. Each has its categories and each its procedures. Instead of helpless individuals being pressed like putty into the cracks of an alien organization, both organizational structures are initially unbending, and will only bend to form new designations where SUSPENSION and reordering are mutual. Once new criteria for success are jointly established, each shares the RISK and responsibility for its own part in non-attainment. The "transfer of hazard" to the poor is inhibited, as are ex post facto blame castings.[3]

How CDC's relate to outside organizations was illustrated when the late Office of Economic Opportunity gave a contract to Abt Associates, the management consultants, for an evaluation of a number of CDC grantees. The consultant had to achieve agreement with the CDC's upon "definitions of success" before beginning his evaluation, and met with the CDC's after the evaluation for an exchange of viewpoints on the adequacy of the evaluator as well as the evaluated.[4]

A major barrier to economic development, then, is the experienced inability to hold within limits the social and symbolic disorder that precedes development. Poor groups will not *voluntarily* RISK and SUSPEND so long as they are engulfed in so much *involuntary* chaos.[5] This argument is consistent with the psychological studies of achieving persons, and group environments that foster the desire to achieve. The achievers take moderate and calculated risks, and do so only when they feel that they have some control over the outcome.[6] The crucial variable is fate control. Paradoxically, people will relinquish some control in order to gain via risk taking, but only if they believe that the intensity of the hazard, and the rewards for hazarding, are, within broad limits, controllable from their vantage point.

It follows that crucial to developmental changes is a constant attention to solidifying one's social base with values so strong and of such quality and universality that you can *afford* to RISK and SUSPEND them.

A most interesting example of nurturing a social base conducive to development was the recent sponsoring by the Harlem Commonwealth Council of the traditional African festival of Kwanza. The festival runs from December 23 to December 30 and celebrates the harvesting of the first crops. The New York *Times* described a local minister instructing children from Public School 68 concerning the straw mat (*mkeka*), the ear of corn (*mutundi*) and the candle holder (*kinara*). The mat symbolizes social tradition on which everything else must rest.

> The kinara, he said, holds seven candles and represents the original stalk—the father—from which all mankind sprang. The ear of corn represents all of us—the offspring of the stalk . . .
>
> As the children sat quietly, the minister explained the seven principles, or the Ngoso Saba of the Kwanza: Umojo (unity), Kujichagulia (self-determination), Ujima (collective work and responsibility), Nia (purpose), Kuumba (creativity), Imani (faith), Ujamaa (cooperative economics) . . .
>
> The good children were rewarded at Kwanza with zawadi —presents representing the fruits of labor of their parents and rewards of seeds sown by the children. Then each child was to tell what good things he was going to do the following year . . .[7]

It is of more than passing interest that the seven principles of Kwanza are exceedingly close to the developmental themes which form the core of this book—a fact suggesting that communities as well as individuals discover that which unites mankind by looking deeply into themselves and expressing values closest to that depth. For, in truth, co-operative economics (Ujamaa) *is* a traditional African concept, so that even the CDC has its origin in black history. W. E. B. Du Bois wrote:

> Yet on the west coast of Africa was perhaps the greatest attempt in human history before the twentieth century to build a culture based on peace and beauty . . . and of the distribution of goods and services according to need.[8]

In ghetto situations risks of all kinds, psychic, economic and physical, generally are much higher with significantly lower rewards, so that bringing risks down and keeping uncertainty within bounds requires organized and simultaneous assaults upon "risk barriers."[9] Co-ordinated actions help to remove the risks of non-reciprocity. Indeed, where there is aggregate decay, only collective ventures can halt this, otherwise it is in each individual interest to escape to some area where risks are lower. Matthew Edel has noted:

> Industries do not make their locational decisions in groups: each individual firm fears for crime, finds its skilled workers have left for the suburbs, and is caught between rising taxes and worsening public services. Individually, each firm decides to flee, and the city and the ghetto as a whole suffer further, also putting more burdens on the few firms that remain, causing them, too, to move in the end.[10]

Only mutual pledges between several institutions to turn the tide, bolstered, perhaps, by federal guarantees, could possibly prevent the ghetto's chaotic environment from paralyzing all further desire to accept hazards. A notable adjunct to risk reduction is the Opportunity Funding Corporation, originally an OEO grantee but expected to survive. It guarantees risky ventures in poverty areas by certain types of organization, guaranteeing against 50 per cent to 75 per cent of any possible loss.[11] In this way, there is just enough risk to require calculation and invite attempts to control outcomes, while the chaos is tamed sufficiently to facilitate some voluntary hazarding.

PROCESS 7   *BRIDGING the DISTANCE*
STRUCTURE VII   *Builds formal alliances and balances the ratio of differentiation to integration*

In Chapter 1 we saw that differences in skin color were not just superficial details, that they warned, and, in most cases, accurately warned, of impending difficulties in reaching someone who was, in fact, DISTANT from one's experience. We saw that whites had little incentive to reach over to blacks, unless the black side of the racial divide had an integrity, importance and culture of its own. The present situation of one-way traffic between "Black Depths" and "White Heights" was oppressive to black people and to the permanent aspects of their IDENTITIES.

Martin Luther King's civil rights campaigns elevated the idea of BRIDGING racial DISTANCES to pre-eminent importance. It is, in fact, an important principle—even more so when it is consistently applied to *all* wide DISTANCES, including those between blacks of different classes and whites of different classes.

The first point to grasp is that shorter DISTANCES are easier to BRIDGE than wider ones, so that any hope of eventually leaping the black/white abyss depends upon the success of large numbers of relatively "shorter DISTANCE" efforts within those communities we know. We learn from loved ones how to engage strangers. Any discernible progress in interracial relationships can only come from the courage, skill and confidence nurtured among intimates, usually of the same color or clan. So-called idealists are often "empiricists of intimacy." They generalize from all the successful relationships they have had on the "inside" to the outside, and ask, "Why not?" Why should not the concern and compassion I have experienced closer to home, also pertain between nations, races, classes?[12] Clearly, then, blacks must first reach other blacks if they are ever collectively or individually to comprehend their relationships with whites.

It is not just a question of learning to crawl short DISTANCES before walking longer ones, but of having shared experiences *worth* communicating. Unless blacks, or women, or Chicanos, or any other oppressed groups have "got themselves together" sufficiently, they will not have any saving knowledge about their own oppression with which to engage the dominant society. As one CDC leader put it forcefully:

> What must be understood historically is that blacks have been made to push integration before we had integrated with ourselves. . . . There are politics that take place in the black ghetto that can only be dealt with by black people on a representative basis. There are militant forces, moderate forces of all colors and shades in the ghetto that must be dealt with by blacks.[13]

Where integration rhetoric is inapplicable to a large mass of black people, it opens up DISTANCES *within* the black community, even as the DISTANCE to whites is being narrowed, and it provokes a situation where the black-white bridge rests upon crumbling foundations at the black end.

There is, unfortunately, a subtle "classism" within orthodox integration doctrine, which gives the upper middle classes, black *and* white, most of the advantages and fewer of the difficulties, while leaving the lower and lower middle classes, black and white, with immense difficulties and doubtful advantages. Let us see how this happens.

The main psychic benefits of integration come from "equal status contact"—that is, where you trust someone as an equal, you SUSPEND optimally to SYNERGIZE his/her perspectives with your own.[14] I know of no evidence to show that a white master is humanized or enlightened by daily contacts with his slaves. Now equal status contact is much more available to middle-class, especially upper-middle-class, blacks, while a substantial proportion of lower-class blacks are beyond and "beneath" the economy itself. They would have to be trained in order to work regularly, and traineeship in white-controlled organizations is *not* equal-status contact. Such "integration" is scant recompense to black communities for the loss of their middle-class talent and potential leadership class to white organizations, where they become tokens of corporate "enlightenment" and are often given liaison, recruiting and personnel jobs which face *back* to the communities from which they came. If a black community wants to confront a major corporation, it frequently finds itself at odds with a black representative of that white corporation, who acts as a shield against and inhibitor of the community's wrath. In order to "get Whitey" you have to beat upon one of your own.

In fact, the difficulties of integration escalate sharply as one goes down the social scale. At the highest levels it is enlightening, even fun. An editor of Dial Press having a literary luncheon with James Baldwin; two black faces at a professor's seminar on racism; Sammy Davis, Jr., hugging Dick Nixon during an election campaign: all these episodes involve blacks of known status and qualifications. At this level, integration has virtually no RISK or SUSPENSE associated with it, and the black percentage among the qualified and certified is 4 per cent or less.

But as we go down the social scale the proportion of blacks rises to 40 per cent or more. Now it is demanded of whites that they permit their social environment to be drastically altered by infusions of large minorities with different norms. Moreover, blackness now begins to signify something which is important to a lot of people. It signifies, on the average, an increasingly lower class composition of a neighborhood. Any persons seriously imagining that Baldwin is an inferior writer because he is black should seek help for their obvious phobias, but someone observing the blackness of several *strangers*, and inferring that this means that his community is in transition to a lower class life-style, will often be correct.[15]

Ironically, then, the requirement of integration is imposed upon poor whites by upper-middle-class liberal whites, and upon poor blacks by middle-class blacks, although the respective middle classes have not themselves had to do or to experience anything comparable by way of culture shock. Since the capacity to BRIDGE wider DISTANCES is generally higher among the educated, the verbal and those organizationally experienced, we have a situation where the psycho-socially relatively COMPETENT command the relatively incOMPETENT to leap wider DISTANCES than the COMPETENTS have themselves achieved! No wonder integration policy has cut off liberal Democrats from their blue-collar base, and black dramas depict middle-class blacks, Ph.D.'s and assorted clergy, groveling on their knees chanting, "We Shall Be White."[16]

Even blacks who are integrated "fairly" into white corporations would have equal status contact mostly in the washroom and around coffee percolators. Lilly White, Incorporated, would have no reason to change its organizational ethos just because it had a 10 per cent assortment of individual blacks. In experimental conditions even the raising of the black ratio to 50 per cent, and the equalizing of status, conditions hopelessly unrealizable in the immediate future, was still not enough to create equality of influence and process. When a number of biracial problem-solving groups with two blacks and two whites in each were carefully observed, it was found that

> Whites made more remarks than did blacks.
> Whites spoke more to one another than did blacks.
> Blacks spoke more to whites than did whites to blacks.
> Blacks spoke more to whites than to one another.[17]

If *that* is integration, it is a disaster for black people.

The CDC goes a long way to overcoming the disaster of present integration policies. Within the cohesion of an organized black community, blacks speak more to blacks, until they are convinced of their thesis, and then start speaking confidently and articulately to whites, secure in the representation of their constituency and its consciousness. The CDC thus links blacks to whites at the level of interorganizational relationships. If we are serious about equal status contact, then we have to bring into contact those equal in the sense that they each represent organizations. A further source of equality comes from the two organizations being differentiated like apples and oranges, so that discussion of which is "higher" becomes foolish, and each must SUSPEND its own assumptions to explore the novelty and significance of the other.

The CDC also makes it possible for blacks to "integrate" extensively with whites near the top and peripheries of their respective organizations, so that the middle-class elements, with most to gain by contact, can have it; those nearer the bottom of the socio-economic hierarchy can minimize contacts, if they wish. Yet the CDC would not be separatist in philosophy as much as independent, since the leadership would be demonstrably and daily in contact with the white world. It is probably more developmental for an impoverished CDC member to identify vicariously with the equal status contact of his community's leaders with white leaders, than for that member to suffer personally unequal encounters with white authorities. It is probably better for middle-class blacks to represent an entire community when they negotiate with whites, than merely their own aspirations for mobility.

A CDC helps its area residents and staff *balance the ratio of differentiation to integration* in their community life. This balance between differentiation and integration is a key to the whole helical process of development. Insofar as people need to BRIDGE DISTANCES to others in order to survive, they must have some control over the structural width of that DISTANCE, and this process is integral to the control of the RISK and SUSPENSION levels already discussed.

The CDC controls "structural width" in a number of ways. It sets up norms which contain an acceptable range of deviation, beyond which community pressure mounts upon the deviant individual. There are also collective agreements on which outsiders are reachable by whom, and which are beyond the pale. Where DISTANCES are too narrow, parochialism sets in. Where they are too wide, alienation, fragmentation and breakdown occur. Under the present circumstances of the poor, this latter condition is far more prevalent. In any event, the people themselves, and *only the people*, know what DISTANCES they can stand, and where to set limits.

Economic organizations are especially valuable because they contain divisions of labor, with differentiated activities requiring integration if the enterprise is to function. Extensive research has documented that the creativity and productivity of commercial enterprises depend upon an optimal balance between differentiation and integration. In unbalanced situations every incremental piece of DISTANCE subtracts from the capacity to BRIDGE it, and vice versa. Yet there is a "Twilight Zone" wherein activities are DISTANT enough to be really interesting and important, yet close enough to enable a BRIDGE of communication to link them. Hence the most successful enterprises (in those environments demanding creativity) are *both* highly differentiated *and* highly integrated, and they grow by extending this optimal balance of opposites.[18]

PROCESS 8   *SELF-CONFIRMATION & SELF-TRANSCENDENCE*

STRUCTURE VIII   *Confers social benefits, fuses social and material rewards into a symbolic system, and becomes a repository of meanings*

By definition, a true community is SELF-CONFIRMATION writ large. Building a community is also a form of SELF-TRANSCENDENCE. The creativity of its members is poured into the foundation of semi-permanent structures, rules and systems which become "reality" for thousands in that community and beyond. The CDC is a public testament to the capacity of the poor and their leaders to create a social architecture that signifies something. If the oppressed are ever to help change society, they must initially master their own environments, and demonstrate in microcosm the social possibilities of their beliefs.

There is a case for arguing that the development of persons presently poor requires a symbolic system which is substantially different from the signaling system of the larger society. For one thing, the mass media of the dominant society teach "consumer traineeship," *not* hard work or struggle. There issue from TV sets and magazines invitations to indulge, spend, lick, snuggle, bask, masticate and devour. Whatever asceticism and self-denial were needed to build giant organizations in the first place[19] are now detriments in training consumers to covet products in an affluent society.

To the poor such titillations are poison. They cannot afford the scale of consumption presented, and still less can they afford the suckling psychology of privatized enjoyments. Before them is a Barmecide feast that triggers all the "relaxation responses" associated with ingestion, *and* the "frustration responses" associated with gagging on an unfilled gullet. No wonder there is rage and violence. I am told that peptic ulcers arise from digestive juices being secreted into empty stomachs of persons craving nurture. If so, poor communities must be awash with raw stomach acid, evoked by our media. Extensive research into motivations to achieve have established that achievers do not work principally for money. Rather imaginations are afire with as yet unrealized ambitions and fantasies long before money becomes involved.[20] When money is offered as an incentive to groups including high and low achievers, it mainly galvanizes the low achievers.[21] The "highs" are already mobilized by the challenge offered, and by the fact that significant others have defined this particular challenge as a test of their achievement.

Research that content-analyzed children's readers and contemporary American folk literature over the last century and a half found that "achievement fantasy" had literally raged within small communities, some decades prior to the great industrial feats. Since the last century, achievement imagery has been failing inexorably from decade to decade.[22] It has left organizational monuments to itself, except in poor communities. Today these organizations utilize "consumption imagery," but the poor and especially the black were excluded from the "achievement era" and cannot now afford the "consumption era." In every sense they have the worst of both worlds.

The problems in the ghettos today—which are really intensifications of wider cultural problems—are that: (a) the community "incubators of achievement" are no more; (b) achievement would anyway need redefinition so that it describes a process of social development in the context of poverty; and (c) the accumulation of money no longer signals or measures social benefaction, as it once did, and new "signaling systems" are required.

It should be obvious by now where the CDC, with its strong social base, fits into these equations. Only an organized community can incubate achievement motivation in sufficient strength to shut out mass media appeals to residents to roll over like spaniels, in the (false) expectation of being tickled. Only a strong community has the power to define what achievement shall consist of in its own peculiar and oppressive circumstances. People with little money *have* to reward each other mostly with love and solidarity. It's beautiful—but it's also obligatory.

But even were there three times the money, and no accompanying organizational change, a signaling system that said, Personal Income = Contribution to the Community, would lead to grotesque errors of symbolization. We are talking of a subculture in which drugs are marked up over 1000 per cent.[23] Whatever Carnegie's fortune may have signified to Main Street during the last century, a high income in Dope Alley signifies how many members of your community you are keeping on the needle, for private profit or to feed your own habit. The true benefactors of poor communities must usually make do with emotional riches and material impoverishment, while the exploiters are affluent and alienated. It is all part of the crucifix.

Nothing short of a CDC with its socio-economic mandates could work out ways of symbolizing, measuring and rewarding those who genuinely benefit their communities, and distinguishing these from the blood suckers. What is needed are systems of social accounting that give achievers what it seems they must have, bench marks against which to rate themselves, and ways of approximating to their community's definition of success.[24]

However, it would be a mistake to think of community development as the War on Poverty envisaged it, as a kind of perpetual consensus, holding together the elements of a Democratic alliance, with city halls, social agencies and the poor locked into the appearance of unbroken mutuality by the conditions of the grant. It simply does not (and did not) work that way, for you cannot mandate integration at the expense of differentiation. Consensus may only be possible after one small group has acted decisively on its own to find the "winning combination" which the community then applauds. Martin Luther King, for example, was highly controversial among other black leaders until the Montgomery bus boycott had succeeded. Roy Innis was particularly scornful on the issue of consensus planning for CDC's. He told a group of senators:

> As to whether we are seeking consensus, no we are not. No place, no time in the history of mankind has anything important in society been done by consensus . . . the Madisons, the Jeffersons, the Hamiltons, the Ben Franklins did not in any way seek consensus. They had some solutions to the needs of the American colonies, and they packaged these solutions, and ran ahead with them . . . and they created the most powerful nation in the history of mankind. I do say, they did not stop for consensus. They were very sensitive though, to the feeling of a broad spectrum of the American colonies.[25]

What research on achievement has shown is the meaningfulness to achievers and their audiences of the tasks undertaken. One way to turn a poor community from a handicap into an advantage is to understand how desperately needful and grateful such a community could be to its achieving sons and daughters. The very fact that your work is for persons you know, whose needs you know, can give every increment of productive output a significance totally lacking in a GM factory, or other institutions dedicated to force-feeding the already fat.

To the extent that the surplus from productive activity is spent on community benefits, each target met could signify an additional facility, with community celebrations; for the new playground, the clinic, the scholarship fund, the credit union. That is SELF-TRANSCENDENCE, too, when the work of mind and hands becomes a gift to those you love.

Indeed, the whole experience in pioneering with a new social structure, of being part of a movement that, if successful, could conquer poverty in our century, is a potentially transcendent one. Such explorations of Social Space could ultimately be more meaningful[26] than the flights of astronauts.

PROCESS 9   Dialectic *leading to SYNERGY*

STRUCTURE IX   *Provides arena for conflict resolution between laterally structured, interdependent groups requiring a multiple synthesis of ends*

Let us first consider the definition of SYNERGY as the fusion of different aims and resources to create MORE between interacting parties than each had to begin with. This requires the conception of community or a similar sum of relationships to which "the More" accrues. If there is some institution charged with the creation of surplus value, and which synthesizes a whole more valuable than its parts, then SYNERGY is further facilitated. There must also be some composite index which registers "the More."

Or consider the notion that SYNERGY is multifaceted, creating common allegiance, not because it means exactly the same to everyone, but because there are "faces" to which almost everyone can relate. A synergistic *system* must contain those "faces," but it is little more than a variegated lollipop unless those relating to one "face" are led by the system to comprehend *other* "faces" to which different persons are attracted. Again, this is a question of system design.

A CDC, which is a social institution, *and* a business one, *and* political one, *and* an educational one, etc., and which employs, tutors, pays, empowers and unites its members, is potentially synergistic as well. However, there is nothing accidental or mystical in this process. There must be real connections between the facets so that they work with (syn-ergo) one another in a process of mutual enhancement. Members have to discover for themselves that the facet which initially drew them into participation is enlarged and enriched by the facets enjoyed by others.

Gar Alperowitz, testifying in favor of the Community Self-Determination act, explained the importance of such designed convergences:

> Here the notion not only of "coming together," but more precisely of "synergism" is important. The notion that one part might reinforce the other part is the heart of this bill. It is the concept I would emphasize above all others. There is, in the first instance, a hope that minimally taxed profits developed from one side can flow over and help the other side. But second . . . there is a hope that there will be a new dimension in the relationship of one side to the other.[27]

Alperowitz goes on to discuss the HELP CDC in Albuquerque:

> Specifically, in New Mexico, I have seen and talked with a number of people who have been carrying out a simple literacy training program *which leads,* in the next step, to a simple woodworking program, *which in turn may lead* to a self-help housing program which inculcates skills, which lead to a housing development program [and then a contracting company] . . .[28]

Two years later the Watts Labor Community Action Committee was able to describe the following "SYNERGIES" within a strategic deployment of institutions:

> The poultry ranch supplies the produce farm with fertilizer; the products of both entities are transported on trucks fueled and serviced by the W.L.C.A.C. gas stations and repair center; the Elite Supermarkets and the new general hospital serve as outlets for the products of both ranch and farm . . . Moreover, the training components built into W.L.C.A.C. enterprises are linked to the community union's youth organizing arm, the Community Conservation Corps.[29]

The disciplines of economics and finance have their own analogues of SYNERGY which can be designed to dovetail with the psycho-social processes. Among these are multiplier effects, economies of agglomeration, demonstration effects, leadership effects[30] and the concept of leverage. The multiplier effect comes from the additional jobs created by the spending of newly employed workers. Agglomeration economies occur when the presence of one business lowers the cost of establishing others because they share public facilities, sell services to each other at lower cost, act as outlets or create the need for additional services. The demonstration effect refers to the galvanizing of ghetto residents by the visible success of their neighbors and to the attraction of business from the outside. The leadership effect refers to the retention within the community of its most talented residents as well as influxes of such talent.

Extensive use of financial leverage was suggested to CDC's and other minority enterprises by Ted Cross, a Wall Street lawyer and advocate of "Green Power." With initial paid-in capital of $150,000 plus unsecured notes from the Small Business Administration, and 90 per cent SBA guarantees on additional bank loans, as much as two and a quarter million dollars can be raised.[31] The method has some obvious drawbacks, a very high debt equity ratio reducing flexibility and adding heavy debt servicing costs. Other criticisms have been made,[32] but clearly the "synergies of finance" should be utilized wherever possible.

There are other resolutions we have not yet covered. One very damaging series of polarities is the manner in which the entire debate on racism, poverty and inequality takes place between liberals and conservatives. One combatant champions the public sector, the other the private, and the poor become mere objects of a joust between giants. Both conservatives and liberals accuse the other of secret designs to enslave the poor—either through economic royalism or welfare paternalism. Both make insistent preachments about individualism, although only the poor are genuinely individual in the sense of being institutionally unsupported and lacking a "sector" of their own.

The historical result is that the liberal thesis and conservative antithesis have torn apart the necessary principles of a developmental philosophy and have seriously corrupted several key concepts. For example, the notion of a universalism of just laws and federal guidelines spreading across the land from Washington is opposed by a conservative emphasis upon the local community, and neighborhood school, free from federal interference. Liberal bureaucrats pronounce that the poor need their help; conservatives rejoin that the poor should help themselves. The poor thus find certain components of what they need championed by one rival faction, only to be rejected by the other, and in allying themselves either way, the necessary synthesis alludes them.

In fact, the polarities are lethal in another way as well. When conservatives say, "Let the poor help themselves," this is usually, if not always, a code word for rejecting completely their aspirations. It means, "*We* are not going to help *you*." When conservatives extol community, it is usually, if not always, those communities who are resisting the demands of the black underclass. Similarly liberal "help" can often be translated as "more jobs for us helpers in targeting you."

All these corruptions become possible because the poor are being talked *about*, instead of talking for themselves. When CDC spokesmen talk about self-help, it is not a code word for abandonment. When they talk about *being* helped, it is no request for a passive receipt of services. When they advocate community, they do not mean their servitude beneath the White Citizens Council. As the poor gain control over the terminology in which their fates are argued, corrupted slogans become transformed into reconcilable terms, facilitating synergistic resolution.

Gar Alperowitz has argued that the concept of community economic enterprise resolves the sterile East-West debate between centralized bureaucratic socialism, versus multinational, oligopolist corporatism.[33] Both these systems suffer from an increasing centralization of power and the alienation of citizens from vital decisions affecting their lives. In effect, the CDC helps to put the freedom, especially the capacity to originate businesses, back into economic enterprise, by altering the criteria that justify economic activity. Similarly, it takes some of the principles of socialism, and brings to them a life they have rarely enjoyed by permitting local communities to define social benefit, rather than using an arbitrary definition of the People's Will to bludgeon specific people. This new synthesis of community autonomy, with national patterns of aid and trade between community-owned enterprises, Alperowitz calls a Pluralist Commonwealth.[34]

You cannot SYNERGIZE a whole society, without "intermediate SYNERGIES" at the local level, and such localities train their residents best for national and international co-operation, if the neighborhood is a synergistic microcosm of nationwide issues. Alperowitz notes:

> In order to break down divisions which pose one group against another and to achieve equity, accordingly, the social unit at the heart of any proposed new system should, so far as possible, *be inclusive of all the people*. . . . the minorities, the elderly, women, youth—not just the "workers" who have paid "jobs." . . .
> The only social unit inclusive of *all* the people is one based upon geographic contiguity. . . . In a territorially defined local community, a variety of functional groups must co-exist, side by side. Day by day communication between them is possible and long-term relationships can be developed; conflicts must inevitably be mediated directly, by people who have to live with the decisions they make.[35]

CDC's with neighborhood governments would also reduce the contradiction between the interests of owners, manufacturers, workers and other direct beneficiaries upon the one hand, and the polluted, unfairly taxed neighborhoods chopped up by highways to serve industries. Indeed, the whole series of dichotomies between private affluence and public squalor becomes resolvable when local, democratic publics own wealth-producing facilities and decide how much or how little pollution, highways, taxes and other effects *their* industry will give or take from *their* community.

A CDC movement could become a desperately needed corrective to the liberal ideology of "interest group pluralism." The failures of this ideology are yearly more apparent. For interest groups are rarely democratic internally and they frequently exist to boost a particular technique. Just as sociology, psychology and mental health have "oppositional paradigms" designed to discredit the assumptions of rival disciplines, so are hundreds of professional, industrial and union organizations designed *against* SYNERGY. These include groups with "special interests" in poverty itself, in which the poor *have* no "special" interest but a "common interest of liberty, equality and prosperity . . . [which] cannot afford the costly competition of the pressure group process."[36]

Theodore Lowi has described the early planning for the War on Poverty when Walter Heller, head of the Council of Economic Advisors,

> issued a formal request to all heads of domestic Departments and major independent agencies to examine their existing programs as a means of generating new program suggestions. . . . The response to Heller's request was overwhelming, and probably not a little distressing. More than 100 distinct proposals were made. However, each agency tended to see a new war waged by expansion of its own programs. . . . The question here, then, becomes, how do interest group liberal policy makers go about their jobs when there is a large substantive (one is tempted to say *critical*) issue, rather than several discrete *incremental* issues. The answer is *incrementally just the same, which means they make no substantive decisions at all.*[37]

It was the Community Action Programs located in ghettos and rural enclaves, upon which dozens of "incrementalizing," self-aggrandizing special interests suddenly converged.[38] The poor residents, without even majority representation on poverty boards, were seriously expected to co-ordinate these warring interests, each spouting its own professionalese and similar mystifications. It was this job of actually making a decision that had been ducked in Washington and all the way down the line, illustrating the dictum that society pushes its social contradictions and irresolutions down the socio-economic ladder, where they are solved by force, at the expense of the weakest. The War on Poverty was the only war arbitrated by privates, third class.

Now let us turn to the third (interdependent) definition of SYNERGY, that it is a process growing out of a dialectical, dialogical process of balance, justice and equality between persons and groups and between the ideas and resources they represent. While no kind of social structure can actually guarantee SYNERGY, structures can still point the way and increase the probabilities of mutuality. Where different groups have relationships officially defined as equal, co-operative and interdependent, and where there is an arena and procedures for the peaceful reconciliation of conflict, SYNERGY is more likely to be achieved.

Conversely, SYNERGY is impeded by structured inequalities, one-way communications, the pulling of rank as routine, rather than as last resort, and a dozen kinds of power plays. But we cannot be purists on the subject of equality and dialogue, because no organization can debate its decisions for indefinite periods, and must make certain decisions by act of authority, if necessary, if it is to survive. To make unilateral decisions harder without making synergistic ones easier and better will only increase tensions, postpone decisions and polarize "freedom" against "law and order" in political rhetoric.

But assuming that SYNERGY can be facilitated through reconcilable terminology, humanistic social science, designed convergences, etc., it becomes very important to insure that groups make every effort to reconcile differences, before solutions are at last imposed. As a rule, the struggle and mutual SUSPENSION needed will not even be attempted where techniques of domination are easy to use. For this reason the CDC needs laterally organized groups within its structure, and relationships with outside forces that are as equal as the corporation can make them. The rationale for disorders and demonstrations is that they produce, simultaneously, a solidarity of equals within the ghetto, and something for the community to bargain with (a return to order) in relationship to outside forces.

Given the "great changes" in American communities over the last few decades,[39] which have seen the structural domination of once sovereign cities by the now "down town" business districts that annexed them in the name of efficiency,[40] the CDC movement can be seen as a long overdue struggle for neighborhood rights and justice.

PROCESS 10 *FEEDBACK ORDERED into COMPLEXITY*

STRUCTURE x *A system of authoritative and legitimate expectations based on neighborhood sovereignty. A marshaling and deployment of community resources*

Much as the individual ORDERS the FEEDBACK from his interpersonal relationships into a mental map of expanding COMPLEXITY, so does a community create its own coherent structure. This structure brings about a record of shared experiences and expectations, and an historical continuity which imparts a sense of moving forward through time, and passing on to one's children's children an accumulating body of knowledge.

For this there must be institutional repositories of knowledge. The National Congress for Community Economic Development has begun to collect case studies of its members, and in the last few months of OEO's existence, "education" courses were funded. In the absence of any agreed body of knowledge, the process was begun of generalizing from concrete cases of successful operation. The Center for Community Economic Development—an advocacy and support group—has computed a library of CDC affairs.[41] Among CDC's, CIRCLE, Inc., has set up the Roxbury Institute of Business Management, which runs extensive classes and traveling seminars. Twentieth Century Fund has a task force report on community economic development written by Geoff Faux,[42] the former Director of Economic Development at OEO. CDC's were also extensively evaluated by Abt Associates.[43]

Abt found that 50 per cent of CDC ventures were either above break-even point, or projected by the consultants to break even within the first five years. This compares favorably with the 80 per cent failure rate of new businesses in general, and does not take into account the "social profits" from ventures showing financial "losses," and the obligation upon CDC's to employ neighborhood residents rather than the best talent available. For example, 20 per cent of CDC employees were previously unemployed, 12 per cent were previously on welfare or receiving unemployment compensation. The average CDC evaluated was paying its staff some $57,000 more than they had received in previous employment, and 50 per cent of all managers had been upgraded in responsibility, while 70 per cent of non-managers had upgraded skills. Over 200 per cent leverage has been obtained with seed money provided by the Special Impact Program.[44]

Community control and community support were surprisingly good compared with past experience. A study in Newark in 1965 found no single "leader" or group with a community recognition factor of more than 20 per cent.[45] In contrast, 73 per cent of residents in the target areas recognized the CDC's existence, 50 per cent valued specific things they were doing. However, little progress has been made in distributing stock to the community, and with the exception of citizens' boards of directors, found to be highly representative of area residents, elective processes were not much in evidence. It is perhaps unreasonable to expect wide citizen participation until there are surpluses for distribution. CDC's have made a good impression on most of those they dealt with in public and private institutions. Only 21 per cent of those polled regarded CDC leadership as deficient, and most of the rest praised it—a surprisingly good showing considering the anger and demonstrations amid which many CDC's were founded on average only twenty months earlier.

However, CDC's can never be fairly evaluated until better indices are developed for estimating social benefits. Some way has to be found of building the necessary social base, without it showing up as "loss" on the balance sheet.

Some promising and creative ideas have come from Bernard Gifford, ex-president of FIGHT:

> One of the terms we've been throwing around without defining it is "profit." In Rochester, we had to explain to both the black and the white community what FIGHT meant by "profit." Our definition is at variance with the traditional definition. For instance, if we take 10 welfare mothers off the welfare rolls and these mothers work for us for a year, we state very emphatically in our profit and loss statement, under "special category," that we saved the Monroe County Department of Social Services $50,000 because we took 10 people off welfare onto our payrolls. We have about 18 brothers working with us who were ex-cons. If you go by the statistics, you'll find that about 75 percent of the brothers who leave the slam get remanded in less than nine months. We found out that nobody with us went back to the slam; those who left us went on to better jobs. So we put that in our profit and loss statement, saying, "Based on the statistics, 75 percent of these people will go back to the slams costing the correctional institutions so many thousands of dollars."[46]

More recently Peat, Marwick and Mitchell have worked out a complex scheme for evaluating CDC's against their own yardsticks. The scheme was accepted by OEO and its grantees, but all is now in suspended animation. The right to organize experience and measure one's own progress in ways that suit an unusual situation and a particular ethnic-cultural life-style, can make quite astounding differences in actual performance—not to mention changes in the way that existing performance is valued by others.[47]

My own attempts to ORDER the COMPLEXITY of Chapters 1, 4, and 5 is presented in Table 6. Here all the ten principles of process and the ten principles of structure form a coherent and integrated whole. It is a General Systems Theory, for those concerned with nomenclature, an open, self-transforming, holistic, "field" system. It does not tell the poor *what* to think and do specifically, but suggests the form that any choice must take if development is to result.

It would be tempting to end my book on this high note. Go forth and develop! CDC's are it! Unfortunately I have become convinced over the last few years that crucial elements in the "developmental mix" are still missing—while others have been seriously distorted. In plant growth, a single missing element of sun, water, soil, temperature can blight a harvest; so in the growth of human institutions. The argument so far has selected some of the best examples that illustrate development principles. It has shown what CDC's, at their best, *can be,* not what they mostly are. Let me briefly review some of the remaining unsolved problems.

Winning recognition for the new institutional IDENTITY
If many readers had not heard of CDC's before picking up this book, or if what they knew had failed to fire their imaginations, then they are not alone. There has been a curious failure among its advocates to put the CDC's virtues across to the public at large—curious because black groups have shown in the past considerable penchants for publicity and rhetorical skills.

In part, the problem may lie in the decision to subcontract the advocacy function to white, middle-class grantees, such as the Center for Community Economic Development. I am not reflecting upon its competence, so much as objecting to the division of labor, whereby CDC's "get on with business" while whites talk and write about it. Such divisions overlook Cruse's point that communications *are* a business, one excellently suited to the black cultural heritage, and the least of a CDC's rights must be the day-to-day control of the projection of its own image.

This mistake probably arose as a reaction against the civil rights phase of the struggle, immediately preceding the creation of CDC's. This was a period of "media leaders" and symbolic progress belying economic stagnation. Yet to swing to the opposite extreme, to immerse oneself in the nitty-gritty of economic enterprise without educating a market as new as the CDC, is a continuation of the historical flip-flop from extroversion to introversion and back again.

It is also a serious error, I believe, to ignore the white constituencies of conscience, to which Martin Luther King appealed, in favor of doing "strictly business" with Middle America. There was once a tactical advantage in snubbing the more sympathetic whites, because it was felt that their very sympathy might break up black solidarity, and it was noticed that their sympathy had no substantial economic benefit behind it. It was fashionable to allege a total hypocrisy among these very whites who had suffered alongside blacks in civil rights struggles. The tone was set by LeRoi Jones agreeing on television with Tony Imperiale, a right-wing vigilante, that SDS had started the Newark riots!

The alleged "hypocrisy" of white civil rights activists and sympathizers can be traced to a totally different source. They are themselves rhetoricians, writers, communicators, clergy, students, etc. They gave black civil

TABLE 6

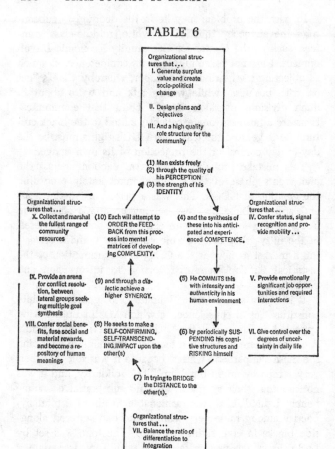

Organizational structures that ...
I. Generate surplus value and create socio-political change

II. Design plans and objectives

III. And a high quality role structure for the community

(1) Man exists freely
(2) through the quality of his PERCEPTION
(3) the strength of his IDENTITY

Organizational structures that ...
X. Collect and marshal the fullest range of community resources

(10) Each will attempt to ORDER the FEEDBACK from this process into mental matrices of developing COMPLEXITY.

(4) and the synthesis of these into his anticipated and experienced COMPETENCE.

Organizational structures that ...
IV. Confer status, signal recognition and provide mobility ...

IX. Provide an arena for conflict resolution, between lateral groups seeking multiple goal synthesis

(9) and through a *dialectic* achieve a higher SYNERGY.

(5) He COMMITS this with *intensity* and *authenticity* in his human environment

V. Provide emotionally significant job opportunities and required interactions

VIII. Confer social benefits, fuse social and material rewards, and become a repository of human meanings

(8) He seeks to make a SELF-CONFIRMING, SELF-TRANSCENDING IMPACT upon the other(s)

(6) by periodically SUSPENDING his cognitive structures and RISKING himself

VI. Give control over the degrees of uncertainty in daily life

(7) in trying to BRIDGE the DISTANCE to the other(s).

Organizational structures that ...
VII. Balance the ratio of differentiation to integration

rights forces what they had to give, space, coverage, applause, but in truth, they controlled very little else. However, they are also potential customers, if the CDC's would but make the effort to reach them.

I must sadly report in my observation of CDC's that

they are slowly losing the battle to have themselves measured, appraised and generally regarded in a totally new light, and this is partly because they have aimed their sights at sectors of society who initiate more than they respond and are lacking in social concern. CDC's capacity to influence their environments is still noticeably weaker than the capacity of those environments to influence them. Business consultants with whom I have worked on community problems do not regard CDC's as importantly different from other enterprises.[48] Marketing consultants feed CDC's conventional "business opportunities" with scant respect for issues of cultural integrity or social cohesion.[49] Financial experts lead them into the labyrinths of our system, until they are mortgaged, indebted, hedged around with conditions and ultimately forced to serve those with acceptable credit ratings—who are, of course, middleclass, if not white.[50]

It is at such moments that poverty agencies publicly deplore that the very poorest in the community are not being reached by CDC's and employed in sufficient numbers, even as another department turns down a venture proposal because of the low credentials of those employed within it. As the political heat is turned up, each frightened department and agency purifies its criteria, and offers compassion for the very poorest and venture money for the really qualified. The result is that the poor communities are crucified all over again. This happens because the basic contradiction between business and welfare philosophies has not yet been resolved, much less communicated so as to register with various publics. Business and Welfare are dichotomized. It is rather like a confrontation between a rambunctious gelding and an aging, milkless cow. The union is unfruitful.

But even were CDC's able to look after their own area residents in work settings, there is still no incentive for a consumer of CDC products to consider the social achievements of his supplier. In fact, there is no mechanism to make the consumer even aware of the CDC as a developmental force. And, if those purchasing officers who buy the transformers, and electrical relays which some CDC's make, were to receive social appeals among their technical literature, would they raise fists and shout, "Right on!"? Or are CDC's appealing to the wrong kind of people in the wrong place?

The effect of failing to communicate the potential significance of community development to a sufficiently responsive market breaks down the CDC synthesis into its bare components. The environment will only respond to these "bits," businessmen to the business components, health authorities to health components, and so on.

The bureaucratic slicer

This segmenting process, by which CDC's come to see themselves as a loose assemblage of parts, is also the result of a prolonged relationship with a bureaucratic sponsor. The original idea at OEO was that CDC's would receive their seed capital and go their merry ways within a year or two, at most. It did not happen. Initial injections of capital were so modest that yearly booster shots were required. By this time, the environment had turned against Movement politics, so CDC's settled for a drawn-out "low profile" relationship with OEO and other sponsoring agencies.

In so doing they perhaps avoided sudden death, but at the price of a thousand cuts. For there is an inherent contradiction between innovative enterprise-cum-politics and the procedures of a functionally departmentalized bureaucracy. Each separate function tends to push towards a different professional and/or procedural ideal. Whereas grants for CDC's had initially been scrutinized by only three OEO departments, this increased to ten, and those CDC's that had made themselves known politically came in for the *hardest* scrutiny—a fact that helps explain the reluctance of CDC's to let their lights shine before men.

In one instance five experts had to fly to Washington

from Chicago to explain to OEO's legal department that a housing development plan for a four-block area did in fact include the costs of maintaining white lines in the car park.[51] A mortgage banker assisting North Lawndale Economic Development Corporation, the developer, said he had never in his whole career experienced such niggling. On another occasion the grant for a rural CDC in Hancock County, Georgia, was so late that its president flew up to Washington to explain that if he returned without the money, his life was in danger; his community thought he had stolen it.[52]

A curious system evolved whereby CDC's were "given" investment funds to bank locally, but were not allowed to invest them in business opportunities without additional clearance. Most of the opportunities died while clearance was being awaited, and CDC's knew the profound humiliation of trying to play an ace at the card table, only to have it pulled from their hands, by silent little men seated behind them.

OEO also recreated within its grantees its own split between agency techniques and politics "on the Hill" and in the White House. The United Durham Corporation was almost defunded because southern strategists in the White House and the North Carolina Statehouse did not like one of their board members, a black activist. Fighting the cuts cost $20,000.[53] On another occasion the FBI forbade the Small Business Administration from making a loan to a venture owned by Hough Area Development Corporation.[54] Its manager had attended a conference of the New Republic of Africa. The Internal Revenue Service even turned up at the author's place of work to do an "activity audit" and ask why I was writing about Black Power on an OEO grant. It turned out they were thinking of Charles Hamilton, and were most disappointed by the paleness of my complexion. CDC's have no hope at all, if they are to be denied the rights of free association. As it is, the exhausting nature of their symbiotic ties to OEO drain them of the energy and time needed to make "lateral alliances" at the community level.

The dead hand of interest group politics

It is not fair to blame the foregoing incidents upon personal failures at OEO, or even upon Nixonian machinations. Relationships with other agencies were probably more difficult, and conservatives we have always with us. Rather the pattern is a general one. There seems no escape from the icy processes of liberal, interest group politics. If you are not frozen out, as most are, you are frozen in. Theodore Lowi makes three general observations about the process.[55]

He sees a decay of public control, new structures of privilege and a rapid conservatization of the government interest group nexus. Interest groups will typically become extensions of the government agency concerned, or the agency an extension of the interest group. Together they define each other "in" and the public and other voluntary associations "out." Membership of the interest group ceases to be really voluntary, since it now monopolizes access to the government in its field.[56]

I wish I could say that CDC's have avoided following this pattern. Unfortunately I have witnessed ominous signs: requests to ban new grantees, to concentrate funds among the larger CDC's, and even to downgrade the requirement for democratic processes.

Shortly after their founding, many government-sponsored CDC's stopped the process of fusing with other major constituencies in their areas, groups in media, in cultural activities, etc. Such components were still sought, but as derivatives of, not as equals in, economic development. What was happening was that economic development was becoming another "thing," an additional function, carried out by yet another group, instead of a community matrix.

It is, of course, unfair to expect CDC's to establish much in the way of mutual aid among each other when each is in competition for finite amounts of agency funding. In fact, "business activity" is such an intricate maze that a million-man movement could sink into its interstices, never to be heard from again. What has a hamburger franchisee to say to a stationery supplier that might interest a manufacturer of electrical components? Can CDC's cohere as a movement if they diverge into hundreds of separate businesses having no symbolic relationships to their shared social purposes? It is hard enough, surely, for mattress makers to keep up with stuffing methods and manuals, without ideological and political complications. Only the Chinese have, to my knowledge, addressed themselves to the "dialectics of hairdressing."

Innovation, technology and take-off

But if CDC's cannot diverge in random directions without losing their coherence as a moral alternative, still less can they afford to innovate in the usual sense—that is, through advanced technological complexity. Even if enough minority talent could be found, even if it could be attracted to poverty areas, you cannot organize a community around the significance of low-frequency transducers. And yet it is these kinds of research labs that comprise one of the few ways in which small business can make it.

Hence CDC's face the following dilemma: they need to innovate if they are to succeed, yet they must strain their community base beyond endurance if that innovation is too abstract and technical. There are easy-to-make products, but these are not easy to *market*, since huge corporations muscle out newcomers. But if the CDC does not wean itself quickly from the bureaucratic bosom, the thin mixture of copying powder and correcting fluid that it is forced to suck will doom it to a kind of infantile senility within the space of three to four years. It is a dilemma of considerable proportions, for which there follows a solution.

CHAPTER 6

Social Marketing and the
Organized Poor

*The anger that leads one to strike out aimlessly like a baby is
gone. Black people have learned that the revenge of the night
must give way to the revelation of the morning; that hot explosive anger must give way to the cool determination to build
a community where children can grow up to live the dreams
that we dare not talk about.*

*Fight square, fight on, fight plaza, fight village, and fight
riverfront are only physical manifestations of those dreams.
The moral basis is that we are our brother's keeper; that we
are not isolated animals; that the poor do know what's good
for themselves.*

Bernard Gifford

By "social marketing" I mean the offering of goods for
sale which are labeled and advertised, not on the spurious
grounds of miracle ingredients and acquisitive advantages
to the consumer, but on the basis of the humanity, the
community and the social purposes behind the products,
in this case, Community Development Corporations. The
strategy of social marketing is to create a supplier-
consumer alliance, between the poor organized into CDC's
on the one hand, and on the other hand relatively affluent
and college-educated young, organized into groups, which
give allegiance to peace, civil liberties, ecology, social justice, women's rights, consumerism, etc.

CDC's would invite organized consumers to make socially, politically and ethically motivated purchases, based
on accurate knowledge of what a CDC stood for and the

social purposes which it was accomplishing. In effect it would be a form of "anti-advertising." For while conventional consumer advertising "provides, in the aggregate, a relentless propaganda on behalf of goods in general," in which, "even minor qualities of unimportant commodities are enlarged upon with a solemnity which would not be unbecoming in an announcement of the combined return of Christ and all his apostles,"[1] social marketing would satirize this empty bombast, while stressing that the only important difference lay in the human function, the struggle against racism, and the quest for community, epitomized by a particular CDC.

It would not be necessary in the first few years of operation for a CDC to manufacture for itself the goods it sold. Indeed, if social marketing proved successful, demand could far outstrip the productive capacities of even the best organized CDC's. For rapid expansion, the fullest exploitation of demand and to accommodate the peaks and troughs of political and moral crusading, it would be wise to retail, wholesale or mail-order supplies manufactured by others, but labeled and "brand-managed" by CDC's. Such a strategy would interpose groups of poor persons at crucial points in the distribution network of the economy. If enough organized consumers wanted them there, they could not be dislodged.

Moreover, supplying organizations once welded into the distribution pipeline could in time integrate vertically to take up an increasing amount of the packaging, storing, manufacturing, and raw material production. With an assured market and a full order book, a CDC supplying, say, laundry soap, could first order it already boxed, then start to make and print its own boxes, and later manufacture the soap itself. With numerous lines of merchandise to expand into, the CDC could concentrate on those with the best market, those with manufacturing skills available or trainable within the community, etc. It could use the prices at which goods are being supplied by existing manufacturers as a bench mark against which to measure its own ability to produce the goods efficiently. Such opportunities for expansion and for retention of increasingly large shares of the profit margin within communities would provide a continual incentive for economic growth and development.

The strategy of capturing a segment of the consumer market first could also ease problems of access to capital. Generally speaking, those organizations that can demonstrate customer demand and have backlogs of institutional orders from colleges, churches and voluntary organizations will have less trouble attracting funds and obtaining loans. But would manufacturers cut off supplies to CDC's, the moment that social marketing threatened to become a formidable economic and political force? It is hard to believe they would. In the first place, a number of substantial corporations, e.g., Xerox, the Mattel Toy Co., Kodak, Boise Cascade, are already committed to the success of specified CDC's. Two administrations, Democrat and Republican, have created and maintained some forty CDC grantees under the Special Impact Program of the Economic Opportunity Act. Were a manufacturer to cut off his supply of products to a CDC verging on spectacular success, not only might the opportunity to supply it be seized by a competing manufacturer, but the onus of "cutting the throats of poor people" and the possibility of a boycott by the same consumers who were organized to buy would loom very large.

Any agreements between manufacturers not to supply goods to a CDC are almost certainly illegal. Such agreements would have to include imported goods, along with at least fifty black capitalist manufacturers, which could hardly ignore the pleas of black CDC suppliers and expect to survive. In any event the sudden unavailability of any particular product line would not stand in the way of a social marketing campaign, which could include a very large number of interchangeable consumer products within the compass of its appeal. The system could be demonstrated as workable with the co-operation of less than 1 per cent of the nation's manufacturers.

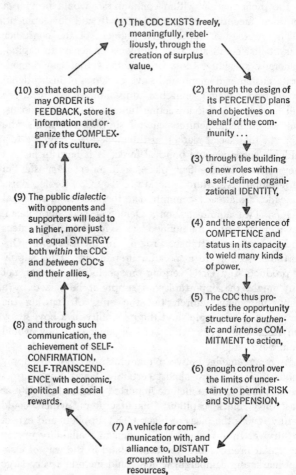

(1) The CDC EXISTS *freely*, meaningfully, rebelliously, through the creation of surplus value,

(2) through the design of its PERCEIVED plans and objectives on behalf of the community . . .

(3) through the building of new roles within a self-defined organizational IDENTITY,

(4) and the experience of COMPETENCE and status in its capacity to wield many kinds of power.

(5) The CDC thus provides the opportunity structure for *authentic* and *intense* COMMITMENT to action,

(6) enough control over the limits of uncertainty to permit RISK and SUSPENSION,

(7) A vehicle for communication with, and alliance to, DISTANT groups with valuable resources,

(8) and through such communication, the achievement of SELF-CONFIRMATION, SELF-TRANSCENDENCE with economic, political and social rewards.

(9) The public *dialectic* with opponents and supporters will lead to a higher, more just and equal SYNERGY both *within* the CDC and *between* CDC's and their allies,

(10) so that each party may ORDER its FEEDBACK, store its information and organize the COMPLEXITY of its culture.

Social marketing—along with much of the rest of this book—was designed with the helical model of psychosocial development in mind. Here is the overview and structure, for the argument in this chapter.

1. *The CDC EXISTS* freely, *meaningfully, rebelliously, through the creation of surplus value*

In arguing for CDC's in Chapter 4, I stressed the importance of poor people, organized into groups to share meanings, freeing themselves from pre-programmed advice and exhortation. Even if the professionals were broadly right about what the organized poor "ought" to do (and they seldom are) the concrete existential choice in the actual situation has to be made by the poor themselves—not because they choose better—but because choice is a developmental necessity, without which one remains "poor" in every sense of that word. Community choices can best be achieved when each CDC becomes its own origin of *surplus value.*

Heretofore, surplus value has had a restricted meaning, referring only to the economic wealth generated by an enterprise over and above its own needs for survival. With social marketing, however, this source of wealth becomes one of *meaning* and *value.* The CDC and its area inhabitants live in and by these values and project them out into the society as an inseparable part of its merchandise. Hence the level of existence—of outward-thrusted meaning —is immeasurably increased. The CDC's can present themselves as a source of new life-styles, as pioneers in a new conception of fighting poverty, as redefiners of the very terms "wealth, excellence, social responsibility, justice," etc. When they meet and negotiate with others, *they* will have defined the subject matter, shaped the agenda, listed the priorities. There are infinite degrees of freedom and choice for a poor community. They can choose to employ welfare recipients, rehabilitate convicts, help mental patients, extol Black Power, rebuild the ghetto, fight racial injustice, build free schools, create safe streets—the list is limited only by the limits of imagination within the CDC and among responding customers, and by the amount of activity that can be subsumed beneath the supply of each increment of product or service.

For the most part, conventional corporations barely consider the meaning of their work at all. How many Kellogg's employees sigh with satisfaction at the day's end, thrilled by the avalanche of Cornflakes and Rice Krispies that will reach tomorrow's breakfast tables? If they are few, and if the vision is less than exalted, might this not derive from the cultural limitations of snapping, crackling and popping in preference to more adult forms of communication?

Social marketing nourishes rebellion in the best sense of that term—a redefinition of one's life, values and social purpose from the roots up. Because someone somewhere must confirm the new, rebellious vision by buying the products that carry its meaning, this kind of radical existence meets the criteria of Albert Camus:

> In order to exist, man must rebel, but the rebellion must respect the limits it discovers in itself—a limit where minds meet and, in meeting, begin to exist.[2]

Hence every new projection by the CDC of its own spirit is aimed at an idealistic human response, somewhere beyond that community itself. Because the projection never for a moment ceases to be an act of attempted communication, it is a "rebellion for growth," not destruction.

Social marketing also aims to cut the gordian knot, strangling innovation in the marketplace. Just try to get a new detergent into a supermarket, or a new can of fruit. The "entry costs" are prohibitive, requiring price concessions to the supermarket which border on bribery. The basic homogeneity of rival products is no accident. So long as products are virtually identical, the competitive emphasis falls upon sheer commercial weight and push—all of which favors the big supplier against the small. Everywhere we find bottlenecks with thousand-man sales forces and millions in advertising used to push the strongest through and squeeze the weaker out.

Typically, a big manufacturer will set up "competition" between his own brands so that he straddles the limited choices within a product field. Not only does this alert him to shifts in taste, but one of his lines will stand to pick up the losses of another. Brute strength is, as always, the kissing cousin of basic uniformity and restricted opportunity, in marketing as in politics.

What is needed to cut through this knot is a rebellion against dominating strength and enforced homogeneity themselves. So long as you accept the values by which you lose, the bigger, the slicker and the established will control the market and periodically revise the rules in ways that keep you losing. Social marketing is existential and potentially radical because it alters the underlying premises about Economic Man, as a self-satisfying cash-register-cum-alimentary-tract. Everything we do is founded on values. Change those values and the most formidable, impermeable edifice starts to rock and you discover a truly amazing strength within yourself.

Consider . . . You cannot be squeezed out of a market by "superior hucksterism" and sheer advertising volume, if enough consumers are united in opposition to hucksterism and market domination. Hour upon hour of corporate monologue could only repel an audience dedicated to dialogue. Where CDC's appeal as underdogs and victims of racism, then the very use by top dogs of their powers of vindication will only emphasize their top dog status. A dominant culture that worships quantity, size and relative standing upon predetermined yardsticks can yet be flummoxed by qualitative changes militating against the linearity itself. What can a corporation chairman with three houses and two swimming pools do about a CDC which says it needs the money more than he does? Once the consumer agrees to consider the needs of the supplier in addition to his own, the whole basis of "competition" is altered. It's a totally new game.

One advantage of a conceptual revolution is not only that the quantity of a particular value may become irrelevant, once it is overturned, but that, like a skilled jujitsu artist, one can turn the strength of a deflected enemy in one's own preferred direction. Hence the cigarette commercial "I'd rather fight than switch," featuring the Tareyton smoker with a black eye and machismo sentiments, can be turned into a peace slogan "We'd rather switch [to CDC products] than fight." Even the noisy repetition of commercials can be used against them. Imagine a TV screen divided into quarters, within each square an earnest, white-coated gentleman lecturing you on thinly disguised equivalents of Excedrin, Bayer Aspirin, Anacin and Bufferin. Four seconds of hectoring confusion, as they all speak at once, all claim superiority, all quiver with sincerity; then the volume is reduced to a mutter, and you hear a Voice Over:

> They're lying, you know. There's no difference. The FTC has said so—four times. The FDA has said it, twice. We're fed up with having our airwaves *polluted* with this silly babble when there are so many urgent problems. We make aspirin too, just aspirin, no better and no worse than those four. But while we make it, we build a community, bring hope to thousands who never had hope before, and we're going to make our part of the city a livable place again, with safe streets, decent homes and self-respecting people. Think about that—come and visit us—you may even get fewer headaches, when you see what we're doing. But when you *do* get a headache—remember our brand. It's called "Just Aspirin." To you that might mean aspirin, pure and honest. To us it means a just society, with social and racial justice. When

you reach for JUST ASPIRIN you reach beyond pills to free us, you reach beyond things to people, and people need each other. Right?

2. *Through the design of its PERCEIVED plans and objectives on behalf of the community . . .*

Any significant measure of success for social marketing would not only allow CDC's to plan for cleaner streets, better schools, improved services, expanded sales, etc., but the community would become a veritable treasure house of economic, social and political intelligence. While in-depth studies of teen-age gum-chewing habits may be useful to Wrigley's Chewing Gum in a narrow economic context, such information lacks cultural and political significance. Such compartmentalization of knowledge into narrow veins is partly responsible for the seeming cultural deprivation of the business community, and helps to explain the tendency in our culture for organized insensibility to rule over less organized, more human sensibilities.

But under social marketing there would be developed information which synthesized cultural, political, ethical, social and economic facts and preferences. The CDC would gain access to priceless information concerning the socio-political pulse of American people, their philosophies, ideas, opinions and propensities. A steady stream of such information, if shared among CDC's, could make of them the best-informed, most intelligent and humanly sensitive social movement in American history.

Nor would this superior perceptiveness have to await the full flowering of social marketing. From the very outset CDC's could easily possess themselves of socio-economic intelligence that would be the envy of a sophisticated market research group. For the great advantage of appealing beyond materialism to deeply held social, political and moral beliefs is that most of the "market research" has already been done. We already know the proportions of liberal, conservative, populist, radical, pro-black and anti-black votes for thousands of wards and constituencies across the country. We know how different areas voted on dozens of referendum issues. Canvassing reports detailing house-by-house the support for particular candidates are probably obtainable. There are literally hundreds of political, social and voluntary organizations with highly articulated public positions—and membership lists. Progressive forces in the American middle class are inveterate petitioners, letter writers and joiners.

Such persons also concentrate themselves geographically around campuses, in urban centers, in key suburbs and in certain occupations. More open than suspicious, more garrulous than withdrawn, they would readily volunteer the names of their friends and associates for a cause they regarded as worthwhile. In comparison with the ease of locating such persons, one can only commiserate with Young and Rubicam, who conducted a survey for General Foods entitled "Exploratory Interviews to Uncover Conscious and Latent Consumer Needs in the Grilled Sandwich Area."[3] Whereas social marketing has only to discover the more intelligent and articulate beliefs of the more intelligent and articulate consumers, Y&R must hunt down the furtive sandwich eaters, grilling and masticating unseen in a million kitchens.

The effect upon a poor community of attaining access to such a broad array of socio-economic and cultural intelligence as social marketing can provide would be profound. We saw in Chapter 1 that young people mature conceptually by comprehending, first, their immediate family, then their local community, then their larger urban environment, their state, nation and the world.[4] This growth "by widening conceptual circles" was crucially dependent upon the quality of the links between one circle and another. Hence, if the head of the family was jeered at on the street, if the neighborhood was humiliated by the indifference of city hall, if the city was powerless in national affairs, major defenses would develop against a comprehension of "the wider circle," and ghetto adolescents would remain fixated at "street level," or lower, regarding the world of work beyond the ghetto as a treacherous and humiliating sphere.

The combined effect of bringing the world of work into the ghetto along with a stream of sophisticated information about friends and allies "out there" could transform the perceptual, informational and conceptual learning of poor communities. Social marketing would become a "bridge of knowledge" to the outside, a map of how the political economy can work on behalf of the disadvantaged.

I have also argued that developmental perception aims straight for the contradiction between "is" and "ought," the real and the ideal, the status quo and the realizable. It attacks the feeble euphemisms which paper over the social anomalies and the absurd excuses. There are so many contradictions faced by the poor—in fact, poverty is a "crucified" state of being nailed between opposing pressures—that only a few can be discussed here.

One major contradiction is that American culture consists of two opposing streams, a deeply conservative economy, and a surface layer of liberal humanism, a thin warm stream above a deep cold one. Near the surface is a substantial segment of the *rhetorical leadership,* who are often vehemently on the side of the poor, while at a deeper level, the real economy holds the poor in its grip. Thus a book that moves one to tears by describing the plight of the poor is actually enriching a publisher and perpetuating the lopsided distribution of wealth. A talk show wherein a spokesman of the poor confounds utterly some platitudinous bureaucrat is but a surface victory. Who is making money from the show itself? Why Platitude Programmers, Inc.!

In fact, the self-expressive skills of the liberal middle class are, under the present system, of very limited use to the poor. A tiny proportion of the self-expressers have

ever met a payroll. For years they have held their noses
in the presence of businessmen, yawned at engineers, and
shuddered genteelly at the world of marketing and selling.
What can a CDC do with an English Lit. major? A soft
social scientist? You cannot eat the six thousand annual
denunciations of racism in dissenting periodicals which
are mostly read by the converted anyway.

Another way of thinking about this contradiction is that
it polarizes business and politics, economics and civil rights.
This is a crucifix for the whole Movement, so much so
that Jesse Jackson had recently to resign from the Southern
Christian Leadership Conference on the grounds that his
emphasis on economics distracted from civil rights. To be
an effective political spokesman for the poor one has to
break with the current social order. But can a struggling
CDC break with its bank, creditors, consultants, program
analyst, venture capital approval analyst, the IRS, local
businessmen? Not often, and not easily. No sooner does
a CDC become established than a very conservative pre-
occupation grips it—survival (reputedly the most popular
course taught at the CDC-run Roxbury Institute of Business Management).

The contradiction is most frequently found in the persons recruited for jobs in CDC's, where the ex-organizers
and politicians confront the managers and accountants,
two distinct subgroups, with two distinct philosophies and
precious little in common. The schizoid character of many
CDC's is not helped by the disproportionate approval
among blacks for teachers, clergymen, organizers and politicians, to the detriment of business-related persons.

Social marketing could make a giant stride towards the
reconciliation of these contradictions. First, because it asks
the liberal self-expressers to act in the marketplace, the
one, significant, non-verbal manner of which they are all
capable, and which will affect economic reality. It also
enlists the liberals' undoubted communication skills—but
again on behalf of concrete products and cash proposi-

tions. Let their passionate rhetoric change the patterns of economic distribution, rather than blowing the dust from speakers' rostrums. Once CDC's are into the business of book clubs, publishing houses, record companies and speakers' bureaus, the tens of thousands of liberal artists and writers can put their careers where their mouths are —so that audiences are moved emotionally and economically on behalf of the poor.

Social marketing is also an answer to the conservative-radical polarity between the businessman and the politician within the poor community. Political and social skills become the basis on which the CDC appeals for customers. Blacks do not have to change their positive evaluation of preachers, politicians and organizers. They have only to make these values apparent and salable to others, while rewarding the businessman for taking those "controversial" risks that must be taken if CDC's are to alter their relationship to external institutions. Politicized business is conducted by new rules, which fuse the skills of each specialist.

3. *Through the building of new roles within a self-defined organizational IDENTITY*

The character or IDENTITY of the CDC would clearly shape the roles within that organization, and the significance accorded to each position. Yet both character and roles within it are themselves dependent on the *product* strategy.

At least two strategies recommend themselves. The first is to supply mostly "dull" and homogeneous types of mass-produced products, e.g., Just Soap, Just Aspirin, Just Stationery. The idea is that the people behind the product are seen to their best advantage, where the product itself competes minimally for attention, and that homogeneous products are those most irritatingly and artificially differentiated by advertising, so that where you have a basically dull product, you will have a basically annoyed consumer, hoping for surcease. Moreover such products are often simple to make, taxing minimally the community's technology and facilitating a common understanding of shared work. Another advantage of a nondescript product is the many degrees of freedom which the CDC has to define a character more significant than its product. In the whole realm of healing, teaching, building community, fighting racism and struggling for justice, the CDC can be anything it wishes to define.

A second strategy would demand products so meaningful in themselves that they express community intentions. There are fewer possibilities here, but some very significant ones. For example, posters expressing political and social convictions are purchased in large numbers by young middle-class consumers and these could portray the consciousness of various communities and the ideals of social marketing. It is especially advantageous to be able to sell your own advertisements. Films or video cassettes made by residents to explain particular experiences, techniques, and dramas, e.g., The Trouble with Social Workers, The Landlord Without a Face, Running a Drug Clinic, could be sold to universities, social agencies and public television. A CDC could run a Social Justice Book Club, pressing those authors who hawk their social conscience, to waive royalties on books sold to the club, and encouraging their publishers to be similarly generous. Writers who research and interview among the poor should be reminded of the rights of their "raw material." In time a successful book club could grow into a major publishing venture.

Other examples of products that express community sentiment are black or Chicano studies programs, creative playthings to raise the intelligence of infants, cable TV franchises, community radio stations and educational supplies. A number of surveys have shown that blacks identify very strongly with the whole area of education, so that a scholastic supply house could be both the pride of a community and provide products useful to middle-class student allies of community development. For IDENTITY is not a small container, tossing on turbulent oceans, it is location in a world of meaning, to "stand for" education is a vital source of self-establishment. To have a role in rebuilding America, refurbishing its values, and educing its humanity is to find oneself and one's nation at one and the same moment.

Once we have de-emphasized the importance of the product itself (or, as in strategy 2, emphasized the human communication through the product), then product-related roles such as product inspector, lathe operator, finished assembler, machine maintenance man, etc., tend to submerge themselves in favor of "community builder," "rap leader," "organizer," "brother," "teacher." Now, the traditional view, which social marketing could alter forever, is that these latter roles are peripheral and "female" support activities to "real" production.[5] Hence the manufacture of plastic cocktail swizzle sticks is "productive," while teaching and healing are "burdens" upon hard-working swizzlers. But suppose that the product is supported on the marketplace chiefly because of the healing and teaching activities? In that case, the status and the evaluation of these latter roles rise sharply in comparison to product process roles, which, under strategy 1 or 2 become merely media for the expression of community character and values, much as the film technician is there to convey the film director's purpose.

We saw in earlier chapters that the vast bulk of "participative roles" offered to poor people in Model Cities, Community Action, and mental health legislation were dead-end, untransferable jobs, supervised by professionals and chronically dependent upon the good behavior and refunding of that particular program. Even the New Careers program put extra rungs beneath professional ladders, so that in several years (provided you went back to school) you could then start at the bottom! Of course, by then, several more rungs will have been added above you. Professional status must be constantly elaborated.

There is simply no future for the disadvantaged in climbing professional ladders, and bureaucratic hierarchies, since they are designed to narrow progressively at the top, so as to exclude more and more people. Frustration is built into the system, quite purposely, as is relative poverty. You have to invent your own roles and structure, if poverty is to be conquered—roles that are not subordinate and identities that are not a disgrace. Social marketing would permit a CDC to create as many roles as there are identifiable human needs, to boast of a lateral rather than a hierarchical structure and to get paid for the difficulty of resolving conflict without pulling rank.

4. *The experience of COMPETENCE and status in its capacity to wield many kinds of power*

Just as a community's perceptiveness can be greatly enhanced by the fusion of economic with social and political intelligence, so does COMPETENCE or strength depend upon an adequate synthesis of powers. Social marketing adds persuasive, moral and benefactory COMPETENCES to that synthesis of powers represented by the CDC itself.

Without social marketing CDC's will probably continue to lack dramatic impact or communicate clearly the novelty of their social purpose. Without social marketing the CDC can come to regard itself as socio-economic and cultural-political, but the environment will slice through the hyphens by its atomistic response to a composite formulation, and in denying the larger synthesis it denies the novelty in the synthesis. Yet to gain the response of a socio-economic, cultural-political market is to be confirmed in one's new creation. Consider what social marketing might have done in the heyday of the civil rights campaigns. Suppose that after each triumphant confrontation, wherein white oppressors disgraced themselves with brutal clumsiness, products had been available to liberal sympathizers. Suppose that the half-million mourners who came to Martin Luther King's funeral had, instead of enriching airline companies, paid $100 for products bearing his message, and commemorating his sacrifice? That would have meant $50 million passing through the hands of his followers, and along with it would have come huge increases in bargaining power, the cohesion of paid staff, the funds for fresh publicity and production. Of all the different kinds of power, economic power is essential to long-term cohesion. Unlike political, moral and persuasive powers it can more easily survive a leader's death, or the transient moods of national guilt and momentary sorrow. It is the glue that holds the other powers together. It can "cash in" on temporary crises, leaving behind something more tangible than a memory, namely, the means of perpetuating that memory by laying the foundation of new institutions.

CDC's, using social marketing, could manage this synthesis of powers, concentrating especially on those areas where conventional corporations are woefully weak, moral, political and persuasive competencies of an open and democratic kind. But what cripples poor people almost more than anything else is that they have nothing to give that others want, in short, no *benefactory* powers. In the final analysis a man's work and life are his gifts to others, his way of earning their love and approval. One way of understanding a riot, strike or boycott is to see them as desperate attempts to create a "benefit" with which to bargain. The "benefit" being a return to order, a return to work and a resumption of purchase. Yet it is easy to stir up hatred for "disruptive" strikes and "riotous" mobs, and the public usually blames the most proximate cause of any disruption. Hence workingmen and the poor have mostly "negative powers," which they exercise only in crises and at the cost of public disfavor.

Social marketing would eliminate this serious disadvantage by providing poor communities with positive forms of benefactory power. Consumers would be "buying" an alternative to riots, a positive philosophy, and, before long, the reality of social development and a renewal of America's values.

For a 10 per cent minority group like Black Americans, political power, gained by majority votes for representatives, would require the support of anything up to 40 per cent of the rest of the electorate. Even in cities like Cleveland a black mayor needs 15 per cent or more of white votes, and what he gains is a city with shrinking tax base and deteriorating housing, increasingly dependent on Washington or on white-controlled metropolitan government.

But with social marketing a black community which gained only 5 per cent of the national market for some popular consumer item would be a "community millionaire." Were black leaders to gain in the marketplace the same proportions of white voter allegiance they have *already* achieved in politics, they could transform a dozen ghettos or more.

5. *The CDC thus provides the opportunity structure for* authentic *and* intense *COMMITMENT to action*

I have argued that the poor are robbed of authenticity. Permitted to threaten, bluster and employ the rhetoric of revolution, they are nonetheless barred from the actions that could make them honest men. Even authentic acts of rage are turned inwards upon the community, so that the poor burn their own districts, rob their own kind and consume one another in their frustration. Leadership is earned through *in*authenticity, through negotiating with whites in deeply compromised ways, learning to repress one's anger, conniving at humiliating terms in order to have a little to distribute to one's followers. For there is liberation in telling hard truths to your oppressor, slavery in collusion and the mask of acquiescence.

But would social marketing be authentic in a medium where very little else is so?

The first guarantee of authenticity in social marketing is that its aim is at those already moved by the plight of poor minorities. If there are just 10 per cent to 15 per cent of whites who can appreciate the truth about race relations, then truth can be told with rewards rather than punishments, and we need not doubt that this truth will be emotionally intense. Authenticity and intensity will also be encouraged by the importance of the values being communicated, their personal nature, their human form and by the degree of exposure of a community's "soul" to the world. No sooner does one start to claim something of real importance, for example, that one is healing drug addicts, rehabilitating houses, taking people off welfare, than one's listeners will start to check up. They will have to be satisfied that at least the effort is genuine, and in time they will demand the results.

In contrast, the utter triviality of the claims made by conventional advertisers is quite deliberate and carefully calculated. As long as they keep the level of real COMMITMENT and intensity low, few will bother to check up on their authenticity. So long as it is a *little* lie, delivered by a capering buffoon, we just sigh and occasionally chuckle—while the buffoons grow richer than Croesus by exploiting our relaxed indifference, for those "little" lies, worth five cents apiece, add up to millions.

Hence authenticity and intensity go together. Once social marketing has raised the consciousness of buyers to the critical importance of a choice between CDC's and conventional suppliers, once people understand that they can make or break communities and companies by how they buy, then the opiate idiocy of the singing commercial can never insult our intelligences again. Commercial appeals would become people talking seriously to people, not lollipops dangled before children.

There is an old tradition, dating from the early Marx, that sees man as alienated from the work of his hands. The "authentic bridge" between his craftsmanship and the gratitude of the buyer has been chopped in a dozen pieces by the division of labor. I find this theory attractive, but no longer very convincing. It presupposes the gratitude and admiration of those who receive the crafted product, and in a society loaded down with excess products this ideal relationship of maker and recipient seems obsolescent.

However much the process of manufacture if fractionated, workers and the community can still be united by an authentic and intense social purpose which transcends the physical pieces of their product. If a worker's sole function is to sandpaper a creative plaything he can still understand the purpose of the toy, know that it is a gift from his community to the intelligence of millions of children, that his own children can have a better chance because of it, that Headstart programs have purchased thousands, that its sale finances a day care center which lets his wife go to school, and that thousands beyond his community understand his concerns and share his struggle.

In communications between the CDC and its market, authenticity and intensity have some very businesslike payoffs. Conventional advertising must battle an immense "shrug factor"—the indifference of consumers, who, as they become increasingly affluent, discover that the marginal utility of each additional product falls, even as the value of being huckstered about its miracle ingredients becomes increasingly offensive. During commercial breaks in New York City, there is a serious depletion of the water supply owing to the simultaneous flushing of toilets, in part, perhaps, a critical reflex to the nature of advertising. Whatever the cultural loss, there is still the question of the sheer inefficiency of communicating trivial untruths about boring products.

Now, while there is a great glut of products in affluent America, there is a famine of community, hope, meaning, value, authenticity and COMMITMENT. Hence social marketing would appeal not to the jaded appetites of the already fat, but to a public hungry for genuine values, eager to help if only there was a way. The "marginal utility" of such opportunities would be correspondingly high, the "shrug factor" minimal and the communication remarkably efficient.

One further factor aids authenticity in this context, and makes the CDC more effective than other corporations. When the CDC projects social responsibility in its marketing it is being true to its basic function. Should conventional corporations imitate its social appeal, by subsidizing homes for lost kittens, or by giving three cents for every returned boxtop to the Jimmy Fund, such corporations would be false to their function, which is to make money for absentee owners of capital. Nor should it be difficult to compare the proportions of their wealth which CDC's provide to poor communities with the proportion profit corporations provide. Then we shall see whose social conscience is authentic.

6. *Enough control over the limits of uncertainty to permit RISK and SUSPENSION*

Earlier we saw that the ideal conditions for growth included a voluntary RISK and SUSPENSION of one's "working hypotheses" in the form of values, plans and assumptions. These assumptions are opened up, tested in concrete situations and reintegrated, processes equivalent to segments 6, 8 and 10 of the cycle model. A poor person less often SUSPENDS himself, but typically is SUSPENDED. He enters into an encounter with more powerful forces, the welfare bureaucracy, the housing authority, police, employers, drug pushers, social workers, and discovers again and again that he must SUSPEND his assumption, because it is "mistaken," "pathetic," and/or "morally wrong," and he must listen carefully to what others tell him to do if he wants to survive.

The experience of having one's viewpoint disintegrated by others includes anxiety. It may be sharp and searing when the view is held with some hope or confidence, but often the poor protect themselves from incessant pain by holding views with little conviction, seldom committing themselves to ego-involved action, so that the disintegration of their plans is less traumatically felt.

We saw in Chapter 1 that *control* over RISK taking enables one to hold one's tension level close to a pleasurable level of "excitement," while lack of control produces furious oscillations between extreme boredom (too little tension) and extreme anxiety (too much tension). For the vast majority of poor people, crisis, disagreement and clashes with the dominant culture mean failure, pain, SUSPENSION. They are likely to develop a trouble-avoiding set.

What is liberating about social marketing is that the poor encounter the dominant culture as a collectivity, supporting one another against the disintegration of their viewpoints, and yet agreed upon a controlled level of RISK taking and openness. But above all they can experience crisis, disagreement and clashes with the dominant culture as economically *and* emotionally rewarding. Instead of uncontrollable, compulsory SUSPENSION being experienced as anxiety and failure, controllable and voluntary SUSPENSION is experienced as excitement and success. From a purely economic standpoint, the poor have little or nothing to lose anyway. A public confrontation with an Establishment corporation would enrich a CDC even if spectators split nine to one in favor of the Establishment. The barrier to taking risks is not economic, but psychological and this barrier social marketing helps to overcome.

This brings us to the question of why people risk themselves, and whether there is any difference between Martin Luther King and a stock car racer, both of whom risked death daily. Is there no difference either between the brave and the fanatic—save that the latter is your enemy and the former on your side? The developmental risk taker, the hero, is primarily concerned with the communication and survival of the meaning which he carries. He does not *seek* death, but struggles for a cause that will, if necessary, transcend his death. Social marketing, through the meanings it vests in a community, could give to all its workers meanings worth struggling for, even dying for. Such meanings could be suspended, opened up, and re-examined, because they speak so strongly to the human condition, that they will survive crises to be resurrected. It is in such crises, wherein thousands lose their grip on outworn rules, that the valuable, the situationally appropriate and the eternal principles of man's relatedness to man, are rediscovered, which is why the humane can afford to be open and flexible. In contrast, the fanatic does not wish to survive the destruction of his ideology. It owns and operates him—not vice versa. The stock car racer has found himself "an excitement machine"—a mechanical stimulater.

7. *A vehicle for communication with, and alliance to, DISTANT groups with valuable resources*

The American left has been a frail alliance of unions, intellectuals, certain ethnic and assorted underdogs, conceptually miles apart and seldom far from open dissension. Add to this the tactic of elites to divide and rule, and the easily divided, uncertainly allied have continued for the most part to be ruled. No movement can prosper without the capacity to BRIDGE the DISTANCE between its allies. Social marketing is designed as a BRIDGE between two large groups, far separated by different life experiences, the urban/rural poor and a portion of the middle class, newly liberalized and radicalized at its upper and better-educated fringes. The alliance can hopefully extend before long to migrant workers, blue-collar workers demanding more democracy in the work place, various "un-melted" ethnic groups, organic farmers and back-to-the-earth groups.

But we have to face the fact, and face it squarely, that the vast majority of co-operative type movements in Western democracies, wherein like-minded persons turn in upon one another for support and mutual human discovery, have been less than successful. One important ingredient in these failures has been the tendency for the poor to associate predominantly with the poor, thereby intensifying the existing lack of educational and economic resources. Although successful co-operatism can evoke much of the hidden potential in man, it often fails to grasp those opportunities and creative developments undreamt of in its collective philosophy. There has to be a strong conduit of funds and ideas linking the community with the culture at large. Until recently this would have involved dealing with the "oppressor class," but in the last few years this class itself has displayed considerable disaffection—so much so that perhaps for the first time in the history of powerful nations, radicalism correlates with socio-economic class, so that the opportunity for a non-oppressive economic alliance now exists. With CDC's a system of economic and ideational exchange is now possible with a segment of society well heeled economically, well endowed intellectually and creative in its overall orientation to social and political affairs.

There is an old adage that if one lives in a small community one can be known without knowing, but if one lives in a large city one can know without being known. There seems no escape for middle-class Americans from the dire alternatives of a co-operative parochialism, or an alienated urbanity. Even these unattractive options are denied many poor people who remain alienated and uninformed.

Yet with social marketing there does seem an excellent chance of combining the close ties of real community with a "bridge of knowledge" to the outside world. While the CDC member remains with familiar faces, close, warm, long-term friendships—all to human scale, the very content of this interaction would concern the views of distant persons, the humanity they shared with the community, and how they could be better reached by the CDC's communications systems.

Social marketing helps to resolve the perennial dispute, not only between urbanity and parochialism, but between integration and independence. It does so by prescribing an arm's-length alliance between black and white. Liberals have tended to assume that nothing short of immediate social intimacy could cure racial tensions. Yet it is the intimate encounter that evokes the greatest anxieties. It is not necessary for black people to be loved as individuals by whites in order to start money flowing from affluent to poor communities. Because organized acts of purchase are more abstract and ideological expressions of social concern than hugging and kissing, they can be expressed without "visceral backlash." Instead, social marketing allows whites to come into contact with black ideas, products and emanations. I happen to believe that we are not cured of racism until real intimacy is achieved, but I regard such intimacy as the last step, not the first. If poverty is an additional barrier, adding to the middle-class sense of disgust, then why not cure poverty by an arm's-length exchange and *then* embrace?

Once CDC's began to develop desperately needed skills in the building of community and the abolition of ghettos, further integration would be a matter of enormous advantage to whites, the most open, intelligent and flexible of whom would court the CDC community assiduously, while the bigots would conveniently absent themselves.

At such a time the degree of integration would be a function of mutual respect and desire.

8. *Through such communication, the achievement of SELF-CONFIRMATION, SELF-TRANSCENDENCE, with economic, political and social rewards*

Eighty per cent of a sample of Black Americans agreed with the proposition that "Black people have a special soul which whites have not experienced."[6] And it seems they were right, for another survey found that 44 per cent of whites complained that blacks had a *better* chance in the job market than they did, while 31 per cent said "the same chance." Only 25 per cent of whites could agree that they were relatively advantaged. This after close to a decade of media sermonizing on race relations, dozens of authoritative reports, riots, civil rights campaigns, martyrdom and scores of deaths.

It is arguable that the ringing denunciations of racism on national television and elsewhere only succeed in persuading other groups that their own needs are being ignored relative to blacks. Most whites cannot see that all the rhetoric is something apart from the economy and has done little to assuage racial injustice. They assume that "everyone is for blacks."

Three things emerge from all this. First, black or Chicano CDC's must concentrate on that 25 per cent of "aware" whites, who are enough to constitute a huge potential market. Second, blacks and Chicanos have to continue to communicate and persuade on civil rights. They cannot just concentrate on economic development. Prejudice is still too massive. Third, the process of persuading white America on the facts of discrimination and the suffering of the disadvantaged cannot remain apart from the economics of daily life. The present separation gives a false appearance of victory, and stirs the jealousy of other victims, when there is nothing in fact to envy.

Only social marketing could fuse movement rhetoric with *actual* economic gains. If it can be made to work, customers will not be accepting just a product, but confirming, rewarding and understanding a community, its message and its soul. This is vastly more significant to interracial understanding than a female who purchases a face cream, incidentally produced by a black capitalist, so that she can discover "a lovelier you." The one is narcissism; the other, human understanding.

There are reasons to believe that social marketing would compare favorably with traditional marketing as a technique of communication and for sheer efficiency of impact. The evidence comes from communications research. First, it has been found that better-educated people prefer two-sided arguments to one-sided arguments.[7] Second, it has been found that when young people are confronted with two conflicting claims upon their allegiance, one stressing the rightness of egoism and personal satisfaction, the second stressing satisfaction achievable through helping others, they will choose the second, and the more the issues are clarified through debate, the greater is the conversion to this option.[8]

Third, it has been found that a medium is effective in carrying a message to the extent that its character is congruent with a particular message.[9] For example, the advertising of a wart-removing substance in the pages of *TV Guide* has to reckon with the fact that no programs feature warts and less than 2 per cent of the readership are "wart-conscious" as they flip the page—and yet it still pays to advertise. How much more would it pay to make a socio-political and commercial appeal in the pages of a left-wing journal, immediately following a moving article on the possibilities of community development? Here congruence would be high and advertising readership could climb as high as 80 per cent of total readership. The ratio of replies to circulation for mail-order advertising could be unprecedented.

Fourth, there has been considerable revision of the notion that the mass media stimulate the masses, who twitch individually to their appeals. In fact, messages are crucially mediated by the social network in which the individual has a place.[10] After receiving a message he checks with his relevant reference group, especially its leader upon that particular topic. It has been found that appeals are most effectively disseminated by the social network and acted upon by members (a) when the appeal is congruent with the purposes of the social network, (b) the leader is known, respected, articulate, (c) the social network is active and cohesive, (d) the network is urban, secular, cosmopolitan and educated.

Fifth, there has been considerable research on recall and retention of messages, and on brand loyalty.[11] Recall is much higher if (a) the hearer envisages himself passing the message on to a friendly audience, (b) the message engages deeply held socio-political attitudes consistent with the message, (c) the message is part of an organizable whole, (d) it provides a role for the hearer to play, (e) he can act upon the message quickly, (f) he sees the material within the message as being useful in argument. Once again, social marketing has distinct advantages on these criteria. Brand loyalty is much harder to break when (a) a purchasing habit becomes a fundamental aspect of belief and character, (b) one's reference group uses the product, membership is related to the use of the product and one is seen by one's group to use it, (c) use of a product is subject to rational analysis, conscious choice and reflection. Once social buying becomes a habit, consumers who had nudged social history in a self-chosen direction would not lightly regress to suckling on the latest taste sensation. For the vulnerability of traditional marketing is that brand loyalty is often weak, based upon unreflective, semi-automatic habits and prejudices, fleeting, subliminal reactions and attitudes as foolish as the commercial appeals that fostered them. To make purchasing choices a matter of critical scrutiny and reflection is to direct a searing light upon the compensatory fantasies, the faddishness, narcissism and "incest" of man-product relationships.

A word should be said about failures, because there will be some. Almost certainly some CDC's will overpromise and then try to fudge results. With large amounts of money suddenly available to people who have had so little, for so long, some corruption is inevitable, some idealistic promises to the consuming public will be tragically marred and broken. It is a crucial part of the system design that when gangsters seize control of a CDC they find themselves with the lion's share of nothing. Consumer support depended upon idealism, upon honest endeavors, however faltering, to fight poverty and build community. If such promises are broken the market will collapse, and the citizens' board will purge the corrupt executives—not just because they are corrupt, but because they are unsuccessful and cannot even pay off their cronies.

The Mafia can infiltrate American business and wholesale corruption can continue because the consumers do not care about the origin of the Popsicles they suck. This gives criminals their chance to move into the vacuum of our uncaring. We owe it to poor communities to discourage mutual exploitation by systematically rewarding internal democracy and civic virtue, and giving those communities that move strongly against corruption another chance, and another, so long as a learning process is in evidence.

Social marketing can also unleash one of the most powerful motives in man, that of SELF-TRANSCENDENCE, the desire for one's visions, acts and communications to pass from one's own identity to enrich the lives of others beyond one's lifetime. Do not laugh at revolutionary immortality. The flesh and blood of Asian peasants has proved stronger than our technologies, our people-sniffers, electronic battlefields, and laser-guided rockets. SELF-TRANSCENDENCE can inspire death and sacrifice as well, and is not necessarily developmental. But it becomes so when harnessed to creativity and its expression in human values. For this, social marketing, which buries the product within the humane concerns of its originators, is an ideal vehicle.

9. *The public dialectic with opponents and supporters will lead to a higher, more just and equal SYNERGY, both within the CDC and between CDC's and their allies*

Social marketing contributes importantly to the synergistic process of creating abundance. Using communications media, a value-full context of ideas, imagination and information can enrich the several participants in different ways. Add ten dollars to ten dollars and you have a mere addition. Compete over who gets most of the twenty dollars and you have an atmosphere of hostility and psychological scarcity—a zero sum game—delightful for statisticians but a jungle for all caught up in its concrete reality. But where images are combined with images, ideas with ideas, and the whole orchestrated into a symphony of values, then one creates more than the sum of the ingredients, and the whole transcends each of the individual parts as well as their totality.

For example, take a poster drawn by the young daughter of a CDC member, which is printed by the community and sold to a university student. What do the parties have? The girl and her community get to express themselves, they get money for the poster and there is no need to fight with the group of consumers about shares of money, because all money flows one way—from middle-class customers to the poor. The CDC also communicates via the poster the idea of social marketing, the spirit and values of the community and the availability of additional products. It may even succeed in harnessing one SYNERGY to another SYNERGY. For example, the poster may explain that the community seeks consumer co-operation based on specific internal co-operative tasks it is performing. In this event the kindness and skill of one ex-junkie in healing an addict produces "spontaneously" the desire of consumers to buy the poster. Two formerly separate acts of concern are now synergized.

What does the buyer of the poster get? She or he gets the feeling of having helped the designer and the community and of having responded to and confirmed the message. By displaying the poster she expresses her own convictions, social, political, ethical, decorates her room, and satisfies her aesthetic sense. By paying for the poster she supported an idea she approved of, and "voted" for a social and economic direction for her country. Notice that a single act of purchase and sale has taken on a much heavier loading of meaning than is usually the case.

Or consider the idea of SYNERGY as justice, equality and balance between parties and elements. There is SYNERGY in moving money from the middle class to the poor, since each dollar is usually worth more to a poor person than to a middle-class one, so that equality increases the amount of positive evaluation of each dollar.

But there is a more fundamental opportunity for SYN-ERGY; different viewpoints, needs and activities can only be fused if they are weighed equally in the process of attempting a reconciliation. Social marketing, with its high informational and visual content, by its capacity to thrive economically off controversy, its ability to use the mass media to explore rival issues and its consistent advocacy of equality and social justice, is an excellent vehicle for balancing the demands of consumers and suppliers.

It would be essential for organized CDC's to deal as equals with organized groups of consumers. Such an alliance could be gradually expanded and experientially deepened by "encounter group type" soul searching and mutual revelation. Where deep *needs* instead of righteous and moralistic *goals* and *demands* are revealed, there is a considerable increase in the "synthesizability" of motives.

For goals specify, often rigidly, how a need should be met, while a "naked" need can be met by a number of different goals.[12] Ultimately, dialogue is a far more sensitive and intelligent form of communication than monologue and manipulation. We have only to make product appeals sensitive and human to reap the benefits of dialogue, and expose the crudity of monologue, while traditional advertising must strive to keep its materialism crass in order to nullify the advantages of dialogue.

If whites wish to reform relationships within the ghetto, then the point of easiest leverage is not an army of social workers urging mental health morality on thousands of domestic relationships, but a move to relationships of dialogue and equality between poor communities and the wider culture. Make this relationship profitable and just and the leading residents will soon internalize the style by which they gain their bread and their influence. Social marketing does this and more; it pays CDC members for treating each other with justice and consideration. The demonstrated decency of brothers and sisters to one another is the basis on which consumers are attracted. SYNERGY interpenetrates the different levels.

I am no sentimentalist about "hidden democracy" among poor people. I believe that the arts of SYNERGY have to be learned, that the learning is difficult, and that the habits of deprivation die hard. I also note that men will stand up to their knees in blood and entrails in a slaughterhouse to earn a living wage, that many recruits are sickened but persist and learn, and I don't believe that living synergistically is as hard as that! I also believe that there are greater intrinsic rewards in SYNERGY than in slaughter, even if both are undertaken, in the first instance, to make a buck.

We have already touched upon numerous contradictions that "crucify" poor people, and which it is the function of SYNERGY to resolve. There is the tension between "is" and "ought," between knowing that you are oppressed and countenancing the shame and disgrace. There is the conflict between needing to make some money, and the need to confront the (white) source of your survival, and the fact that your white "allies" are mostly impotent to help you, while your white opponents sit upon the resources you need. There is the contradiction that you "win" at the level of symbolic politics, but lose on bread-and-butter issues, so that liberal "victories" give them a sense of righteousness but leave you empty and angry. There is the conflict that you need to separate yourself from middle-class whites to achieve independence, yet the bulk of the resources are on the other side of the divide. You have to qualify to get a good job, but most qualifications are exclusionary by design.

I have argued that social marketing helps to resolve *all* these contradictions and many more, by redefining polarized alternatives until they merge. In fact, a close look at the principles of the development model will reveal that they are themselves potential opposites. To exist rebelliously is to differentiate oneself, while to find SELF-CONFIRMATION is to integrate. To SUSPEND is an internal differentiation or disintegration, so that one can better reintegrate oneself internally. All segments of the cycle are variations on differentiation and integration and the whole cycle integrates differences, and differentiates integrities in an endless sequence.

It was Marx's insight that the relationship between labor and capital was the chief shaper of cultural consciousness. I believe this has changed with the decline of mass production as a cultural deity and the rise of consumerism. Surely it is truer to say that we are shaped by hundreds upon thousands of commercial transactions from the toy store to the stock market. TV as one medium of this commercialized consciousness is watched, on average, for 3,000 days between the ages of two and sixty—roughly nine full years of life.[13]

If social marketing can alter the meaning of the buying-selling relationship and our mass-communicated culture we shall have wrought a transformation. The traditional commercial relationship is the lowest possible form of SYNERGY —an *egotism à deux*.[14] The customer, eyeing the shelves, thinks, "Gimme that." The salesman, eyeing her purse, calculates what he can extract.

Now, social marketing works by inviting the consumer to care about the supplying organization, its people and its soul. The consumer satisfies not just material wants but social, political, relational and world concerns. It would "shape" people entirely differently, evoking their humanity instead of drilling it out of them.

10. *So that each party may ORDER its FEEDBACK, store its information, and organize the COMPLEXITY of its culture*

I have argued that CDC's can become storehouses of vital skills, resources, information that are imperative to a sense of movement and continuity in the organized life of poor people. Social marketing with its continual projection of a community's life-style, aims and achievements is a perfect means of building a community history, a coherent set of images, a cultural matrix accumulating over time, movement in the best sense of the word. If, as is often claimed, poor minorities have had their cultural traditions expunged, and their collective sense of ethnicity uprooted, here will be a chance to gather and restore the fragments into a whole, to make history and record it.

The social intelligence gathered by CDC's would be quite different from the "social bookkeeping" of large federal and private agencies. The former would obtain knowledge about equal relationships, full disclosure of intentions, the most creative ideas and the most productive SYNERGIES. It would thus stand in marked contrast to organized social science with its pitiful piles of fractured findings. We could begin to witness the collapse of artificially and pathologically differentiated disciplines. Instead of boxes labeled economics, psychology, sociology, philosophy, political science, medicine, etc., we would have an integrated, problem-centered, human-centered and ultimately relevant information on which *political* and *ethical* images elicit which *economic* gains and what kinds of *sociological* systems grow from and respond to such action.

The disgrace of social science in our time is not just in its refusal to help the poor, for in truth it has little to give to man qua man.[15] For social science has all but banished man himself from the center of life's stage, to become a detached observer skulking in the wings, and regarding actors as the derivatives of the props and facades. All knowledge accumulated by this means is useful only to men similarly detached and alienated from events, men who are "liberal" in direct proportion to their distance from the problem. Voyeurism has become the cornerstone of the "scientific method" applied to social affairs—Peeping Toms watching Uncle Toms through slits in the ivory tower, the impotent methodically measuring the impotence.

What social marketing promises, through a redefinition of social knowledge as the product of COMMITMENT, are large numbers of social indices by which the conquest of poverty and discrimination can be measured. One problem is that a bottle of aspirin would have little room on its tiny label for the history and ambitions of its CDC supplier. What will be required are readily identifiable indices of achievement. If we want men of achievement to fight poverty, we have to replace traditional success symbols with indices that more nearly reflect humane accomplishment.

CDC's could publish the mean earnings of their employees, along with ratios of top-to-bottom earnings, to give an equality index, an assurance to the consumer that his support was not going to nouveau riche poverty hustlers; indices of minority hiring, percentage of surplus spent on,

CHAPTER 7

Orchestrating Social Movements: Some Middle-Class Allies for CDC's

The inescapable conclusion is this: At the bottom of the whole question of backward cultural development of America the cultural banality, the cultural decadence, the cultural debasement of the entire American social scene, lies the reality of racism—racial exclusion, racial exploitation, racial segregation, and all the manifestations of the ideology of white superiority. . . .

For this fundamental reason the Negro civil rights movement, at this late stage of its development, cannot go any further, it cannot transform itself into a movement with a revolutionary set of ideas unless it incorporates a cultural program along with its economic, social, and political program.

Harold Cruse, *Rebellion or Revolution*

Specifically, with which current groups of middle-class reformers might CDC's ally? We must beware of simply appealing to "white sympathy" for "black oppression." It is humiliating for blacks to be objects of sympathy, or to believe that whites are striving "unselfishly" for them. It is equally cynical to claim that people only feather their own nests, and that all moral statements can be reduced to a core of egoism.

The aim must be to resolve the selfish-unselfish dichotomy, so that helping others is an extension rather than a negation of the self, and each reform movement realizes its own ambition via the enhancement of others.

In order to design such SYNERGIES and orchestrate the parties to the alliance, it is necessary to search the motives and aims of some contemporary movements. The following discussion of the critics of mass culture, the youth rebellion and peace movement, the women's liberation movement and those concerned with ecology, cannot pretend to be comprehensive. I am solely concerned with those of their aims that are synthesizable with a social marketing—CDC—strategy.

The critics of mass culture

These range all the way from the outraged sensibilities of what the *Wall Street Journal* calls the new "mass intelligentsia," to the many more who feel that commercial media insult their personalities. Actually, there can be no non-violent change in our social institutions without some measure of change and control by progressive forces of the means of persuasion and communication. Before reaching the age of eighteen an average child has watched television for 22,000 hours, longer than it takes to study for a bachelor's degree. One becomes what one beholds.

It has been argued forcefully that each one of us who connives at oppression at home and bombing in Vietnam diminishes himself culturally and humanly. Could many of the tragic events of the last few years have happened had we not been tranquilized and mesmerized by a "culture of foaming nonsense"? Attempts to televise various threats to our civilization bring furious protests at the interruption of soap operas. In fact, there is a major communicational pathology at the very heart of our entertainment industry. Until it is cured we cannot as a nation really talk to each other in a way that resolves other issues. We have slipped into a technocratic definition of the democratic process, which claims *it is democratic to know in advance, and to supply audiences with the programs that most will watch*. Such a proposition directly attacks principle 6 of our developmental model, the need to RISK and SUSPEND oneself in communication to others. It assumes that programmers have little or nothing to learn from the reaction of their audience, because they can make a "sure-fire" impact. The process resembles a phonograph record stuck in a single groove.

To be certain, or near certain, that an audience will watch a program, one would have to sacrifice all democratic values inherent in the cycle model: (1) any creativity likely to surprise or annoy the audience, (2) any respect for the audience which might make you overestimate its intelligence, (3) respect for one's own uniqueness, which distinguishes one from the audience, (4) any belief in one's COMPETENCE to enlighten the audience, (5) any personal COMMITMENT or fervor greater than that of the audience, (6) the chance to change one's mind as a result of communicating with them, (7) the chance to introduce to audiences unfamiliar experiences to which their reaction is not known, (8) the opportunity to be CONFIRMED as an artist, a leader and an innovator, (9) the chance to create new shared bonds and to renew human co-operation and mutualities, and (10) the chance to expand public consciousness through shared viewpoints and thus create a complex and aesthetic culture. The sacrifice of these values is precisely what television, commerce and popular culture have achieved.

This explains why the Golden Age of television was at the very beginning of its postwar operations, before Nielsen ratings had accumulated and mass reactions were known, and why its quality declined precipitously as techniques for reaching audiences were perfected. Social learning is partly a function of uncertainty and of periodic error.

Because large advertising revenues ride upon a single program, every effort is made to secure the largest audience at the lowest risk. With so much economic risk, existential RISKS that imperil the "delivery" of an audience are all but eliminated, and fierce contests in sameness ensue, with "different" programs milking the same few cultural udders with a brutal energy.

Accompanying genuine existential RISK taking is the experience of tension which increases to the point of anxiety. Yet traditional program policy forbids anxiety-inducing material that might cause us to SUSPEND cultural shibboleths. Since tension at the level of excitement—but not at the level of anxiety—sells soap, the "solution" is to portray conflicts that the viewer knows will be resolved for him seconds before the program ends. He can get excited about the near success of stereotyped villainy, safe in the knowledge that some embodiment of Red-Blooded Americanism or Muscular Christianity will administer "righteous" beatings in the nick of time.

Not only does that viewer associate the reliable raising and lowering of his tension with the see-thru freshness of Baggies, but with the use of greater force, authoritative force, and righteous force, which solves his problems and reduces his tension as a concomitant of solution. As the program ends, he is "set up" for the commercials that follow, once more relaxed so that he can swallow physically and mentally the substances processed for him. "Relax, eat up, the police and the Marines are taking care of it . . . See Wholesomeness return in shining white . . ."

However, the system has cracks in its edifice and they are widening. For commercial mass media are caught in a hopeless contradiction. The amount of money spent on advertising tends to be inversely proportionate to any real difference between rival products. Advertising's function is to differentiate artificially what is basically homogenous, like laxatives, cigarettes, soft drinks, aspirin, toilet paper and so on. To insist shrilly upon the distinction of the indistinguishable and undistinguished is its central technique. Caught between a desperate fear of losing customers through genuine innovation and losing customers through the intrinsic dullness of the product, advertising's "tigerish" solution is an ersatz novelty perched precariously upon a limp conformity, the dildo of its socio-emotional impotence.

Whatever meaning was once present in marketing tends

now to diminish with increasing affluence, for that meaning derived from physical necessity. The consumer balanced the purchase of one good against that of another, his usually rational choice spurred by unsatiated physical wants for health and survival. Today the principle of declining marginal utility makes every "new" product incrementally more boring than the last one, and the harsh discipline of survival is replaced by foolish whimsy of "dreamy softness, Lux in four colors to mix, match and have fun with." John Kenneth Galbraith has even prophesied a day when "the voice of each individual seller may be lost in the collective roar of the all together . . . Silence interrupted perhaps by brief, demoniacal outbursts of salesmanship will ensue."[1]

Social marketing could be the answer to many of the complaints of the culture critics. First, there are significant correlations between aesthetic appreciation and general social concern.[2] Since aestheticism also correlates with education, and the educated are the most disenchanted by TV fare,[3] they could enjoy a higher standard in CDC-sponsored programming. Genuine human differences between CDC's would be offered in the place of artificial product differentiation.

For much that is present in good art and entertainment is present in the logic of the social marketing appeal. Both emphasize true experimentation and originality, respect for human subject matter, subtle characterization and the evocation of the audience's full potential for intellectual and emotional participation in the drama of events. A market appeal that wants consumers to ingest passively can afford no entertainment that arouses them to critical scrutiny and action, but an appeal that seeks to evoke COMMITMENT and concern for forgotten Americans must command the whole realm of art and literature that has stirred men's souls.

In time the "social market" could come to represent a kaleidoscope of human ideas and life-styles. CDC's representing many approaches to community building, along with Daytop Villages, Synanon Houses, organic food farmers, Hippie communes, artists' co-operatives, New Towns, therapeutic communities, Free School Co-operatives, film-making and video colonies, Indian reservations, utopian communities, etc.

Sizable existential risks could probably be taken in programming and messages sponsored by CDC's and their organized consumer allies. Poor people have little to lose economically, while having everything to gain by a desperately authentic message that changes the attitude of audiences. Even an audience that split seven to three against a CDC's viewpoint would bring them increased custom and more support than they now enjoy (perhaps *only* poor people can risk the telling of hard truths). Because the whole attempt at community development is a pioneering venture, full of RISK and drama, it is probable that programming would reflect such heady experiences.

Social marketing could be of great economic advantage to the left-wing viewspapers like the *New Republic, New York Review of Books, Nation, Ramparts,* to the underground press and to specialist media. By and large such media get little advertising support, which drives up the cost of the publications and restricts them to intellectual audiences. A potential boon to the economics of dissenting journalism, social marketing could increase the size and circulation of all publications aiming at a socially responsive public. At present advertising departments are albatrosses around the necks of many writers. Dr. Benjamin Spock could get no mass circulation magazine to publish an article on peace until he was indicted. The then Senator Joseph Clark found that even a man of his prominence could not get such magazines to accept an article on truth in advertising. When NBC exposed the conditions of migrant farm workers in Florida, exploited by the Coca-Cola Company, the latter moved more than a million dollars in advertising to CBS and ABC.[4]

Social marketing could help end the pathological split between moral and economic forces. The progressive press and various movements would gain funds but only by putting their money where their mouths were, and joining their financial futures with that of poor people's corporations. The "Verbal Left" would face the challenge of building economically viable counter-institutions to potentiate whatever moral leadership it now claims.

The youth rebellion and peace movements

Although campus disorders have subsided and the conventional wisdom pronounces a return to the feckless style of the fifties, the roots of the tension have not gone away. As I wrote in *Radical Man,*

> One principal cause of student rebellion lies not in *their* discontinuity but in a strange unevenness within American cultural traditions. Coming to this country from England, early in the sixties, I was almost immediately struck by the strength of developmental and humanist themes in American educational and child rearing philosophies, and the relative weakness of these same themes in commerce and in politics. . . . It has long seemed to me only a matter of time before the developmental themes in American life confront the repressive themes, and before those students nurtured in the better homes and schools come to regard the opportunities offered by business and government as an insult to their achieved levels of psychological development.[5]

In effect, the youth rebellion is part of the war between the Two Cultures, the humanistic-idealist culture on the one hand, and the technical-scientific on the other. Campus rebels were drawn disproportionately to the liberal arts and softer social sciences at the more prestigious universities. The Movement was one favoring self-expression and self-fulfillment through social change, and it was far stronger among those who viewed their education as an expansion of cultural horizons, as opposed to those with instrumental attitudes towards education. For these reasons the Movement was preponderantly upper-middle-class.

For tens of thousands of students studying non-technical, non-professional subjects there is simply nowhere to go after graduation. Theirs is a crisis of role-lessness. Truth and beauty may be contemplated—but nowhere can they be realized—least of all with a B.A.'s qualifications. Attempts to solve this crisis are rarely successful. One method is to enter the communications field, but this only adds to the surfeit of liberal rhetoricians, over the doers and movers of more conservative cast. Another device has been the creation of temporary idealistic jobs such as VISTA and the Peace Corps, along with civil rights and organizing jobs funded by the "philanthropoids"— Ford, Carnegie and other foundations. These have served only to postpone the role crisis until mid or late twenties.

Another device has been to give whole sections of the disaffected generation an indefinite moratorium and a kind of cultural sandbox in which to play. When a federal blacklist was uncovered a few years ago, it was found only to apply to policy committees. "Poor security risks" were actually encouraged to do basic research, immerse themselves in their laboratories, while loyal Americans made selective use of their discoveries. On the same principle young people can write books, make speeches, demonstrate peacefully and strike a million postures of COMMITMENT, while the machinery of commerce grinds on, selling their rhetoric at a generous profit to itself, and distributing red armbands, rebellious tracts, beads, bells and other playthings.

Consider that the Vietnam War continued long past the time in which at least 30 per cent of the population was *implacably* opposed. Now, if that 30 per cent had been workers, executives or government officials, the war could not have continued. If one third of industry had struck, instead of one third of the universities, during the Cambodian invasion, the shock waves would have paralyzed the war effort. But who constitute anti-war forces? They are students, old people, housewives, clergy, teachers, writers, artists, intellectuals and poor minorities,[6] in short, precisely those who are creatively or forcibly detached from institutional mechanisms. Among the middle class the wellsprings of compassion and protest are a function of insulation-with-affluence, and such insulation is a privilege. Yet the price of insulation and "enlightenment" is practical impotence. For me the Berrigan brothers are psychologically tough, even heroic, but sociologically they are powerless and accepted that condition when entering upon a life of cloistered virtue. "Verily I say unto you, the children of darkness are more worldly than the children of light."

Few would deny that the advertising copywriter is deeply compromised as an artist. But what about those beautiful people cheered to an echo in literary salons and cathedrals of culture? What of the integrity of those well paid for their wit, artistry and criticism, who yet know their words cannot feed a poor family, or halt a slaughter? Of course, the talk show audience will clap dutifully when the sign lights up—it sounds so good anyway, and a few liberals will get elected because their personalities are engaging, but their audience simply cannot afford to emulate them. For it is tied by one foot and one hand to an economic and cultural meat grinder from which the speaker is freed. In fact, a closer look would reveal that the speaker is sponsored by the surplus generated from the meat grinder. He has used the system to insulate himself from it.

Social marketing could put an end to the practice of selling one's practical potency for cultural and spiritual sensitivity. It discovers within necessary consumption a potent source of influence with immediate effects. Selective purchase could be the first among many steps towards a re-engagement with, and alteration of, the dominant economy by millions who are currently becalmed in an extended moratorium.

Another role that middle-class supporters could play,

especially those at or around universities, is to vest CDC's with their creative productions and inventions, like books, records, tapes, designs, films, patents, etc. The universities are vast storehouses of unutilized prototypes; even if CDC's were in no position to exploit certain ideas, they could still act as agents for the inventors. In fact, a Social Justice Book Club could precede a publishing house, and a record club a full-blown recording business. Once alternatives were available, the pressure upon "enlightened" artists and writers to benefit the poor would be overwhelming. There is no good reason why a future Joan Baez (who began in a Cambridge cellar) and future Beatles (who began in a Liverpool one) should reach their own generation via RCA or giant recording companies. And those who write *about* the poor could hardly deny their CDC's the right to handle sales, once an effective sales organization was set up.

Yet another role that middle-class consumers could play is to take over the marketing and advertising functions of CDC's. There would be a new division of labor, with CDC's manufacturing and supplying, and consumers acting as agents, advisers and promoters on the best way of reaching other middle-class consumers like themselves. One way to insure that women are not insulted in the marketplace is to employ them to act with respect towards their own sex. The advantage of this idea is that it allows dissenters to do what they do best—write, dramatize, communicate, create, but in a way that *really* changes society because it alters distribution patterns.

Robert Lifton has described segments of the middle-class counter-culture as "protean man," collectors of experience and multifaceted identities.[7] Not for them, the long, obsessional career path, with its accumulation of personal power. If he is right, then such people would choose to do something different every few years, and they would be excellently suited to temporary, creative and self-expressive work on behalf of CDC's. One survey has shown that many of these young people have parents in mass media occupations,[8] and in entertainment, so communicating is very much their heritage, although the style is radically different.

I have argued that what bedevils the relationships between the poor and middle-class career bureaucrats in the "helping" professions is that the latter still aim to succeed in the traditional way. No one with such ambitions will readily link his fate to that of a poor person; rather he will arrange things so that he gets promoted independently of any emancipatory process.

In contrast, protean men, seeking a series of novel, intense, experiential and temporary relationships, might find an alliance with the poor adventurous rather than distasteful. They might be the first middle-class group in America capable of truly devolving their own abilities onto others without envy or the need for competitive subordination.

Above all, some of us would become *whole* men and women, instead of outraged hawkers of a conscience that few will buy. We may then see a pause in the process of radicals turning upon liberals, excoriating them for a cowardice that is more an impotence; in demonstrators hurling themselves against institutional walls, in a desperate attempt to put their bodies on the line with their convictions and to defy for a few moments the society which has lured them into playgrounds of perpetual preparation. For without counter-institutions of the kind social marketing could provide, insurgent leaders have to strive to maintain a crisis atmosphere, lest their unpaid followers drift off to another barricade and their movements "die" in the intervals between each new outrage.

Nor is the left as uncontaminated by consumerism as it likes to think. We consume causes like products, blacks one year, ecology the next, then back to imperialism. "I'm into the peace and conscience bag this year—how about you?"[9]

There is considerable scattered evidence that middle-class student consumers desire alternate information and supply systems and have even gone to the trouble and difficulty of setting them up for themselves.

The Yellow Jersey Bicycle Coop at the University of Wisconsin, along with the People's Beer have enjoyed considerable patronage and success. The North American Student Cooperative Association has 314 member co-ops in thirty-two states and six Canadian provinces. The *Wall Street Journal* reports:

> Many of those who support such institutions prefer to do so for ideological reasons. "We're sick and tired of the restrictions and hassles dumped on young people by the establishment," declares a University of Michigan Coed who belongs to a coop in Ann Arbor. "We want to get our own ideals and values in practice."[10]

Other highly successful co-ops are North Country Food in St. Paul, Minnesota, and SOB (Students of Berkeley), which has sprouted into a retail conglomerate, adding store after store, and supports day care centers and minority living programs. Credit unions have sprung up at least in a score of university communities. The Isla Vista Community Credit Unions sponsors its own Department of Justice.

The Boston *Globe* recently announced the launching of Video Frontier in local coffee houses, offering "wild, noncommercial, sometimes raunchy and always anti-establishment tube fare." New York and several other cities have witnessed the same phenomenon. "Groove Tube" specializes in satirizing commercial TV, while carrying announcements of local events, rock concerts, nature food restaurants, etc.[11]

In the meantime, there is a falling away from traditional marketing appeals. "The Great Youth Market is a bubble that has burst," complained the Research Guild of Chicago. Instead young people "have turned to fighting pollution and poverty," which "eventually have to have an effect on products." Status has moved "from conspicuous consumption to a posture of non-materialism. . . . Another alarming trend is the failure of "youth-directed advertising and sales promotion. . . ." With such "erratic social attitudes . . . mothers [who] used to curb their daughters' fashion impulses now must plead with them to buy." The "back to school" promotions and college-crested products "have taken on a sickly cast . . . as passe as hope chests." Marketeers have found some comfort in a booming do-it-yourself and "creative" market. Where Avon representatives used to offer free advice to high school girls on "make-up and dating," they have had to switch to "women's rights and the 18-year-old vote."

Daniel Yankelovich, Inc., has even instituted a social service to businesses so that they will not "underreact to trends that threaten their business." Trends potentially threatening as well as exploitable include "social and cultural improvement," "personal creativity" and "reaction to business hypocrisy."[12] Ironically, Yankelovich's findings are a near perfect argument for social marketing. His samples representing more than six million students demand precisely those changes by those means which social marketing could provide.[13]

An alliance with poor people in CDC's who are in genuine physical need could rescue the current youth culture from its self-indulgence, pseudo-primitiveness and tendency to cultishness. It desperately needs to live for a purpose beyond itself.

The peace movement is unlikely to make much progress either, unless it makes inroads into the mass media to prevent the promotion of violence. We have already seen how anxiety is reduced by righteous force. By the same process guilt about violence is assuaged by giving "redeemed" criminals special and impossible missions against a bestiary of foreigners.

The violence is the result of a basic dilemma. How do you impress people with bland conventionality, total lack of originality and the absence of authentic COMMITMENT? The answer is to *jolt* them with violence, sudden death, increased volume, sheer repetition, gimmicks and incidental humor. A genuine dramatist can spellbind his audience by an incident as small as a raised eyebrow. The hack has to mow down Germans, explode buildings, crash cars and show hospital patients or legal defendants hovering perennially between life and death if he is to stir, slightly, our jaded appetites. Like the sadist, the voyeur, the exhibitionist and the object fetishist, popular film and TV are driven to excess by the beast of their own nothingness. Especially in films we have an escalation of the *technical* virtuosity with which cruelty is depicted; bodies dance more convincingly as bullets shred them, blood spurts more dramatically from wounds, the suffused face and protruding tongue of the garroted man is more lovingly explored by the camera. As conservatives discovered long ago, you cannot go on extolling motherhood and apple pie; people will yawn in your face. Only a Monstrous Foreign Plot against mothers and pies can make your advocacy of the latter plausible. It needs a Mission Impossible in order to save our precious right to Hee Haw (for what would Hee Haw be worth if it wasn't endangered?).

The peace movement needs to go beyond piety to the exercise of a power short of physical force. An answer is surely economic power. Had there been CDC sources of supply when half a million marched in Washington, had the marches broken up into buying demonstrations, switching their patronage away from those who opportunistically fueled the war machine, the war would have been over in months. CDC's would today be recognized "peace organizations," teaching the arts of conflict resolution at the community level, and exemplifying the advantage of having a corporation whose owners are visible and responsive to social demands.

Ultimately, there can be no peace in the world unless human conscience is placed at the helm of our bureaus and machines. For this we require social and ethical proposals as well as responses. For powerless conscience conjures up its monstrous opposite, conscienceless power. I shrink to say it—but I think Gandhi and Martin Luther King fell into the error and innocence of Billy Budd, and helped to create the masters-at-arms that killed them. "The world cannot stand much perfection," Herman Melville noted. Perfect Goodness enrages those morally eclipsed.[14]

We have to create systems like social marketing so that goodness is never "pure" and hence polarizing. If I buy ice cream made by a CDC, then who is to say whether I am noble or merely hungry? Is not the answer to be *both*—or, in other words, human? Then can the CDC dwell upon the treat it has given me and I can be glad I helped its residents, and neither of us need sag beneath moral indebtedness.

The Consumer Movement

The great weakness of the consumer movement at present is that it is content to react *after* the event of sale and purchase. So long as manufacturers dictate the range of products, the price structure, the informational context in which goods appear, and the significance of their very appearance, they remain the overwhelmingly dominant force. The consumer advocate can only rush to the scene in a horse-drawn fire wagon after the alarm has sounded. If the consumer movement wishes to be potent, rather than pure and uncontaminated by commerce, it will have to intervene at the time that products and their presentations are planned.

The clowning, self-mocking quality of so many commercials is designed to disguise their power and unilateral influence. A small cheat in a commercial or a product— say, the large wad of cotton in an aspirin bottle—is trivial to each consumer, but is worth millions to one manufacturer. We cannot mount a demonstration against cotton balls! In effect, we have ceded power to the manufacturer when we let him make the whole issue into a giggle. Only if there are social issues at stake, which transcend cotton balls, can we make consumers sit up, take notice and see their acts of purchase as significant COMMITMENTS to a different corporate form. By explaining to the consumer how a community is wrestling with the problems of urban living, the consumer is given real, multiple choices concerning ways of life and ultimate philosophical issues. Now he can choose to help people who personify many interpretations of justice, healing and community, or people who personify bigness and egoism. Hence, when a consumer buys, he votes for a life-style, helps to direct the future of American life and champions a moral principle in a way that helps to universalize it.

A traditional rationale for our economy was that it constituted "a marketplace of ideas" chosen by "dollar ballots." Alas, thousands of jostling appeals on the level of "Quaker Oats cereal is a love-pat for tiny tummies" are less than elevated ideas. But with over one hundred and later perhaps thousands of CDC's searching for better ways to live we *might* have a contest of ideas, of unfolding social and ethical experiments, inviting intelligent scrutiny and support.

The Women's Liberation Movement

Consumer power is also a potential lever for women's liberation, as we shall see. But first let us consider how the present organization of mass communications and advertising now dooms women to subordination.

The current selling techniques have an enormous stake in the passive, in-taking function and domesticity of women. "I'm a housewife and I'm proud of it," simpers Madison Avenue's answer to women's liberation. "I'll always be a good little Maxwell Housewife," purrs another, upon discovering that coffee-klatching has overcome her loneliness. It is not unusual to see young women, their arms wrapped around their limbs, caressing their own body stockings while whispering huskily about their tactile qualities. Rarely, outside of a lunatic asylum, can one witness such autistic frenzy and curious willingness to converse with one's own thighs.

It is not just mass media who have a vested interest in woman as a force-fed goose. Her ultimate receptiveness is demanded by men, whose work is often so routine, ruthless and meaningless that *she* has to consecrate its significance. He works for *her*. Her omnivorous appetite for trivia must be pumped and primed, so that he can dedicate his loot to the family, and feel cleansed each time he returns from the jungle. It is the peculiar distinction of the mass media to have locked their idealized women into isolated domestic compartments, there to gush with sweetness about boy-girl problems, family relationships and suburban peccadillos, all mediated by mouthwash or similar products. Not just women, themselves, are so encapsulated, but all those saving characteristics that Americans associate with women: generativity, intuition, sincerity, spontaneity, warmth, receptivity, flexibility, compassion and co-operation. Shut off from such characteristics, the worlds of business, politics and international relationships turn ugly and malevolent, through lack of falsely "feminized" virtues. Shut away from practical applications in the wider world, these same virtues become mawkish and platitudinous, serving, like women themselves, a mostly decorative function in public life.

Millions of women in non-communicating private homes must service their male counterparts, providing each with those resources missing in the idealized male psyche. The suburbs ring the cities as the camp followers ring the battlefield, and each night the warriors "tank up" with enough affection to see them through the fray. Instructions to women on how to feed and resuscitate their warriors are issued by the male-dominated communications networks, which co-ordinate the isolated households of their dependents. By this method calculation controls spontaneity, power controls co-operation, practicality rules over ideals, corporations control consumers and the purified image of man controls the purified image of woman.

Just as the consumer is turned in upon herself by most advertising, so each family is invited to turn away from the outside world into an "incestuous," domestic embrace. While the streets outside fall beneath the sway of hoodlums, each family shrinks into a huddle around its tube, hardly talking to each other but suffused by an electronic glow. In the meantime, the world's bridges collapse, the gaps widen, democracies die through our indifference and even by our help, and the ghettos become more sharply delineated and desperate.

Having allowed UNBRIDGEABLE DISTANCES between huddled households to develop, the advertising fraternity then exploits the ensuing loneliness by manipulating DISTANCE. First, advertisements pander to those who want to place an UNBRIDGEABLE social DISTANCE between themselves and others, then advertisements cater to those who want desperately to close the DISTANCE by conformity. Marketing plays off the two groups against each other, exemplifying the dictum of William Hazlitt, "Fashion is gentility running away from vulgarity, and afraid of being overtaken." The "beautiful people" get access to the latest fashions in clothes, travel and entertainment at a price. Later these are "traded down" to the mass, who scramble pathetically to be "with it," while the beautiful people move on to something else.

Beneath all the "happy neophilia" of the marketplace is the sharp spur of loneliness. Like Alice Through the Looking Glass, one has to run very fast to stay in the same place, and twice as fast to get anywhere. It is this that imparts to so much of American life its drivenness and perpetual insecurity. As for the poor, they *have* been left behind in disgrace, as a warning to laggardly workers.

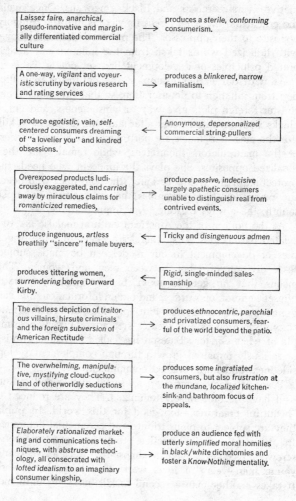

Laissez faire, anarchical, pseudo-innovative and marginally differentiated commercial culture → produces a sterile, *conforming* consumerism.

A one-way, *vigilant* and voyeuristic scrutiny by various research and rating services → produces a *blinkered*, narrow familialism.

produce egotistic, vain, *self-centered* consumers dreaming of "a lovelier you" and kindred obsessions. ← *Anonymous, depersonalized* commercial string-pullers

Overexposed products ludicrously exaggerated, and *carried away* by miraculous claims for *romanticized* remedies, → produce passive, *indecisive* largely *apathetic* consumers unable to distinguish real from contrived events.

produce ingenuous, *artless* breathily "sincere" female buyers. ← Tricky and *disingenuous* admen

produces tittering women, *surrendering* before Durward Kirby. ← *Rigid*, single-minded salesmanship

The endless depiction of *traitorous* villains, hirsute criminals and the *foreign subversion* of American Rectitude → produces ethnocentric, *parochial* and privatized consumers, fearful of the world beyond the patio.

The overwhelming, *manipulative, mystifying* cloud-cuckoo land of otherworldly seductions → produces some *ingratiated* consumers, but also *frustration* at the *mundane, localized* kitchen-sink-and bathroom focus of appeals.

Elaborately rationalized marketing and communications techniques, with *abstruse* methodology, all consecrated with *lofted idealism* to an imaginary consumer kingship, → produce an audience fed with utterly *simplified* moral homilies in *black/white* dichotomies and foster a *Know-Nothing* mentality.

It is important to understand that the relationship between corporate merchandizers and consuming households is astonishingly similar to the relationship between dominative/aversive racists and Black Americans. Once again the crucifixion dilemma forces its victims into the category opposite to their oppressor. The pattern is laid out above, with italicized words taken from the inflated and deteriorated principles of development first set out in Table 1.

As with our earlier examples, the oppressor may flip-flop from inflation to deterioration, so that programs about sinister foreign plots give way to winsomeness, and curvy chicks with tip-tilted noses alternate with licensees-to-kill. For the most part males are portrayed in idealized likeness of the manipulators themselves, while females are their idealized opposites. She plays the innocent who needs the protection of the righteous killer, the consumer who needs the persuader. She personifies the open mind, the open mouth, the always trusting, ever impregnatable.

At the bottom of the American cultural malaise are two related pathologies. First, there is a belief that the principles of development in our model can be made subject to a division of labor between men and women. This means that *he* gets to EXIST, be COMPETENT, COMMIT himself, BRIDGE DISTANCES, and ORDER information. *She* SUSPENDS herself, CONFIRMS him, provides him with TRANSCENDENT orgasms and creates SYNERGY. This is an example of what Gregory Bateson has called "schismogenesis," or seriously impaired growth through complementary lopsidedness and impoverished communications.

Peace, ecology, consumerism, social justice and culture —all have become falsely feminized. They are reduced to "beautiful creatures"—too good for this world. In public they are subject to pious tribute and ceremonial deference. In private, and in practice, they are prostrated and screwed. It takes a woman almost two decades to rear a young man—years of love, worry and sheer hard work. It takes another man a second to kill him. Not until men are taught nurture and women are encouraged to confront their would-be Defenders can peace and justice come.

The great advantage of social marketing is that it reverses every part of this chauvinist dynamic. Its ideal is what Virginia Woolf pleaded for, the androgynous mind, the synthesis of "male" and "female" characteristics. For when articulate, assertive females lay siege to male bastions, the great danger is that they will be assimilated one by one into a vicious masculine ethos, and discover that every aspect of traditional "femininity" proves a handicap in the jungle.

In contrast, the empowerment of those characteristics now feminized may be the only hope for our world. We need millions of "Nervous Nellies," "Bleeding Hearts" and "Nigger Lovers." For what is false about traditional femininity is the powerlessness that makes it safe and cuddly. There is nothing wrong with authenticity, compassion or co-operation, that empowerment cannot cure by making it whole and balanced.

Woman power exercised through the now despised roles of shopping, advertising and marketing, is like Black Power that builds itself upon the once despised status of being black and separated. With social marketing, the act of purchase takes on new significance, just as the CDC turns de facto segregation into cohesive community power. Each victim transforms the significance of a stigmatized role.

Through social marketing upper-middle-class feminists can sit down with the poor and black women in CDC's to work out a strategy that unites classes. Feminists may discover that poor mothers would love to be full-time housewives, instead of cleaning the offices where the former do their work!

Social marketing would turn each family, and each community, outwards into "long-distance" but caring relationships with CDC's and assorted underdogs. Along communication channels now dedicated to "chewing your little troubles away" would come detailed human viewpoints of highly differentiated people, with big troubles.

Women could emerge from their homes to form powerful and influential consumers' clubs which would not only support CDC's, boycott defense contractors and control the image of woman in the mass media, but could also patronize corporations according to published indices of their treatment of women employees. The fashion parade could be undermined by attracting consumers back towards the poor instead of away from them.

The Movement for Ecology and a Human Culture

Ecology is used here both in its narrower and broader senses. Narrowly it refers to a preservation of a balanced natural environment vis-à-vis man as despoiler; broadly, it merges with the whole concept of SYNERGY, the orchestration of values, along with justice, balance and reconciliation. You cannot have a natural balance without a human one, or Nature's guardians will be subordinated and the environment will share their fate.

It is arguable that the Community Development Corporation is itself an ecological breakthrough, because it overcomes the split between private and public property, with the latter as the former's spittoon. Since CDC's hold much of their local land collectively, the residents care for the whole ecology of the community, and the land is experienced with the intimacy of private land but without excluding others from enjoyment. Several rural CDC's, especially those run by American Indians, have respectful attitudes to communal property. Senator Gaylord Nelson is one prominent advocate of the ecological benefits of community development.

Social marketing would allow CDC's to televise and present the beauty of lands they have preserved. It would permit them to introduce, with the help of expert allies in the universities, products designed and packaged to minimize ecological damage.

But all these techniques are palliatives unless the ingrained habits of mounting production and voracious consumption can be changed. Social conflict in America has been "solved," if at all, by proclaiming that there is enough for all combatants and then grinding up a hugely disproportionate share of the world's resources to assuage each domestic combatant. We cannot continue like this, and social marketing that gives material sustenance to the poor while satisfying the affluent with the abstract, ideational and human qualities of necessary products is a vital first step in getting people off the materialism bandwagon.

In its broader sense, ecology is a balance of concepts, ideas, and feelings; a balance of people's relationships to people, whether in communities, cities or nations. From this comes a reverence for all life. Televised communications are an excellent opportunity to present opposed viewpoints, and because of the nature of the medium, to dramatize the potential fusion of different images and perspectives.

Just as subordination and containment are implicit within all unresolved contradictions, with the "masculine" polarity ruling over the "feminine" polarity, so through dialectic can each oppressed half first gain an antithetical equality, followed by an optimal synthesis. Some of the numerous SYNERGIES which social marketing could achieve are summarized in Table 7.

SYNERGY is, of course, the true meaning of democracy. At the moment, America is critically overcentralized, with a federal logjam of competing interests in Washington. Instead of government redistributing unjust shares of wealth, it more and more reflects the lobbying that money can buy, in an anti-synergistic win-lose game. Social marketing could decentralize important spheres of decision making and influence, into thousands of small communi-

TABLE 7

"Productive" activities, e.g., the manufacture and marketing of things,
    subordinate, contain
"Unproductive" teaching, healing, helping and sustaining people.
→ Success at healing and helping people becomes the main rationale for buying otherwise mundane products.

Self-interest, acquisitiveness and business-as-usual,
    subordinate, contain
Charitableness, altruistic concerns, United Funds, Community Chests and other ways of keeping the poor "grateful."
→ Concern for others fuses with the need to maintain oneself, so that everyday business and consumption empower those in need.

Mechanical techniques and organizational imperatives,
    subordinate, contain
Human processes and affective interchanges.
→ Human affective processes of mutual support are projected through communications by authentically committed CDC's.

The logic of means and increased efficiency,
    subordinate, contain
A logic of ends, encompassing reason, the enrichment of human goals.
→ The customary ends of consumption and possession are immeasurably enriched by additional purposes, while still utilizing latest means.

The conscienceless power of those hyper-actively pulling political and economic strings in the "real world,"
    subordinates, contains
The powerless conscience of those enjoying Everlasting Moratoriums, Intellectual Reservations and tot-lots for Urban Sophisticates.
→ Writers, intellectuals, students, housewives and "mass intelligentsia" come into shared power through the organized purchase and marketing of CDC goods and services.

The economics of expansionism and imperialism,
    subordinates, contains
The rights of other nations and the needs of world ecology.
→ Issues of justice and balance between man and man, man and nature are negotiated between organized consumers and suppliers with ties to the Third World.

The "masculine" ethos of politics, science, commerce, competition and "tough-minded" realism,
  subordinates, contains
And labels "feminine" the ethos of home, the humanities, community, co-operation, culture and tender-minded idealism.

→ Co-operation, community and other falsely feminized virtues become motives for conduct of practical and commercial affairs.

Empiricism, objectivity and risk-less obsession with milking the status quo,
  subordinate, contain
Imagination, yearning, visions and risk-full attempts at creative transformations.

→ The people's imagination and creativity become the source of what is marketed, purchased, observed and evaluated.

The value relativism of the economic market place and the value freedom of the social sciences,
  subordinate, contain
The growth of a viable system of human ethics, a value-full truly human science.

→ Values, while relative to different situations, e.g., justice, ending suffering, etc., make strong claims upon organized consumers, who respond in patterns that could lay the basis for a moral science.

Trivial and clownish mendacity about homogenous products, along with pseudo-innovation,
  subordinate, contain
Genuine product innovations and awareness of the real social impact of business corporations.

→ The very fact that so many products are dull and mundane becomes an opportunity to address the underlying social achievements of the CDC

The calculated creation of demand and the maintenance of psychic scarcity and deficiency motives,
  subordinate, contain
Genuine wants among the hungry and deprived and the consciousness of abundance among the affluent.

→ A psychology of potential abundance is created by middle-class consumers opting for psychic and ideational "riches" while material and economic substance flows toward the poor and needy.

ties, which will be judged by the "size" of their ideas and values and their capacities for mutual enlightenment.

It is the function of CDC's and social marketing to orchestrate this SYNERGY of values, to create a rationality of ends, an ecological balance of human needs, and a philosophy of encompassing reason—in fact, what Matthew Arnold defined as a *culture:*

> Culture seeks to make all men live in an atmosphere . . . where they may use ideas, as it uses them itself, freely— nourished not bound by them. This is the *social* idea; and the men of culture are the true apostles of equality.[15]

of twenty million, with a paid circulation of 8.5 million, according to figures released today by the National Congress for Community Economic Development.

First started in 1972 by the New World Coalition with only forty advertising pages supplied by a dozen CDC's, the half-catalogue, half-manifesto has increased in size and circulation each subsequent year. Its once unique formula combines articles written by well-known writers and spokesmen for CDC's, descriptions of the life-style and achievements of CDC's, alongside advertisements for their products. It is distributed through trade book channels, by youthful street vendors, through CDC retail outlets and storefronts, and by mail to over four million subscribers. On campuses it has largely replaced now defunct college yearbooks as evidence of student membership. It makes frankly ideological appeals to a quality readership to support the rights of the dispossessed, the spirit of community and the values of equality.

The 1983 edition has thrown open its editorial pages to eight different explanations of the catalogue's meteoric success. Most are uncharitable, illustrating the dictum that financial success—of any kind—has few literary friends. William Buckley opines that justice *is "an easy atonement for the massive failure of integration," a "lightning-rod for the highly charged guilt of affluent suburbanites, unable to acknowledge their own basic conservatism." Noting "a nominal participation by established ethnic groups," he senses "a false charity" which disguises "a hatred of Middle America and all but the most oppressed of ethnics. . . . Once again the top-dogs have joined with the bottom dogs in an attack upon the socio-economic groups in between." Robert Nisbet criticizes "the communal fantasies of middle-class youth so addicted to anarchy that they can only dream of communities formed by others more peaceful and law-abiding than themselves. . . ."*

The CDC is "the lost home of the affluent rebel, exiled from human decency by his own excesses, separated from home and community by his passionate state of mind, he helps to finance a vicarious community to which he can never truly belong." Social marketing is "a pathological twist in the perennial quest for community." Three other contributors argue among themselves as to whether social marketing follows Marxist principles. One sees it as the emerging consciousness of "a student proletariat—the new class of intellectual laborers." A second sees "a reactionary return to the social idealism of Hegel" and a third denounces it as "typical bourgeois mystification aimed at obscuring the student-worker alliance . . . mawkish in its middle-class morality, as when a boy says to his Dad, 'Gee, I'm going to hold my breath until you're nicer to those colored folks.'"

It says much for the strength and security of the CDC movement that it now feels able to sponsor self-criticism— of whatever merit. The whole movement received a considerable shot in the arm in the late seventies, with the run-away success of CDC Consortium's chain of "Best Buy" Consumer Centers. The Consortium was the pioneer of the now commonplace practice of retailing selectively only those products judged as superior by various consumer organizations. The legal costs of fighting both the Consumer's Union, angry at the "commercial desecration" of its image, and leading manufacturers seeking to protect their dealership systems, came close to breaking the Consortium in 1976. Yet it survived, and has to date invested close to $70 million in organized communities. The Consortium also sponsors an interdisciplinary research publication *The Journal of Moral Science and Social Economy*, which analyzes the pattern of market responses to various ethical appeals by CDC's. It aims to unify the social sciences around moral schema.

"GARIBALDI BRIGADE" TO DESCEND
ON EAST BOSTON
Boston *Globe*, Tuesday, May 5, 1983

For the fourth year in succession six hundred Boston area students will spend an "Italian Summer" in East Boston, building a "People's Park" and rehabilitating a four-block area. The project, jointly organized by the East Boston Community Development Corporation and graduate students from M.I.T.'s department of landscape architecture, has drawn hundreds of volunteers from Bay Area colleges. Called the Garibaldi Brigade, after the six hundred followers of the famous nineteenth-century Italian revolutionary, the student work force will plant hundreds of trees and flowering shrubs, partly purchased and partly donated by local nurserymen, and will help rehabilitate sixty buildings.

The park will be formally opened a week before Labor Day by the mayor of Boston. In all, sixteen residential streets have now been closed to through traffic by erecting a barrier in the center to make two cul-de-sacs. Trees and shrubs are planted both beside these streets, at the end of them, and in the gardens of co-operating households. Area residents have formed block clubs to protect the flowers and trees from vandalism.

The close ties of friendship that have sprung up between students and local residents of predominantly Italian descent have surprised everyone but the organizers. "When I first saw them with their rough clothes and long hair, I didn't want to leave the house," said Mrs. DaMincio, a widow, and now proud owner of a repainted house and a blooming front yard, "but when I saw those beautiful flowers and what they were doing for the neighborhood, I changed my mind completely. I'll miss them, I can tell you."

The summer's work will end as usual with an Italian Festival, a large rally against the extension of Logan Airport, and a regatta opposite the waterfront property recently developed by EBCDC. A float entitled Noise Pollution, flying the flag of the Boston Port Authority and covered with red tape, will be ceremoniously rammed by the U.S.S. Risorgimento, symbolizing an aroused community. Plans by students to create a deep sea monster entitled Untreated Sewage have been shelved after residents complained about its stark realism.

HOUSEHOLDERS' SERVICES POP UP
LIKE MUSHROOMS
New York *Times*, Sunday, June 18
Business and Finance Section
by A. R. Haskin

The six-year-old CDC-Consumer Alliance, already renowned for its fertility, has recently sprouted more than thirty Combined Household Service Associations. These consist of a single switchboard which when called will dispatch a carpenter, plumber, plasterer, electrician, locksmith, repairman (but no domestics) to your house, usually within the hour.

For example, CHSA Rochester, an affiliate of Fighton, guarantees workmanship, explains charges, and offers prompt, honest and courteous service. As the brochure, distributed door to door by a commando sales force of University of Rochester students, puts it, "You are served not by a fly-by-night operator, but by a self-disciplined community, proud of its members and their work, determined to give you satisfaction."

Many associations run their own arbitration office with public and CDC representatives. Some 80 per cent of complaints are settled out of court in these offices, to which either customers or CDC workmen, disciplined by their community, can appeal.

The associations are credited with putting to work some twenty-five thousand "hard-core" jobless trained by Dept. of Labor, Manpower programs in ten cities. In the past there was serious discontinuity between training and obtaining jobs. Programs often resulted in little increase in wages and spotty employment records. But where CDC's run both the training program and the Service Associations, and where student volunteers are available to expand the demand, street by street, the transition to higher-paid work is smooth and effective.

HALF A MILLION HIGH SCHOOLERS MARCH
SCHOOL COMMITTEES IN UPROAR
Washington *Post*, March 20

What began more than a decade ago as ultra-respectable, church-sponsored "Marches Against Hunger" are now threatening the economic status quo in more than four hundred communities. Three Southern Californian school districts have officially banned high school marches "aimed at socialist goals" and "inspired by collectivist ideology." A spokesman of the Southern Baptists Association, an original co-sponsor of the Atlanta March, has denounced what he called "the sinister subversion of our original intentions." In their initial form the Marches Against Hunger would organize schoolchildren to ask parents, friends and neighbors to donate approximately twenty-five cents each for every mile marched, so that a child might collect as much as four or five dollars a mile for a twenty-five-mile march.

Over the years there have been growing complaints against the "symbolic suffering of marching." "Poverty and hunger are results of maldistribution of economic resources and are not miraculously cured by blistering our feet and passing the collection plate," declared a flyer put out last year by the high school division of the National Students' Association. Consequently, a new kind of march is rapidly replacing the old. Children ask parents and neighbors for detailed shopping lists covering items from foodstuffs to cleaning products, to hardware, garden supplies, automobile accessories, etc. As many lists from as many households as possible are solicited. The children then march no more than five miles, meeting with representatives of half a dozen or so local CDC's along the line of march, where they hand in the appropriate list. In the next few days the items are delivered by the CDC to the various households, and continued delivery service is solicited.

It is the last feature that has drawn the ire of many parents and school officials. "I do not send my children to school in order to have my business confiscated," complained Hew Bellows, Vice President of Target Stores. New Hampshire's vitriolic Manchester Union Leader has referred to "rampaging Red Guards holding Main Street to ransom." But the children themselves, never slow to spot flaws in their mentors, have proved difficult to discourage, continuing to organize marches as extra-curricular activity. 17-year-old Anne Selby of Del Mar, California, spoke for many of her classmates when she confronted a recent PTA meeting. "You seem to be saying that action against hunger and poverty is acceptable if it has no permanent effect upon our lives and our economy." Disputing the continued efficacy of the traditional Marches she said, "We do not seek an education in order to make pitiful and inadequate gestures of moral awareness, so as to cement the smugness of our society. If there is something noble in suffering for twenty-five miles, then why can't you suffer changes in your economic relationships that will cure injustice, instead of displaying the piety of your children like praying Pharisees along the street?"

Similar sentiments were echoed in a petition signed by 1,000 students in the Wellesley public schools. "We are sick of 'Sunday morning Christianity' which attempts to rectify with dimes and divinity the injustices of the working week. True concern for others requires that we alter our way of conducting business. We are weary of atoning in long marches for the economic avariciousness of our elders."

Last night Gabriel O'Rourke, chairman of the Boston School Committee, described as "impertinent" a request from a delegation of black school children that the Boston public school system purchase its school supplies from the Roxbury Action Program. He declined to elaborate on his statement made last week when the Boston Globe's "spotlight" investigation revealed that three no-bid contracts for classroom furnishings had been awarded to his nephew's company, Fahy and Groves, Inc. On that occasion O'Rourke had said, "I believe in community, too—my own."

SCANDALS ROCK CDC MOVEMENT
MORAL HYPOCRISY EXPOSED
Chicago *Tribune*, April 29

Two CDC directors of Gary's (Ind.) Northside Organization were indicted today on twenty counts of bribery and extortion charges. Special prosecutor William X. Hogan alleged that Ahmed Moboto and Hastings "Wilkie" Wallingford of the Gary Brotherhood had conspired first to bribe and later threaten city officials in order to obtain an exclusive franchise for catering at the new Malcolm X Raceway. Lawyers for defendants denied all charges, claiming "political harassment" of their clients.

This scandal coming on top of the shooting death of the

*crippled president of the Citizens' Development Associa-
tion of North Syracuse has cast grave doubt over the whole
future of the CDC movement, touted as a "moral alternative" to the normal conduct of the nation's business.*

*Senator Samson Creakle of Arkansas has called for an in-
vestigation committee to examine "this orgy of leftist hypocrisy" which has "the gall to appeal to God-fearing
Americans on the grounds of conscience." The National
Congress of Community Economic Development could
not be reached last night for comment. Two members of
its board of directors are awaiting trial in connection with
a violent demonstration outside the South African embassy.*

DEMAND HEAVY FOR LIBERTEX INSTALLATION
Washington *Post*, July 27

*The old Nielsen company used to have trouble getting
their meters installed in sample households but thousands
of requests have poured in for Libertex, a "feedback loop"
which enables the viewer to register up to a dozen kinds
of verdict upon his television viewing. A row of buttons
on the Libertex can either be punched periodically to register a verdict on each sixty seconds of viewing time or in
cases of high emotion the button can be held compressed
for several seconds, which will show up on the recording
device. A five-dollar deposit is being asked for in view of
damage caused to the mechanism by irate viewers during
earlier tests.*

*Negative verdicts range from B for boredom and D for
disbelief to H for hustle and I for insult to intelligence, but
it also has an A denoting approval and E for educational,
and a C for creative. In addition, viewers can label programs V (violent), P (pornographic) and S (sanctimoni-
ous), and several more.*

Libertex, the brain child of Caltech students and the Bay Area People's Institute, is built upon the success of Zap!, a gadget that not only cuts the sound on TV but produces a temporary disturbance of the visual image. Viewers have described as "extraordinarily pleasing" the ability to disintegrate the visual image and verbal flow of certain hucksters and pundits. A reporter visiting Sunset Homes, a retirement colony for Cook County democratic workers of the machine of the late Mayor Richard Daley, watched "wizened old men, cackling with delight as they 'zapped' video cassettes of their ex-boss."

Libertex has aroused considerable interest because of the suggestion by presidential aspirant Senator Edward Kennedy that the networks should compete for a $100 million federal grant to be shared among them according to their relative ratings upon "a quality and creativity index." Libertex is known to be lobbying for such a use of its ratings. "There appears to be a considerable difference in what people will merely watch and what they will vote for as high in quality," reports pollster Zachary Poole. "One fools even less of the people, less of the time, if one asks them to exercise discriminating judgement."

COURTS REFUSE PRIOR RESTRAINT
Talk Back Launched Amid Furore
Variety, September 15

A Federal Appeals Court today reversed a lower court injunction sought by the Advertising Council which enjoined Community Publications, a subsidiary of the National Congress for Community Economic Development, from launching their premier issue of Talk Back—a new TV program guide.

The offending article, entitled "The Celebrity Meat

Market—What Price Sincerity?" purports to publish the secret list circulated among advertising agencies, stating the price at which various celebrities will vouch for any commercial product. In some cases scruples are mentioned, along with the price at which they might be overcome. For example, "Miss _____ prefers wholesome products with images of purity and cleanliness, advertisers who risk compromising her image must expect to recompense her above the stated figure." The article includes names from a $1,000 list, a $2,000 list, and upwards to $10,000.

It is this last feature that seems to have alarmed a number of celebrities who have threatened to sue on grounds of defamation. What concerns them is the publicizing of their market price as compared with other celebrities. "It is absolutely untrue that I have done commercials for $2,000," said Lulu Galosh from her Beverly Hills home last night. "I'm finished in this town if that lying list is published." Recourse is often had to commercials by celebrities in a lean period. Their price tends to be higher if they once portrayed "sincere characters" such as Moses, President Roosevelt and Ulysses S. Grant. The list draws attention to such "credibility points." It also makes suggestions as to the kind of products that an actor's image might enhance, for example, "Rock Cunningham, who played Atlas in The Whole World in His Arms, might be suitable for a heavy duty household cleanser or a fork-lift truck."

Other innovations promised by the publishers of Talk Back are weekly indices of the degree of Male Chauvinism, Sado-Masochism, Authoritative Violence and FTC complaints against advertisers. Sponsors will be rated according to their Minority Hiring records and War Complicity. There will be an Obscenity-of-the-Week feature and an Inside Report on Network censorship and muzzling of program participants. As far as possible, index figures *and outrageous incidents will be traced directly to the sponsor's product. For example, "Cockette for the cuddly femme" brought you five muggings, one rape, two "righteous beatings" by lawmen and was given three Contempt-of-Women citations by the magazine's panel. It rates five percentage points below the national average on its Racist Quotient and was nominated in July for a "Nanny" (officially the Inanity Award given by the Citizens Council for Better Broadcasting). The publication has also purchased the rights to carry the monthly Libertex ratings.*

WAVE OF STUDENT "BUY-INS"
HIT NATION'S CAMPUSES
New York *Times*, October 1

Fifteen years ago it was the Vietnam War and Black Studies. Twenty years ago it was Civil Rights. Today the target of student pressure is the purchasing policies of colleges and universities around the country, and nearly everywhere administration resistance is crumbling.

It all began quietly, at first, with the now famed Ann Arbor Statement, which demanded that the University of Michigan order its scholastic and stationery supplies exclusively through Community Development Corporations. Refusal led to the notorious "Michigan Bonfire" and ex-President Nixon's "sign-of-the-swastika" speech.

The California Textbook Strike pitted three prominent publishers of textbooks against students and professors demanding that the publishers subcontract their binding operations to ghetto corporations. When the publishers gave way, the California Regents fired thirty prominent professors who had signed a statement promising to switch texts. This dispute is still in the courts, as is the suit against five students who produced three thousand pirated textbooks on a Xerox copier and sold them in aid of the strike.

More recently student organizers from the University of Wisconsin have been credited for substituting Afro-fizziac for Coke and Pepsi on more than one hundred campuses. Divinity students from Drew University have formed a three-hundred-man sales force that regularly descends upon clergy who make public utterances on poverty at high levels of abstraction. The students ask for economic deeds to match pious words, and have been known to pray publicly for the souls of the inconsistent. One result has been a sixty-thousand-a-week candle factory in Newark, N.J.

Angry state legislatures, long used to the plums of political patronage surrounding their institutions, are struggling with more than a dozen "Right to Sell" bills which make it a crime for state-supported institutions "to discriminate in terms of color or wealth" against traditional corporations.

One of several hold-outs against student pressure is Oral Roberts University—founded by the popular evangelist. "There is only one criterion of purchase at ORU," the evangelist told his television audience. "That is Christ's Criterion, service to mankind. If a supplier gives us good Christian service, then we are not switching to someone else, merely because they happen to be black or socialist."

Few colleges have taken the line of Harding College, Arkansas, which has described social marketing as "the vampire of America's life-blood, sucking out of our national arteries the precious fluid of self-interest." In direct contrast, the president of Coolidge College, a small liberal arts school in Vermont, put himself up for mock auction in a potato sack emblazoned with CDC mottoes. He fetched $3.75—less than the school janitor. Not all the students were enthusiastic. "It's pathetic, isn't it?" remarked one coed. *"Just like my parents on New Year's Eve—forced jollity, and drunken humor. No sense of dignity." "We were enjoying ourselves before that clown got in on the act,"* grumbled an organizer.

CHRISTMAS '83 TO HAVE SOCIAL GOSPEL ORIENTED TO THIRD WORLD
from "The Reporters," WGBH, Channel 2, Boston

Campaign Third World jointly sponsored by the New World Coalition, the National Council of Churches and the National Congress of Community Economic Development will aim to "bring Christ back into Christmas." It could, in time, significantly alter Christmas shopping as we know it.

At least one hundred university "Coops" (co-operative stores run with university participation) and three East Coast department store chains will feature large displays of crates and boxes containing food, fertilizer, implements, and medical supplies, etc., for underdeveloped countries. On the walls behind the displays continuously running, rear-projection films will portray the plight of many of the world's peoples, the impact upon the communities of the receipt of the goods displayed and the products being put to use. Shoppers are invited to pay for the contents and freight of one or more crates, designating the country of their choice, and enclosing a written message.

A campaign is being prepared to announce "simultaneously from 5,000 pulpits," the week after Thanksgiving, that adults should give gifts on behalf *of each other to Third World countries, rather than to each other. Special Christmas cards will be available by which to inform friends or relatives that gifts have been sent in their name. The cards contain a warning described by some critics as "Christmas lobbying," which reads:*

*It is not enough to give gifts to under-developed
countries, we have to respond to them by buying
the products they manufacture. Write to your
Senators and Congressmen urging an end to those
import quotas discriminating against poor countries and their infant manufacturing industries.*

Most of the films that will accompany the campaign
were previewed here last night. They struck this reporter
as excruciatingly poignant. You'll need strong nerves for
"The Children of Bin Dihn," a view of Vietnam's largest
children's hospital, and the second generation of the war's
victims. Birth defects caused by defoliants are graphically
depicted along with the growing list of victims from the
estimated sixty thousand tons of ordnance unexploded at
the war's end, which has taken a remorseless toll year in,
year out.

In stark contrast is a satirical film of an affluent American
family up to their knees in gift wrapping paper and rib-
bons, desperately trying to remember who sent what to
whom so they can remember to thank them. A neurotic
aunt who is thanked for an electric nutcracker when in
fact she gave an electric back scratcher is dissolved in
tears and runs into her room to pop tranquilizers. In a
climactic scene the family laughs drunkenly over a musical
toilet roll, commiserates with Dad over his third "executive sandbox for the man who has everything" and presents
Uncle Max with a statue of The Thinker, whose head pops
open to light a cigarette. Then mother insists that they
"carry all this junk out to the yard," while the children
force-feed the family dog his "doggie-variety-yums-yums"
from his "Santa's Stocking for Four-Footed Friends." The
closing shot shows a garbage can loaded with glittering
litter, the retching sound of a dog being sick, and the face
of a small Indian boy, his eyes huge in a face shrunken
with hunger, stares from the crumpled page of newspaper
sticking from the can.

CORPORATE GIANTS FIND CDC's
HARD TO CO-OPT
Miami *Herald*, December 12

Faced with a surge of CDC "social marketing" America's largest corporations struck back with $75 million worth of what Madison Avenue calls "humanads" or "the bleeding-heart blitzkrieg." "One would have thought," remarked Advertising Age, *"that Humble Oil's sole function in the economy was to finance Harlem Prep and to film its graduation exercises." The campaign came to a sickening end when Citizens for Better Broadcasting won the right to equal time and presented the fractions of one percentage point which leading advertisers actually spent on social projects. In three cases, more had been spent on "humanads" than on humans. Even before this denouement, polls had shown that viewers were skeptical about this streamlined version of corporate conscience.*

Since then several corporations have offered CDC's exclusive rights to wholesale and retail their goods in specific areas. Some, like Xerox and Mattel, have been foster parents to CDC's since the earliest prototypes of the sixties and have had little trouble communicating their social concern, but some Johnny-Come-Latelies on the social scene have found CDC's choosy about their patrons, and "problem children" once adopted.

Fears that CDC's could be reduced to a mere front by corporate patronage have proved illusionary. In a world increasingly communications conscious and sensitive to hypocrisy, the "front" tends to commit the whole body. Recently ten so-called "captive" CDC's demanded increases in their wholesale and retail margins for the second time in a few months. The manufacturers acceded rather than risk a shattering blow to their carefully contrived image as "the poor man's friend."

Extract from Television Script of *The Masticators*
A Documentary Sponsored by the California
Regional Congress of CDC's

Video	Audio
FADEUP ON STATUE OF LIBERTY. ZOOM IN FOR C.U. ON INSCRIPTION.	
	Announcer *Give me your tired, huddled masses yearning to breathe free.*
CUT TO AMERICAN CRUISE SHIP LEAVING NEW YORK HARBOR. ZOOM IN ON SUNDECK AND PAN ACROSS ACRES AND ACRES OF AMPLE OILED FLESH BROILING IN SUN. C.U. ON HAND SCRATCHING BELLY.	Announcer *The teeming refuse of your wretched shores.*
HAND GRASPS CHOCOLATE MILK SHAKE WITH STRAW. LIQUID MOVES UP STRAW. TILT UP TO SUCKING JOWLS.	*Slurping noises.* Announcer *An estimated four million Americans still go to bed hungry. One third of the world's population suffers from malnutrition.*
TWO LARGE MATRONS PLAYING DECK QUOITS GIGGLE GIRLISHLY AT CAMERAMAN.	*Yet the greatest problem for Americans is obesity. There are simply too many tempting foods and liquids for our bodies to absorb.*

WHITE SMOKE PUFFS EMERGE FROM CRUISE SHIP'S FUNNEL.	*Leave it to American Know-How to devise a solution. The food industry has now given us their answer— expectorate!*
CUT TO MAN LEANING OVER RAIL OF CRUISE SHIP SPITTING CHOCOLATE MALT INTO SEA.	*No, he doesn't dislike it. He's saving on calories.*
CUT TO SUPERMARKET. PAN ALONG SHELVES. AND SHOW CARDS. "TV SNACKEROO, THE IN-BETWEEN MEAL FOR THE IN-IN CROWD." CUT TO DISGUSTED MAN WITHDRAWING STICKY HAND AND CUFF FROM BENEATH LUNCH COUNTER.	*Today we have an increasing number of expectorant foods, as the industry likes to call them, "disposable foods." There are those intended to be chewed and spat out—so that instead of finding those sticky blobs of chewing gum beneath your seat—you may now find the best part of a Television Snack.*
PAN ALONG SHELVES TO PICK UP "FAT-FREE HOMOGENIZED CHICKEN," "JELLO SUCKITS," STARCH-FREE POTATEEN— SQUARES FOR EASIER STORAGE.	*Then there are those foods once nutritious and whole, but carefully spun, dried, drained, desiccated, disintegrated and reconstituted into fatless chicken, steakless steak, and saccharine-rubber jellies. What is this making of us? What are we becoming?*
DISSOLVE TO TITLE "THE MASTICATORS" OVER BACKGROUND OF COTTON CANDY MACHINE.	*Community Enterprises present* The Masticators, *brought to you by fifty communities who make* JUST *and Liberation products.*

Commercial

GARISH NIGHT CLUB SCENE
WITH LEERING MEN. SMALL
STAGE. TOPLESS WAITRESSES.
SPOTLIGHT GOES ON. DRUM
ROLLS. CURTAIN PARTS. MEN
CRANE NECKS, EYES WIDE, LIPS
PARTED, FACES SHINY WITH
PERSPIRATION. ZOOM TO CLOSE
UP OF COVERED DISH,
SIZZLING. COVER LIFTS TO
WOLF WHISTLES, GRUNTS,
VARIETY OF ANIMAL NOISES, TO
REVEAL ROAST LEG OF LAMB
WITH "SEXY" RUFFLE.

Announcer *Isn't there
something wrong with our
appetite for food or for
sex when these become
things in themselves? Eat
heartily and make love
passionately by all means—*
but to some purpose beyond
yourself.

DISSOLVE TO PICTURES OF JUST
AND LIBERATION PRODUCTS.

*As you buy, as you eat, as you
love and as you live,*
fight for social justice,
renew your own freedom by
freeing others.

Appendix A

SELECTED LISTING OF COMMUNITY-BASED ECONOMIC DEVELOPMENT CORPORATIONS AND CO-OPERATIVES

ALABAMA

Panola Land Buying Association
Route 1, Box 30
Panola, Alabama 35477

Southeast Alabama Community Development Corporation
100 East Academy Street
Troy, Alabama 36081

Southeast Alabama Self-Help Association (SEASHA)
P.O. Box 1080
Tuskegee Institute, Alabama 36088

Southwest Alabama Farmers Cooperative Association
(SWAFCA)
1315 Jeff Davis Avenue
Selma, Alabama 36701

ALASKA

Community Enterprises Development Corporation
503 West Northern Lights Boulevard
Anchorage, Alaska 99503

ARIZONA

Hopi Silvercraft and Arts & Crafts
P.O. Box 37
Second Mesa, Arizona 86043

SPACE, Inc. (Sulphur Springs Agricultural Co-op Effort,
Inc.)
c/o Arizona Rural Effort, Inc.
377 Main Street
Yuma, Arizona 85364

ARKANSAS

Arkansas Community Investment and Development, Inc.
El Rock Building
1015 Louisiana Street
Little Rock, Arkansas 72202

Eastern Arkansas Community Development Corporation
P.O. Box 709
Forest City, Arkansas 72325

Jefferson County Progress, Inc.
204 East Fourth Street
Pine Bluff, Arkansas 71601

CALIFORNIA

Action Industries
1607 Pacific Avenue
Venice, California 90291

East Los Angeles Community Union
1330 South Atlantic Boulevard
Los Angeles, California 90022

Green Power Foundation, Inc.
1150 South San Pedro Street
Los Angeles, California 90015

Neighborhood House, Inc.
321 Alamo Street
Richmond, California 94801

Operation Bootstrap
4161 South Central Avenue
Los Angeles, California 90011

Rural Action Groups, Inc.
c/o Tulare County Community Action Agency
P.O. Box 1069
Visalia, California 93277

South Central Improvement Action Council (IMPAC)
8557 South Broadway
Los Angeles, California 90053

Venice Community Improvement Union, Inc.
617 Broadway
Venice, California 90291

Watts Labor Community Action Committee
11401 South Central Avenue
Los Angeles, California 90059

West Side Planning Group
707 North Fulton
Suite A
Fresno, California 93728

COLORADO

Denver Community Development Corporation
4142 Tejon Street
Denver, Colorado 80211
Federation of Southern Colorado Peoples Enterprises
P.O. Box 76
La Jara, Colorado 81140

CONNECTICUT

Freedom Now, Inc.
270 Grand Avenue
New Haven, Connecticut 06513

DISTRICT OF COLUMBIA

Fairmicco, Inc.
c/o MICCO
920 U Street, N.W.
Washington, D.C. 20001
KOBA Enterprises, Inc.
1631 14th Street, N.W.
Washington, D.C. 20036
Peoples Development Corporation
c/o Peoples Involvement Corporation
2146 Georgia Avenue, N.W.
Washington, D.C. 20001
Youth Enterprise, Inc.
1028 Connecticut Avenue, N.W.
Washington, D.C. 20036
Youth Pride Economic Enterprises, Inc.
c/o PRIDE, Inc.
1308 Pennsylvania Avenue, S.E.
Washington, D.C. 20036

FLORIDA

Everglade Progressive Citizens, Inc.
324 S.W. Fifth Street
Belle Glade, Florida 33430

Seminole Employment and Economic Development
    Corporation
P.O. Box 2076
Sanford, Florida 32771

GEORGIA

Appalachian Enterprises
P.O. Box 66
Mineral Bluff, Georgia 30559

Crawfordsville Enterprises, Inc.
Route 2, Box 80A
Union Point, Georgia 30669

East Central Committee of Opportunity
Central Administration Building
Mayfield, Georgia 31059

Model Neighborhood, Inc.
940 McDaniel Street, N.W.
Atlanta, Georgia 30310

New Communities, Inc.
P.O. Box 1904
Albany, Georgia 31702

HAWAII

Lokehi-Pacific Corporation
726 South Kihei Road
Kihei, Hawaii 96753

Maui Economic Opportunity, Inc.
189 Kaohumanu Avenue
Maui, Hawaii 96732

ILLINOIS

Neighborhood Commons Corp.
1874 North Freemont Avenue
Chicago, Illinois 60614

North Lawndale Economic Development Corporation
3324 West Roosevelt Road
Chicago, Illinois 60624

Pilsen Neighbors Community Corporation
1850 South Blue Island Avenue
Chicago, Illinois 60608

True Peoples Power Development Corporation
1328 East 47th Street
Chicago, Illinois 60653

The Woodlawn Organization
1135 East 63d Street
Chicago, Illinois 60637

KENTUCKY

Council of Southern Mountains
Berea, Kentucky 40403

Grass Roots Economic Development Corporation, Inc.
1125 Main Street
Jackson, Kentucky 41339

Job Start Corporation
Rural Route 5, P.O. Box 879
London, Kentucky 40741

LOUISIANA

Floridana Economic Development
104 South Second Street
Amite, Louisiana 70422

Grand Marie Vegetable Cooperative
P.O. Box 17
Sunset, Louisiana 70584

Southern Cooperative Development Fund
P.O. Box 3005
Lafayette, Louisiana 70501

MARYLAND

Ebony Development Corporation
c/o Council for Equal Business Opportunity
1102 Mondawmin Concourse
Baltimore, Maryland 21215

Model Urban Neighborhood Demonstration (MUND)
2133 Maryland Avenue
Baltimore, Maryland 21218

MASSACHUSETTS

CIRCLE, Inc., and New England Community
    Development Corporation
90 Warren Street
Boston, Massachusetts 02119

East Boston Neighborhood Council, Inc.
144 Meridian Street
East Boston, Massachusetts 02128

Freedom Foundation & Freedom Industries
3401 Washington Street
Roxbury, Massachusetts 02119

MICHIGAN

> Accord, Inc.
> 2889 West Grand Boulevard
> Detroit, Michigan 48202

> Black Star Economic Development Corporation
> 7525 Linwood
> Detroit, Michigan 48206

> Inner City Business Improvement Forum
> 6072 14th Street
> Detroit, Michigan 48202

MINNESOTA

> Midwest Minnesota Community Development Corporation
> 200 East State Street
> Detroit Lakes, Minnesota 56601

MISSISSIPPI

> Adams-Jefferson Improvement Corporation
> 709 Franklin Street
> Natchez, Mississippi 39120

> COAHOMA Opportunity, Inc.
> Clarksdale, Mississippi 38614

> Delta Foundation
> 819 Main Street
> Greenville, Mississippi 38701

> Milestone Cooperative Association
> Lexington, Mississippi 39095

> Mississippi Fish Equity, Inc.
> 146 Center Street
> West Point, Mississippi 39773

> Miss-Lou Farmers Cooperative
> Route 2, Box 119
> Liberty, Mississippi 39645

> Mound Bayou Development Corporation
> Mound Bayou, Mississippi 38762

> North Bolivar County Farm Cooperative
> P.O. Box 134
> Mound Bayou, Mississippi 38762

> Poor Peoples Corporation
> P.O. Box 3193
> Jackson, Mississippi 39207

> West Batesville Farmers Cooperative
> Batesville, Mississippi 38606

MISSOURI

The Black Economic Union Community Development
Corporation
2505 Prospect Street
Kansas City, Missouri 64127

Bootheel Agricultural Services Incorporated Cooperative
(BASIC)
Box 233
Hayti, Missouri 63851

Union Sarah Economic Development Corporation
4526 Olive Street
St. Louis, Missouri 63108

Upgrade Enterprises, Inc.
East St. Louis, Missouri 63102

NEW JERSEY

Black Peoples Unity Movement
201 Broadway
Camden, New Jersey 08103

Greater Newark Enterprises Development Corporation
78 Peabody Place
Newark, New Jersey 07104

MEDIC, Inc.
287 Washington Street
Newark, New Jersey 07102

People's Development Corporation
605 Broad Street
Newark, New Jersey 07102

NEW MEXICO

Del Sol
Albuquerque, New Mexico 87108

Home Education Livelihood Program, Inc. (HELP)
933 San Pedro, S.E.
Albuquerque, New Mexico 87108

Zuni Craftsmen Association
Pueblo of Zuni
Box 368
Zuni, New Mexico 87327

NEW YORK

Bedford-Stuyvesant Restoration Corporation
1368-90 Fulton Street
Brooklyn, New York 11213

BUILD
339 Genesee
Buffalo, New York 14204

Community Cooperative Center
1310 Atlantic Avenue
Brooklyn, New York 11216

Economic Opportunity Commission of Nassau County, Inc.
320 Old County Road
Garden City, New York 11530

El Barrio Economic Development Corporation
105 East 106th Street
New York, New York 10029

Fighton, Inc. (originally FIGHT)
65 Sullivan Street
Rochester, New York 14605

Harlem Commonwealth Council
215 West 125th Street
New York, New York 10027

Harlem River Consumers Co-operative
147th Street and Seventh Avenue
New York, New York 10039

Hunt's Point Community Local Development Corporation
384 East 149th Street
Bronx, New York 10455

We, Ourselves/Black Development Foundation
1308 Jefferson Avenue
Buffalo, New York 14208

NORTH CAROLINA
Farmers Market of North Wilkesboro
North Wilkesboro, North Carolina 28659

United Durham, Inc.
P.O. Box 1349
Durham, North Carolina 27702

NORTH DAKOTA
Standing Rock Industries
Fort Yates, North Dakota 58538

OHIO
CORENCO, Inc.
10616 Euclid Avenue
Room 310
Cleveland, Ohio 44106

East Central Citizens Organization (ECCO)
22nd and McAllister
Columbus, Ohio 43205

Hough Area Development Corporation
7016 Euclid Street
Cleveland, Ohio 44103

OKLAHOMA

CHOICE For Tulsa Project
c/o Tulsa Economic Opportunity Task Force, Inc.
619 East Newton Place
Tulsa, Oklahoma 74106

Northeast Oklahoma Community Development Corporation
P.O. Box 429
Fort Gibson, Oklahoma 74434

Rural Development Program
c/o Oklahomans for Indian Opportunity
555 Constitution Avenue
Norman, Oklahoma 73069

OREGON

Albina Corporation
3810 North Mississippi
Portland, Oregon 97227

PENNSYLVANIA

Business and Job Development Corporation
Highland Building
Pittsburgh, Pennsylvania 15206

Businessmen's Development Corporation
325 Chestnut Street
Philadelphia, Pennsylvania 19106

Forever Action Together
571 Brushton Avenue
Pittsburgh, Pennsylvania 15208

Greater Philadelphia Community Development Corporation
1545 Western Savings Funds Building
Broad and Chestnut Streets
Philadelphia, Pennsylvania 19107

Greater Philadelphia Enterprises Development Corporation
1645 West Thompson Street
Philadelphia, Pennsylvania 19121

Oxford Film Makers Corporation
1550 North Seventh Street
Philadelphia, Pennsylvania 19100

United Black Front
2161-64 Wylie Avenue
Pittsburgh, Pennsylvania 15219

Young Great Society and Mantua Enterprises, Inc.
4040 Locust Street
Philadelphia, Pennsylvania 19106

Zion Investment Associates & Zion Charitable Trust
    (known also as Progress Enterprises)
Progress Plaza
1501 North Broad Street
Philadelphia, Pennsylvania 19122

SOUTH CAROLINA

Santee Production & Marketing Cooperative
P.O. Box 265
Greeleyville, South Carolina 29056

TENNESSEE

The Greater Memphis Urban Development Corporation
P.O. Box 224
Memphis, Tennessee 38101

Tenco Developments, Inc.
809 Union Street
Shelbyville, Tennessee 37160

TEXAS

Las Colonias Del Valle, Inc.
P.O. Box 907
San Juan, Texas 78589

Mexican-American Unity Council
615 Perez Street
San Antonio, Texas 78207

Project MIRA
c/o Economic Opportunities Development Corporation of
    Laredo and Webb County
P.O. Box 736
Laredo, Texas 78040

Self Help Enterprises
P.O. Box 907
Edinburg, Texas 78539

UTAH
>Adela Development Corporation
>465 East 900 South
>Salt Lake City, Utah 84111

VIRGINIA
>Southwest Virginia Community Development Corporation
>401 First Street, N.W.
>Roanoke, Virginia 24016

WASHINGTON
>East Pasco Self-Help Cooperative Association
>Pasco, Washington 99301
>
>The Economic Growth Organization, Inc.
>Seattle, Washington 98117
>
>Lummi Indian Tribal Enterprise
>P.O. Box 77
>Marietta, Washington 98268
>
>United Inner City Development Foundation
>1106 East Spring Street
>Seattle, Washington 98122

WEST VIRGINIA
>Food Services Corporation
>c/o Mingo County Economic Opportunity Commission, Inc.
>P.O. Box 1406
>Williamson, West Virginia 25661
>
>Mountain Artisans
>147 Summers Street
>Charleston, West Virginia 25301
>
>Summers County Economic Opportunity Association
>P.O. Drawer J
>Hinton, West Virginia 25957
>
>West Virginia Cooperative Business Development Program
>c/o Tech Foundation, Inc.
>West Virginia Institute of Technology
>Montgomery, West Virginia 25136

WISCONSIN
>Great Lakes Inter-Tribal Cooperative
>c/o Menominee Indian Cooperative
>Keshena, Wisconsin 54135
>
>Impact Seven, Inc.
>P.O. Box 335
>Turtle Lake, Wisconsin 54889

Livestock Management and Marketing Cooperative
Francis Creek, Wisconsin 54214
Southside Revitalization Corporation
720 17th Street
Racine, Wisconsin 53403

Appendix B

ECONOMIC AND COMMUNITY BUILDING FUNCTIONS OF SELECTED COMMUNITY DEVELOPMENT CORPORATIONS

CDC	For Profit Ventures	Social Ventures and Community Building Activities
Harlem Commonwealth Council New York City Executive Director: Jim Dowdy	Commonwealth Pharmacy Acme Foundry Commonwealth Tours (travel agency) Commonwealth Office Furniture and Equipment Commonwealth Discount Records Commonwealth Terrace Sewing Center Commonwealth Data Services Commonwealth Office Building	Consumer credit program Training facilities and day care centers Commonwealth short-term loan program Technical assistance program and consulting services Sponsorship of the Festival of Kwanza; of the Fiesta de Reyes
Hough Area Development Corporation Cleveland, Ohio Executive Director: Frank Anderson	Martin Luther King (shopping plaza) Community Products, Inc. (rubber injection molding process) Handyman's Maintenance Service (extermination, repairs, rehabilitation) Homes for Hough (construction company) Ghetto East (hamburger franchisees)	Creative Youth Corporation (tailoring, jewelry and export-import co-operatives for younger residents) NOAH (Neighborhood) Organization for Action in Housing) Hough Opportunity Center Hough Community Council Afro Set Association of [local] Community Development Corporations HOPE (Housing Our People Economically)
West Side Planning Group Fresno, California (rural CDC)	Whiskey Barrel Furniture Company (furniture made from discarded barrels) Ana Julies Inc. (candy manufacturer) Three Suns, Inc. (linens, pillows, T-shirts, aprons)	Automobile center (garage, group insurance, spare parts, etc.) Medical Services Center Credit Union Legal Services Center

Progress Enterprises
 	
Philadelphia, Pennsylvania.
	Zion Investment Associates
	Progress Garment
	    Manufacturing Co.
	Progress Aerospace
	    Enterprise, Inc.
	Progress Plaza
	    (17 store shopping center)
	Our Markets, Inc.
		Zion Non-profit Corp. (sponsors
		    scholarship programs and
		    social service centers)
		Opportunities Industrialization
		    Centers (OIC)
		    (now in more than 70 cities)
		Zion Gardens
		    (90 unit garden
		    apartment complex)
		National Progress Association
		    for Economic Development
		    Management Training
		    School

Poor Peoples Corporation
 	
Jackson, Mississippi
	More than forty sewing, leather-
	    craft and toy-making co-op-
	    eratives affiliated to
	    Liberty House, a catalogue
	    retail store outlet
	Flute Publications
	    (publishes black writers,
	    poetry, biography and
	    greeting cards)
		Education and Training for
		    Co-operatives (ETC)
		Southern Media (educational,
		    employee training and
		    publicity films)
		Graphic Arts South (does
		    printing and publicity for
		    Liberty House—also a
		    training facility for artists
		    and illustrators)

Southwest Virginia Community
    Development Corporation
 	
Roanoke, Virginia
    (rural-urban)
    (white-black)
 	
Executive Director:
    Tom Morse
	GEMCO (Gainsboro
	    Electrical Manufacturing
	    Company, Inc.);
	    (custom wire assemblies)
	Botetort Cabinet Corporation
	    (modular kitchen cabinets)
		Impact Housing Corporation
		    (building Cherry Hill
		    Manor Apts.)
		Irongate Water & Development
		    Corporation (building
		    water distribution systems
		    for poor area residents)
		Craig Medical Clinic
		Rural Loan Program
		Social Inventory of "Com-
		    munity Needs" Project

Notes

CHAPTER 1

1. Harold Cruse, *Rebellion or Revolution* (New York: Apollo Books, 1969), p. 104.
2. Ibid., p. 105.
3. *The Crisis of the Negro Intellectual* (New York: Morrow, 1968).
4. *Nobody Knows My Name* (New York: Dell, 1969), p. 73.
5. "Social Origins of Black Consciousness" in *The New American Revolution*, eds. R. Aya and N. Miller (New York: Free Press, 1971), p. 176. Also available in *The Death of White Sociology*, ed. Joyce Ladner (New York: Vintage, 1973).
6. E. H. Hess and J. Polk, "Pupil Size as Related to Interest Value of Visual Stimuli," *Science* 132 (1958).
7. Quoted by Arthur Combs and Donald Snygg in *Individual Behavior* (New York: Harper, 1961).
8. See Jack Newfield in *Partisan Review*, Spring 1968, p. 221.
9. Quoted in *Black Power: The Politics of Liberation in America* (New York: Vintage, 1967), p. 36.
10. See *Poverty and Human Resource Abstracts*, Institute of Labor and Industrial Relations, Ann Arbor, Michigan, for such periodic pitches.
11. *Shadow and Act* (New York: Random House, 1964). Also in Ladner, *The Death of White Sociology*, p. 94.
12. E. S. Greenberg, "The Political Socialization of Black Children," in *Political Socialization*, ed. E. S. Greenberg (New York: Atherton, 1968), pp. 178–90.
13. Here I am indebted to "Identity and the Life Cycle" by E. H. Erikson, *Psychological Issues* 1, no. 1 (1959).
14. Quoted in Cruse, *Rebellion or Revolution*, p. 29.
15. Quoted in Herbert A. Aptheker, *A Documentary History of the Negro People in the United States* (New York: Citadel, 1968), p. 899.
16. See, for example, the discussion in *Negro Mood* by Leroy Bennett (Chicago: Johnson Pub., 1964), p. 49.

17. "Motivation Reconsidered," *Psychological Review* 66 (1959).
18. Quoted in Carmichael and Hamilton, *Black Power*, p. 48, from New York *Times*, July 31, 1966.
19. Robert Coles in *Partisan Review*, Spring 1968, p. 195.
20. Cruse, *Rebellion or Revolution*, p. 114.
21. For a good discussion of Karenga, see Robert L. Allen, *Black Awakening in Capitalist America* (Garden City, N.Y.: Doubleday, 1969), pp. 139–42.
22. Cruse, *Rebellion or Revolution*, p. 114.
23. Cruse, *The Crisis of the Negro Intellectual*, p. 474.
24. Ibid., p. 455–56.
25. "Poems: Paul Lawrence Dunbar," *Freedomways* 12, no. 4 (1972): 334.
26. "Letter from a Birmingham Jail" in *Protest: Man Against Society*, ed. A. Armstrong (New York: Bantam, 1969).
27. *A Rap on Race* (with Margaret Mead) (New York: Delta Bks., 1971), pp. 25–26.
28. Joseph Wolpe, *Psychotherapy by Reciprocal Inhibition* (Palo Alto, Cal.: Stanford Univ. Press, 1965).
29. Milton Rokeach, *The Open and Closed Mind* (New York: Basic Bks., 1960).
30. D. Stein, J. Hardyk, M. Brewster Smith, "Race and Belief: an open and shut case," *Journal of Personality and Social Psychology* 1 (1965): 135–51.
31. W. Wilson, "Rank Order of Discrimination and Its Relevance to Civil Rights Priorities," *Journal of Personality and Social Psychology* 15 (1970): 118–24.
32. Margaret Mead in Baldwin, *A Rap on Race*, pp. 28–29.
33. B. Berelson and G. Steiner, *Human Behavior: An Inventory of Scientific Findings* (New York: Harcourt, 1964), p. 482.
34. "Race-Class Stereotypes" by J. Bayton, L. McAlister and J. Horner, *Journal of Negro Education* 25 (1956): 75–78.
35. There is an especially good discussion of pre-capitalist racism by James J. Jones in *Prejudice and Racism* (Reading, Mass.: Addison-Wesley, 1972), p. 151.
36. A favorite slogan of Martin Luther King.
37. A similar distinction was made by Franklin Frazier; see "Black Nationalism and Human Liberation" in *The Black Scholar* 1, no. 7 (1970).
38. J. Coleman, *Equality of Educational Opportunity* (Washington, D.C.: Government Printing Office, 1966).
39. M. Rosenberg, *Society and the Adolescent Self-Image* (Princeton, N.J.: Princeton Univ. Press, 1965).
40. *A Rap on Race*, p. 15.

41. *The Fire Next Time* (New York: Dial Press, 1963), p. 11.
42. *A Rap on Race*, p. 216.
43. Ibid., p. 12.
44. *Newsweek* poll, October 6, 1969, p. 45.
45. Charles Silberman, *Crisis in Black and White* (New York: Random House, 1964), pp. 9–10.
46. Quoted by Francine du Plessix Gray at the front of *Hawaii: The Sugar Coated Fortress* (New York: Random House, 1972).
47. *Rebellion or Revolution*, pp. 131–32.
48. "A Prison Interview" in *The New Left Reader*, ed. Carl Oglesby (New York: Grove, 1969), p. 231.
49. *Rebellion or Revolution*, p. 107.
50. Ibid., p. 126.

CHAPTER 2

1. R. K. Merton, *Social Theory and Social Structure* (New York: Free Press, 1957).
2. A. J. Ayer, *The Problem of Knowledge* (Harmondsworth, Middlesex: Penguin, 1956).
3. See, for example, the sixty or so research findings summarized by Chris Argyris in the first chapter of *Integrating the Individual and the Organization* (New York: John Wiley, 1963). Even among persons habitually subordinated, their frustration, neuroticism and lack of fulfillment were functions of both formal and informal subordination and inequality.
4. In *Black Drama Anthology*, eds. Woodie King and Ron Milner (New York: Signet, 1971).
5. *Politics and the Ghettos* (New York: Atherton, 1969), pp. 19–20.
6. J. Kovel, *White Racism: A Psychological History* (New York: Pantheon Bks., 1970), p. 54.
7. From the mimeo statement put out in 1968 by Mathew Dumont in his final days at NIMH.
8. James Herndon, *The Way It Spozed to Be* (New York: Simon & Schuster, 1968), Chapter 16.
9. W. W. Mackey, *Requiem for Brother X, Black Drama Anthology*, p. 341.
10. Richard Wright, *Black Boy* (New York: Harper, 1945).
11. See Arthur Kornhauser, *Mental Health and the Industrial Worker* (New York: Wiley, 1965). Poor mental health was at least four to five times more probable in low-skilled, re-

petitive, machine-timed jobs in larger factories. Health was considerably better in those jobs from which blacks are most often banned, e.g., high-skilled, non-repetitive, non-machine-timed work in small factories.

12. *Requiem for Brother X, Black Drama Anthology*, p. 341.
13. Roland L. Warren, "The Sociology of Knowledge," *Social Science Quarterly*, December 1971.
14. Roland L. Warren, "The Model Cities Program," *Social Welfare Forum* 21 (1971).
15. *The Fire Next Time*, p. 47.
16. Ibid., p. 22.
17. Ibid., pp. 42–43.
18. Ibid., p. 49.
19. Ibid., p. 77.
20. Ibid., p. 74.
21. Bargaining opportunities followed by backlashes which occurred during and after America's wars have been detailed by S. M. Wilhelm in *Who Needs the Negro?* (New York: Anchor Bks., 1971), pp. 37–79.
22. Ibid.
23. *Black Drama Anthology*, p. 454.
24. Ibid., p. 470–71.

CHAPTER 3

1. A point made by Robert E. Murphy in *The Dialectics of Social Life* (New York: Basic Bks., 1971), p. 6; an excellent critique of the social sciences.
2. Word used by Thomas Kuhn in *The Structure of Scientific Revolutions* (Chicago: Univ. of Chicago Press, 1970).
3. The admission is by Harvard sociologist George Homans in *Social Behavior* (New York: Harcourt, 1961).
4. Sigmund Koch observed, "Psychology is thus in the unenviable position of standing on philosophical foundations which began to be vacated by philosophy almost as soon as the former had borrowed them." *Behaviorism vs. Phenomenology*, ed. T. Wann (Chicago: Univ. of Chicago Press, 1963).
5. See Richard Sennett's review of *Beyond Freedom and Dignity* in *New York Times Book Review*, November 14, 1971.
6. See also Robert Nisbet's anger with the New Leftists for attacking sociology at the very moment of its receipt of "an honored place . . . in the august National Academy" in

"Subjective Si! Objective No!," *New York Times Book Review,* May 21, 1970, p. 1.

7. *Beyond Freedom and Dignity* (New York: Knopf, 1971), pp. 19–20.

8. Robert Hamblin et al., "Changing the Game from 'Get the Teacher' to 'Learn,'" *Transaction,* January 1969, p. 20.

9. By Reuben M. Baron and Alan R. Bass, Contract No. 81-24-66-04, September 1969.

10. *Rules of Sociological Method* (New York: Free Press, 1964), p. 14. And quoted by Murphy in *The Dialectics of Social Life,* p. 37.

11. *The Dialectics of Social Life,* p. 38; *Rules of Sociological Method,* p. 28.

12. *Rules of Sociological Method,* p. 45.

13. Ibid., p. 104. See also *Dialectics . . . ,* p. 51.

14. *The Coming Crisis of Western Sociology* (New York: Basic Bks., 1970), pp. 51–52.

15. Described by Daniel Patrick Moynihan in *Maximum Feasible Misunderstanding* (New York: Free Press, 1969).

16. Robert Merton, "Social Structure and Anomie" in *Varieties of Modern Social Theory,* ed. H. Ruitenbeek (New York: Dutton, 1963).

17. Richard A. Cloward, "Illegitimate Means, Anomie, Deviant Behavior" in *Varieties of Modern Social Theory.*

18. The formative influence of Merton, Cloward, Ohlin and Nisbet upon MFY and CAP is discussed by Moynihan in *Maximum Feasible Misunderstanding.*

19. See Merton's essay, op. cit., and Moynihan's discussion of how it became policy. See also Herbert Gans, "The Positive Functions of Poverty," *American Journal of Sociology* 78, no. 2 (1972).

20. See Charles Hampden-Turner, *Radical Man* (New York: Doubleday-Anchor, 1971).

21. See Jack D. Douglas, *American Social Order* (New York: Free Press, 1971), p. 16.

22. Gouldner, *The Coming Crisis of Western Sociology,* p. 48.

23. Ibid., p. 294.

24. *The Structure of Scientific Revolutions.*

25. "The Elimination of the American Lower Class as National Policy" in *On Understanding Poverty,* ed. D. P. Moynihan (New York: Basic Bks., 1969), pp. 264–65.

26. Ibid., p. 265.

27. See "Finally, Facts on Malnutrition in the U.S." by F. Glen Lloyd, in *Hunger,* eds. Barbara Milbauer and Gerald Leinward (New York: Pocket Bks., 1971).

28. Miller in *On Understanding Poverty*, pp. 296–97.
29. In Lee Rainwater and William L. Yancey, *The Moynihan Report and the Politics of Controversy* (Cambridge: MIT Press, 1967), p. 18.
30. See William Ryan, *Blaming the Victim* (New York: Pantheon Bks., 1971), pp. 61–64.
31. *The Moynihan Report . . .* , p. 14.
32. Douglas, *American Social Order*, pp. 66–67.
33. For a discussion of this and related issues, see Thomas Szasz, *The Manufacture of Madness* (New York: Delta Bks., 1970).
34. Moynihan, *Maximum Feasible Misunderstanding*, p. 27.
35. See especially Alfred Shutz, "Concepts, Constructs and Theory Formation" in *Philosophy of the Social Sciences*, ed. Maurice Natanson (New York: Random House, 1963), p. 242.
36. Quoted by Henry Winthrop in "Cultural Factors Underlying Research Outlooks in Psychology" (original source mislaid) in *Challenges of Humanistic Psychology*, ed. J. F. T. Bugental (New York: McGraw, 1967), p. 95.
37. "Neutralizing the Disinherited" in *Psychological Factors in Poverty*, ed. V. L. Allen (Chicago: Markham Pub., 1970), pp. 14–24.
38. Carl Rogers in *On Becoming a Person* (Boston: Houghton, 1961) is especially sensitive on this issue; see also Kurt Wolff's "Surrender and Religion," *Journal of the Scientific Study of Religion*, Fall 1962.
39. Moynihan in *On Understanding Poverty*, p. 31.
40. A companion volume to *On Understanding Poverty*, *On Fighting Poverty*, is edited by J. L. Sundquist (New York: Basic Books, 1969).
41. Miller in *On Understanding Poverty*, p. 287.
42. Nisbet, "Subjective Si! Objective No!"
43. Moynihan, *Maximum Feasible Misunderstanding*, p. 142.
44. "The Twilight of Authority," *The Public Interest* 15 (Spring 1969): 9.
45. Perry London, *Behavior Control* (New York: Perennial Lib., 1971), p. 244.
46. Ibid., p. 249.
47. David Bakan, personal communication to Richard Sennett.
48. *The Coming Crisis of Western Sociology*, p. 75.
49. T. S. Langner et al., "Children of the City . . ." in Allen, ed., *Psychological Factors in Poverty*.
50. Ibid., p. 208.

51. *Beyond Freedom and Dignity*, p. 37.

52. London, *Behavior Control*, p. 252.

53. Craig Lumberg, quoted by Floyd Matson in *The Broken Image* (New York: Norton, 1973).

54. In Allen, ed., *Psychological Factors in Poverty*, p. 48.

55. In *Organizational Behavior and Administration*, eds. Paul R. Lawrence et al. (Homewood, Ill.: Irwin, 1961), pp. 26–29; originally in Alexander Leighton, *Human Relations in a Changing World* (New York: Dutton, 1949), pp. 516–61.

56. Ibid.

57. Albert Camus, *Resistance, Rebellion and Death* (New York: Modern Lib., 1958), p. 55.

58. "Social Structure and Anomie" in *Varieties of Modern Social Theory*, pp. 372–73.

59. The classic explication along with the argument that strategic thinking cannot be synthesized with conscience is to be found in Anatol Rapoport's *Strategy and Conscience* (New York: Harper, 1964).

60. Marc Pilisuk et al., "Undoing Deadlocks of Distrust: Hip Berkeley Students and the R.O.T.C.," University of California, Berkeley (mimeo).

61. Here as elsewhere I am especially indebted to Richard Sennett's *The Uses of Disorder* (New York: Knopf, 1970).

CHAPTER 4

1. A good illustration is given by Alan Harrington in *Life in the Crystal Palace* (New York: Knopf, 1958).

2. See Richard A. Cloward and Richard M. Elman, "Poverty, Injustice and the Welfare State," *The Nation*, February 28 and March 7, 1966.

3. Milton Kotler, "Two Essays on the Neighborhood Corporation," *U.S. Joint Economic Committee Report* (Washington, D.C., 1967), p. 185.

4. See Vernon Allen's contribution to *Psychological Factors in Poverty*; and *Do the Poor Want to Work?* by Leonard Goodwin (Washington, D.C.: Brookings, 1972).

5. The broader issue of whether the system is unworthy of the workers' motivation, or the workers' motivation unworthy of the system is addressed by the author in *Workers' Control*, eds. Gerry Hunnius, David Garson and John Case (New York: Random House, 1973).

6. Note especially Moynihan's approving quote of Robert Nisbet that freedom exists in the "interstices of authority." *Maximum Feasible Misunderstanding*, p. 20.

7. For much of the ensuing discussion I am indebted to John Schaar's perceptive essay "Legitimacy in the Modern State" in *Power and Community*, eds. Philip Green and Sanford Levinson (New York: Pantheon Bks., 1969).

8. "The Numbers and the Ghetto" by Daniel Mitchell, Black Economic Research Center. Mimeo distributed by Center for Community Economic Development, Cambridge, Mass., 1970.

9. Jerome H. Skolnick, *Justice Without Trial* (New York: Wiley, 1966).

10. Minutes of resolutions at CDC's meeting in Albuquerque, June 1972.

11. *Community Development Corporations: What are CDC's?* by Matthew Edel. Pamphlet available from the Center for Community Economic Development, Cambridge, Mass.

12. Stewart E. Perry, "National Policy and the Community Development Corporation," *Law and Contemporary Problems* 36, No. 2 (1971): 298.

13. Ibid.

14. For various descriptions of community action see *Citizen Participation*, eds. Edgar S. Cahn and Barry A. Passett, The New Jersey Community Action Training Institute, Trenton, N.J., 1969. Also see Moynihan, *Maximum Feasible Misunderstanding*.

15. However, some Southern rural CDC's claim to have been in existence since the early civil rights struggle, for example, the Poor People's Corporation was founded by SNCC in May 1965, and there was small-scale crafts activity in the wake of this early agitation. The founding dates are taken from *Profiles in Community-Based Economic Development*, Center for Community Economic Development, Cambridge, Mass.

16. Arthur Blaustein and Geoffrey Faux, *The Star-Spangled Hustle* (Garden City: Doubleday, 1972), chap. 4.

17. Ibid., p. 47.

18. *Community Self-Determination Symposium*, Xerox Corporation, Rochester, New York, 1968, p. 47; available also from CCED.

19. Ibid.

20. The book went to press in July 1968, at a time when at least fifty CDC's were in operation.

21. *Radical Man*, pp. 170–78.

22. Ibid. See also Kornhauser, *Mental Health and the Industrial Worker*.

23. Denis Goulet, *The Cruel Choice* (New York: Atheneum, 1971).

24. Ibid., p. 15.

25. David McClelland, *The Achieving Society* (Princeton, N.J.: Van Nostrand, 1961).

26. *Information Exchange: A Conference on Community Based Economic Development*, Cambridge Institute Occasional Bulletin No. 2, Cambridge, Mass., 1969, p. 9.

27. Ibid., p. 11.

28. *Community Economics*, Center for Community Economic Development Occasional Bulletin, Cambridge, Mass., May 1971, pp. 16–17.

29. Personal communication. For inquiries see Tom Morse at SVCDF.

30. North Lawndale Community Development Corporation, Bedford-Stuyvesant Restoration Corporation and MEDIC Enterprises.

31. The phrase is taken from Kuhn's *The Structure of Scientific Revolutions*.

32. *Community Self-Determination Symposium*.

33. Thomas Mayer, "The Position and Progress of Black America" in *Where It's At*, eds. Steven E. Deutsch and John Howard (New York: Harper, 1970).

34. See H. J. Eysenck in *Encounter*, November 1972.

35. "I Don't Mind Failing," quoted in *People's Appalachia*, Morgantown, West Virginia, October–December 1970, p. 14.

36. Oscar Lewis, "The Culture of Poverty," *Scientific American* 215, no. 16 (1966): 19–25.

37. Bennett Berger, "Black Culture or Lower Class Culture?" in *Black Experience: Soul*, ed. Lee Rainwater (New York: Transaction Bks., 1970).

38. McClelland, *The Achieving Society*. See also education materials by McBer Inc., Cambridge, Mass., which applies the "science."

39. Arthur N. Turner, "Work Group Behavior" in *Organizational Behavior and Administration*, eds. Paul R. Lawrence et al. (Homewood, Ill.: Irwin, 1961).

40. Walter B. Miller, "Lower Class Culture as a Generating Milieu of Gang Delinquency," *Journal of Social Issues* 14, no. 4 (1958): 5–19.

41. From Thomas Kochman, "Rapping in the Ghetto," *Transaction*, February 1969.

42. See especially Erik Erikson, *Insight and Responsibility* (New York: Norton, 1964).

43. Irving Lazar, "Which Citizens to Participate in What?" in Cahn and Passett, eds., *Citizen Participation*, p. 291.

44. Ibid., p. 290.

45. For example, the president of the California Dental Association walked out of the meeting when presented with data showing that American Indian women trained to fill teeth had their work judged superior to that of an equal number of licensed dentists *by other dentists*. See Cahn and Passett, eds., *Citizen Participation*, p. 205.

46. (Chicago: Univ. of Chicago Press, 1966.)

47. Quoted by Berger in Rainwater, ed., *Black Experience: Soul*, p. 125.

48. Berger in *Soul*, p. 126.

49. Ibid., p. 123.

50. Robert Blauner in Rainwater, ed., *Black Experience: Soul*, pp. 153 and 157.

51. See Occasional Bulletins 1 to 8, published by the Center for Community Economic Development, Cambridge, Mass.

52. For example, the productivity and morale of one OEO-sponsored work group soared because they all met on the same bus every day. Personal communication with Stewart Perry, Director, CCED.

53. W. E. B. Du Bois, *The Souls of Black Folk* (New York: Signet, 1969), p. 52.

54. Earl Ofari, *The Myth of Black Capitalism* (New York: Monthly Review Press, 1970). He cites Franklin Frazier's *Black Bourgeoisie* (New York: Collier, 1957) as the authority on Chicago syndicates.

55. New York *Times*, Sunday, March 25, 1973.

56. Personal communication with Stewart Perry.

57. Joan M. Nicholson, "Highways—The Bulldozer and the 1968 Hearings," Cahn and Passett, eds., *Citizen Participation*, pp. 216–35.

58. See CCED, *Information Exchange*, for FIGHT's story; and see Jose Rivera's "Community Development Corporations as Institutions for Social Innovation," mimeo, Florence Heller School, Brandeis University, 1971, for a discussion.

59. See chaps. 1 and 2 of *Finding Community*, ed. W. Ronald Jones (Palo Alto, California: Freel & Associates, 1971).

60. See *Shop the Other America*, New World Coalition, Boston, Mass., 1973.

61. CCED, *Profiles in Community-Based Economic Development*, pp. 50–53.

62. Quoted by Sherry Arnstein in Cahn and Passett, eds., *Citizen Participation,* p. 338.
63. From CCED, *Information Exchange,* p. 12.
64. See "Eastman Kodak and FIGHT," Case No. LCH 12H68, Northwestern University School of Business.
65. For a good description of the bill's troubles see Blaustein and Faux, *The Star-Spangled Hustle,* chap. 4.
66. CCED, *Information Exchange,* p. 14.
67. Personal visit.

CHAPTER 5

1. See Cloward and Elman, "Poverty, Injustice and the Welfare State."
2. Quoted by Eunice Shatz in "Patterns of Inequality," unpublished doctoral dissertation, Florence Heller School, Brandeis University, p. 310.
3. For a community-based alternative see Stewart Perry, "A Dignified Community Welfare System," *Center for Community Economic Development Newsletter,* June 15, 1972.
4. The Abt Report is available from the CCED library.
5. Denis Goulet calls this *vulnerability.* See *The Cruel Choice,* chap. 2.
6. McClelland, *The Achieving Society.*
7. New York *Times,* December 22, 1971.
8. Quoted by Earl Ofari in *The Myth of Black Capitalism,* p. 11. Also in W. E. B. Du Bois, *The World and Africa* (New York: International Publishers, 1946), p. 163.
9. To this end the president of Harlem Commonwealth Council acts as community ombudsman; see "East Harlem Medical Tour Shocking" by James H. Dowdy in *Amsterdam News* (reprint), undated, Harlem Commonwealth Council.
10. "Development or Dispersal: Approaches to Ghetto Poverty," mimeo, Center for Community Economic Development, Cambridge, Mass.
11. See OEO descriptive brochure *Opportunity Funding: An Economic Development Demonstration Program.*
12. See chap. 12 of *Radical Man.*
13. *Community Self-Determination Symposium,* p. 26.
14. Jones, *Prejudice and Racism.*
15. This transition is no joke. The National Commission on the Causes and Prevention of Violence has estimated that a person is six times more likely to be a victim of aggravated assault in a community where the average income is below

$6,000. See National Commission on Civil Disorders, *Violent Crime* (New York: Braziller, 1969).

16. LeRoi Jones, *The Death of Malcolm X* in *New Plays from the Black Theater,* ed. Edward Bullins (New York: Bantam, 1969).

17. I. Katz, Judith Goldston and L. Benjamin, "Behavior and Productivity in Bi-racial Work Groups," *Human Relations* 11 (1958): 123–41.

18. Paul R. Lawrence and Jay W. Lorsch, *Organization and Environment* (Boston: Harvard Business School, Division of Research, 1967).

19. For the kinds of attitudes needed to build an industrial base, see McClelland, *The Achieving Society.*

20. Ibid.

21. Ibid.

22. Ibid.

23. Mitchell, "The Numbers and the Ghetto."

24. McClelland, *The Achieving Society.*

25. In *Community Self-Determination Symposium,* p. 42.

26. But see Moynihan's sneers about "middle class aesthetes" and their concern with meaning, New York *Times,* July 2, 1970, p. 24.

27. In *Community Self-Determination Symposium,* p. 7.

28. Ibid., pp. 7–8.

29. CCED, *Profiles in Community-Based Economic Development,* pp. 51–52.

30. Edel, "Development or Dispersal." He cites James Heilbrun and Stanislaw Wellisz, "An Economic Program for the Ghetto," *Urban Riots: Violence and Social Change,* Proceedings of the Academy of Political Science 29 (July 1968), pp. 72–85.

31. The idea is summarized somewhat scornfully in Blaustein and Faux, *The Star-Spangled Hustle,* p. 190.

32. Ibid.

33. "Notes Towards a Pluralist Commonwealth," mimeo, American Friends Service Committee, 1971.

34. Ibid., p. 3.

35. Ibid., pp. 3–4.

36. Kotler, "Two Essays on the Neighborhood Corporation."

37. *The End of Liberalism* (New York: Norton, 1969), pp. 231–32.

38. Theodore Lowi has followed his thesis into the combustion stage in *The Politics of Disorder* (New York: Basic Bks., 1971), p. 35.

39. Over the years this lateral strength has been weakening vis-à-vis authorities external to the community. See Roland Warren, *Community in America* (Chicago: Rand McNally, 1963), p. 9.

40. Milton Kotler is persuasive on how "down town" has colonized its neighboring townships. *Neighborhood Government* (New York: Bobbs, 1969), esp. chap. 2.

41. As of December 1973 this was located at 1878 Massachusetts Avenue, Cambridge, Mass. 02140. Its continuance is imperiled by fund cut-offs by OEO.

42. *C.D.C.'s: New Hope for the Inner City* (New York: Twentieth Century Fund, 1971).

43. Cambridge, Mass., copies may be available from CCED.

44. For a very brief summary of the findings, see *CCED Newsletter*, March 15, 1972, p. 7.

45. Untraceable, I regret. A master's thesis that crossed my desk in 1968.

46. CCED, *Information Exchange*, p. 10.

47. An account of an astonishing increase in scores by African students upon a recall test is told by James J. Jones in *Prejudice and Racism*, p. 64. It was done by placing the items to be memorized within the African oral tradition of storytelling.

48. I worked extensively with a team from Peat, Marwick and Mitchell and spoke to the director of the Roxbury Institute of Business Management.

49. See, for example, the marketing "opportunities" offered to CDC's by the Institute for New Enterprise Development's bulletins, Belmont, Mass., 1971–73.

50. This was the experience of Progress Plaza in Philadelphia; also of Housing Innovations, Inc., in Roxbury.

51. Geoff Faux, "The Bureaucratic Noose," in *Community Economics*, CCED Occasional Bulletin, May 1971, p. 6.

52. Ibid., p. 7.

53. Blaustein and Faux, *The Star-Spangled Hustle*, p. 181.

54. CCED, *Information Exchange*, p. 29.

55. *The End of Liberalism*, pp. 86–97.

56. Ibid., p. 89.

CHAPTER 6

1. John K. Galbraith, *The New Industrial State* (New York: Signet, 1968), p. 219.

2. Albert Camus, *The Rebel: An Essay on Man in Revolt* (New York: Vintage, 1958), p. 12.

3. Samm S. Baker, *The Permissible Lie* (Boston: Beacon Press, 1968), p. 123.

4. Greenberg, "The Political Socialization of Black Children."

5. Personal communication with Bernard Gifford.

6. Quoted by Alan Altshuler in *Community Control* (New York: Pegasus, 1970), p. 25.

7. Irving L. Janis, "Personality as a Factor in Susceptibility to Persuasion," in *The Science of Human Communication*, ed. Wilbur Schramm (New York: Basic Bks., 1963), pp. 57–58.

8. Lawrence Kohlberg, "Education for Justice," Ernest Burton Lecture at Harvard University, School of Education mimeo, 1968.

9. Paul Lazarsfeld and Herbert Menzel, "Mass Media and Personal Influence," in Schramm, ed., *The Science of Human Communication*.

10. Ibid.

11. Joseph T. Klapper, "The Social Effects of Mass Communication," in Schramm, ed., *The Science of Human Communication*.

12. Murray Horwitz, "Training in Conflict Resolution," in *T-Group Theory and Laboratory Method*, eds. L. R. Bradford, J. R. Gibb and K. Benne (New York: Wiley, 1964).

13. Nicholas Johnson, *How to Talk Back to Your Television Set* (New York: Bantam, 1970), p. 7.

14. Erich Fromm, *The Art of Loving* (New York: Harper, 1956).

15. See especially Matson's *The Broken Image*, and Charles M. Fair, *The Dying Self* (Garden City, N.Y.: Doubleday, 1970).

CHAPTER 7

1. J. K. Galbraith, *The Affluent Society* (Boston: Houghton, 1971), p. 173.

2. F. Barron, *Creativity and Personal Freedom* (Princeton, N.J.: Insight, Van Nostrand, 1968).

3. "Television: A Special Report," *Life*, September 10, 1971, p. 43.

4. *Survey of Broadcast Journalism: 1970–1971*, ed. M. Barrett (New York: Grosset, 1971), pp. 11–12.

5. *Radical Man*, p. 419.

6. "American Public Opinion about Vietnam," John D. Robinson and Soloman Jacobson in *Vietnam: Issues and Alternatives*, ed. Walter Izard (Cambridge, Mass.: Schenkman Pub., 1969).

7. "Protean Man" in *Atlantic Monthly*, June 1969.

8. Kenneth Keniston, "A Second Look at the Uncommitted," *Social Policy*, July/August 1971.

9. Personal communication. The insight is Jonathan Kozol's.

10. *Wall Street Journal*, September 8, 1971, p. 36.

11. Boston *Globe*, September 11, 1971, p. 1.

12. "Business Gets a Social Service," Boston *Globe*, November 14, 1971, and *New York Times Review of the Week*, November 22, 1970.

13. *Youth and the Establishment*, John D. Rockefeller III Foundation, 1971.

14. This thesis has recently been advanced by Rollo May in *Power and Innocence* (New York: Norton, 1973).

15. Quoted by Graham Martin in *Discrimination and Popular Culture* (Harmondsworth, Middlesex, UK: Penguin, 1968), p. 74.

Bibliography

Abt Associates, Incorporated. *An Evaluation of the Special Impact Program*. Cambridge, Mass.: Abt Associates, 1972.

Ackerson, N. J., and Sharf, L. H. "Community Development Corporations: Operations and Financing," *Harvard Law Review* 83 (May 1970).

Allen, R. L. *Black Awakening in Capitalist America*. Garden City, N.Y.: Doubleday, 1969.

Allen, V. L., ed. *Psychological Factors in Poverty*. Chicago: Markham Pub., 1970.

Allport, G. W. *The Nature of Prejudice*. Reading, Mass.: Addison-Wesley, 1954.

Alperowitz, G. "Community Development Corporations: A New Approach to the Poverty Program," *Harvard Law Review* 82 (January 1969).

——— (with Staughton Lynd). *Strategy and Program: Two Essays Towards American Socialism*. Boston: Beacon Press, 1973.

Altshuler, A. A. *Community Control*. New York: Pegasus, 1970.

Andrews, L. M., and Karlins, M. *Requiem for Democracy*. New York: Holt, 1971.

Aptheker, H. A. *A Documentary History of the Negro People in the United States*. New York: Citadel, 1968.

Aya, R., and Miller, N., eds. *The New American Revolution*. New York: Free Press, 1971.

Baker, S. S. *The Permissible Lie*. Boston: Beacon Press, 1968.

Baldwin, J. *The Fire Next Time*. New York: Dial Press, 1963.

——— *Nobody Knows My Name*. New York: Dell, 1969.

——— (with Margaret Mead). *A Rap on Race*. New York: Delta Bks., 1971.

——— *No Name in the Street*. New York: Dial Press, 1972.

Barron, F. *Creativity and Personal Freedom*. Princeton, N.J.: Insight, Van Nostrand, 1968.

Bateson, G. *Steps to an Ecology of Mind*. New York: Ballantine, 1972.

——— et al. "Toward a Theory of Schizophrenia," *Behavioral Science* 1, no. 4 (1956).

Bayton, J.; McAlister, L.; and Horner, J. "Race-Class Stereotypes," *Journal of Negro Education* 25 (1956).

Becker, E. *The Lost Science of Man*. New York: Braziller, 1971.

Bell, D. "Meritocracy and Equality," *The Public Interest* 29 (1972).

Bennett, L. *Negro Mood*. Chicago: Johnson Pub., 1964.

Berelson, B., and Steiner, G. A. *Human Behavior: An Inventory of Scientific Findings*. New York: Harcourt, 1964.

Berger, B. "Black Culture or Lower Class Culture?" in Lee Rainwater, ed., *Black Experience: Soul*. Transaction Books, distributed by Aldine Press: New York, 1970.

Berkowitz, L. "The Effect of Observing Violence," *Scientific American* 210, no. 2 (1964).

Biddle, W. W., and Biddle, L. J. *Encouraging Community Development*. New York: Holt, 1965.

Blake, J. H. "Black Nationalism" in *The Annals of the American Academy of Political and Social Science*, March 1969.

Blauner, R. "Black Culture: Lower Class Result or Ethnic Creation?" *Transaction*, June 1967.

Blaustein, A. I. "What is Community Economic Development?" *Urban Affairs Quarterly* 6, no. 1 (September 1970).

—— and Faux, G. *The Star-Spangled Hustle*. Garden City: Doubleday, 1972.

Brower, M. "The Criteria for Measuring the Success of a Community Development Corporation," CCED (mimeo), 1970.

Buber, M. "Distance and Relation." Translated by R. A. Smith in *Psychiatry* 20, no. 2 (1957).

Bullins, E., ed. *New Plays from the Black Theater*. New York: Bantam, 1969.

Cahn, E. S., and Passett, B. A., eds. *Citizen Participation*. The New Jersey Community Action Training Institute, Trenton, N.J., 1969.

Camus, A. *The Rebel: An Essay on Man in Revolt*. Translated by Anthony Bower. New York: Vintage, 1958.

Caplovitz, D. *The Poor Pay More*. New York: Free Press, 1967.

Carmichael, S., and Hamilton, C. *Black Power: The Politics of Liberation in America*. New York: Vintage, 1967.

Center for Community Economic Development, Cambridge, Mass.

Information Exchange: A Conference on Community Based Economic Development. Occasional Bulletin. No. 2, Cambridge, Mass., 1969, p. 9.

Profiles in Community-Based Economic Development. Occasional Bulletin. July 1971.

Community Economics. Occasional Bulletin. May 1971 and others.

Community Development Corporations: What are CDC's? (by Matthew Edel).

Center for Community Economic Development Newsletter, monthly 1971–73.

"Annotated Bibliography on Community Development Corporations." March 1973 (see also Brower, M.; Faux, G.; Morris, J.; Rivera, J.; and Stein, B.).

Clark, K. B. *Dark Ghetto.* New York: Harper, 1965.

Cleaver, E. *Soul on Ice.* New York: McGraw, 1968.

—— and Elman, R. M. "Poverty, Injustice and the Welfare State," *The Nation,* February 28 and March 7, 1966.

Coles, R. "Black Power: A Discussion," *Partisan Review,* Spring 1968.

Combs, A., and Snygg, D. *Individual Behavior.* New York: Harper, 1961.

Cooper, D. *Psychiatry and Anti-Psychiatry.* London: Tavistock Publications, 1967.

Cruse, H. *The Crisis of the Negro Intellectual.* New York: Morrow, 1968.

Deutsch, S. E., and Howard, J., eds. *Where It's At: Radical Perspectives in Sociology.* New York: Harper, 1970.

Douglas, J. D. *American Social Order.* New York: Free Press, 1971.

Du Bois, W. E. B. *The Souls of Black Folk.* New York: Signet, 1969.

Dunbar, P. L. "Poems," *Freedomways* 12, no. 4 (1972).

Dunn, E. S. *Economic and Social Development: A Process of Social Learning.* Resources for the Future, Inc. Baltimore: Johns Hopkins Press, 1971.

Edwards, R. C.; Reich, M.; and Weisskopf, T. E., eds. *The Capitalist System.* Englewood Cliffs, N.J.: Prentice-Hall, 1972.

Ellison, R. *Invisible Man.* New York: New Am. Lib., 1952.

——. *Shadow and Act.* New York: Random House, 1964.

Ennis, B. *Prisoners of Psychiatry.* New York: Harcourt, 1972.

Erikson, E. H. "Identity and the Life Cycle," *Psychological Issues* 1, no. 1 (1959).

Etzioni, A. *The Active Society.* New York: Free Press, 1968.

Fanon, F. *Black Skin, White Masks.* New York: Grove, 1967.

Faux, G. "Politics and Bureaucracy in Community Controlled Economic Development," *Law and Contemporary Problems* 36, no. 2 (Spring 1972).

Femina, J. D. *From Those Wonderful Folks That Gave You Pearl Harbor.* New York: Simon & Schuster, 1970.

Forsythe, D. "Radical Sociology and Blacks" in Joyce Ladner, ed., *The Death of White Sociology.* New York: Vintage, 1973.

Frazier, F. *Black Bourgeoisie.* New York: Collier, 1957.

Freire, P. *Pedagogy of the Oppressed.* New York: Herder & Herder, 1968.

Fromm, E. *The Art of Loving.* New York: Harper, 1956.

Galbraith, J. K. *The Affluent Society.* Boston: Houghton, 1971.

——. *The New Industrial State.* New York: Signet, 1967.

Gans, H. J. "The Positive Functions of Poverty" in *American Journal of Sociology* 78, no. 2 (1972).

Goodman, R. *After the Planners.* New York: Simon & Schuster, 1971.

Goodpaster, G. S. "An Introduction to the Community Development Corporation," *Journal of Urban Law* 46, no. 3 (1969).

Goodwin, Leonard. *Do the Poor Want to Work?* Washington, D.C.: Brookings, 1972.

Gottschalk, S. S. "The Community-Based Welfare System: A Voluntary Alternative to Public Welfare," *Journal of Applied Behavioral Science,* May 1973.

Gouldner, A. W. *The Coming Crisis of Western Sociology.* New York: Basic Bks., 1971.

Goulet, D. *The Cruel Choice: A New Concept in the Theory of Development.* New York: Atheneum Pubs., 1971.

Green, G., and Faux, G. "The Social Utility of Black Enterprise," W. F. Haddad and G. D. Pugh, eds., *Black Economic Development.* Englewood Cliffs, N.J.: Prentice-Hall, 1969.

Green, P., and Levinson, S., eds. *Power and Community: Dissenting Essays in Political Science.* New York: Vintage, 1970.

Greenberg, E. S., ed. *Political Socialization.* New York: Atherton, 1970.

Halleck, S. L. *The Politics of Therapy.* New York: Harper, 1971.

Hampden-Turner, C. M. *Radical Man: The Process of Psycho-Social Development.* New York: Doubleday-Anchor, 1971.

Hannerz, V. *Soulside Inquiries into Ghetto Culture and Community.* New York: Columbia Univ. Press, 1969.

Hare, N. *The Black Anglo-Saxons.* New York: Collier, 1970.

Herndon, J. *The Way Its Spozed to Be.* New York: Simon & Schuster, 1968.

Hollingshead, A. R., and Redlich, F. C. *Social Class and Mental Health.* New York: Wiley, 1958.

Innis, R. "Separatist Economics: A New Social Contract" in W. F. Haddad and G. D. Pugh, eds., *Black Economic Development*. Englewood Cliffs, N.J.: Prentice-Hall, 1969.

Jensen, A. R. "How Much Can We Boost I.Q. and Scholastic Achievement?" *Harvard Educ. Rev.* 38 (1968).

——. "Learning Ability, Intelligence and Educability" in V. L. Allen, ed., *Psychological Factors in Poverty*. Chicago: Markham Pub., 1970.

Johnson, N. *How to Talk Back to Your Television Set*. New York: Bantam, 1970.

Jones, James J. *Prejudice and Racism*. Reading, Mass.: Addison-Wesley, 1972.

Jones, LeRoi. *The Baptism and the Toilet*. New York: Grove, 1966.

——. "The Death of Malcolm X" in E. Bullins, ed., *New Plays from the Black Theater*. New York: Bantam, 1969.

Jones, W. R. *Finding Community: A Guide to Community Research and Action*. Palo Alto, Cal.: Freel & Associates, 1971.

Kain, J. F. *Race and Poverty: The Economics of Discrimination, Race, and Poverty*. Englewood Cliffs, N.J.: Spectrum Bks., 1969.

Kanter, Rosabeth, and Zurcher, L. A., eds. "Alternative Institutions" in *Journal of Applied Behavioral Science*, May 1973.

Kaplan, A. *The Conduct of Inquiry*. Scranton, Pennsylvania: Chandler, 1964.

Keil, C. *Urban Blues*. Chicago: Univ. of Chicago Press, 1966.

King, M. L., Jr. "Letter from a Birmingham Jail" in Armstrong, A., ed., *Protest: Man Against Society*. New York: Bantam, 1969.

King, W., and Milner, R. *Black Drama Anthology*. New York: Signet, 1971.

Kornhauser, A. *Mental Health and the Industrial Worker*. New York: John Wiley, 1965.

Kotler, M. "Two Essays on the Neighborhood Corporation." *U.S. Joint Economic Committee Report*. Washington, D.C., 1967.

——. *Neighborhood Government*. New York: Bobbs, 1969.

——. "The Politics of Community Economic Development." *Law and Contemporary Problems* 36, no. 1 (1971).

——. "The Disappearance of Municipal Liberty." *Politics and Society* 3, no. 3 (1972).

Kovel, J. *White Racism: A Psychological History*. New York: Pantheon Bks., 1970.

Kramer, R. M. *Participation of the Poor*. Englewood Cliffs, N.J.: Prentice-Hall, 1969.

Kuhn, T. S. *The Structure of Scientific Revolutions*. Chicago: Univ. of Chicago Press, 1970.

Ladner, Joyce A., ed. *The Death of White Sociology*. New York: Vintage, 1973.

Laing, R. D. *The Politics of Experience*. New York: Pantheon Bks., 1967.

———. *The Politics of the Family*. New York: Vintage, 1972.

Langer, T. S., et al. "Children of the City: Affluence, Poverty and Mental Health" in V. L. Allen, ed., *Psychological Factors in Poverty*. Chicago: Markham Pub., 1970.

Lawrence, P. R., and Lorsch, J. W. *Organization and Environment*. Boston: Harvard Business School, Division of Research, 1967.

Leinward, Gerald. *Hunger: Problems of American Society*. New York: Pocket Bks., 1971.

Liebow, E. *Tally's Corner*. Boston: Little, 1967.

Lipset, S. M. *Political Man*. New York: Anchor Bks., 1963.

London, P. *Behavior Control*. New York: Perennial Library, 1971.

Lowi, T. J. *The End of Liberalism*. New York: Norton, 1969.

———. *The Politics of Disorder*. New York: Basic Bks., 1971.

Loye, D. *The Healing of a Nation*. New York: Delta Bks., 1971.

McClelland, D. *The Achieving Society*. Princeton, N.J.: Van Nostrand, 1961.

McGinnis, Joe. *The Selling of the President*. New York: Pocket Bks., 1970.

Mackey, W. W. "Requiem for Brother X" in W. King, and R. Milner, eds., *Black Drama Anthology*. New York: New Am. Lib., 1972.

McKissick, F. B. "The Way to a Black Ideology" in *Black Scholar* 1, no. 2 (1969).

Marx, G. T. *Protest and Prejudice: A Study of Belief in the Black Community*. New York: Harper, 1969.

Maslow, A. H. *Motivation and Personality*. New York: Harper, 1954.

———. "Synergy in Society and the Individual," *Journal of Individual Psychology* 20 (1964).

Matson, F. W. *The Broken Image*. New York: Norton, 1973.

May, R. *Power and Innocence*. New York: Norton, 1973.

Mead, Margaret (with James Baldwin). *A Rap on Race*. New York: Delta, 1971.

Merton, R. K. "Social Structure and Anomie" in H. M. Ruiten-beek, ed., *Varieties of Modern Social Theory.* New York: Dutton, 1963.

Miller, K. H. "Community Capitalism and the Community Self-Determination Act." *Harvard Journal on Legislation* 6, no. 4, pp. 413–69, 1969.

Morris, J. "Poor People's Corporation: A CDC Serving a Rural Setting." CCED mimeo, 1971.

Moynihan, D. P. *Maximum Feasible Misunderstanding.* New York: Free Press, 1969.

——. ed. *On Understanding Poverty.* New York: Basic Bks., 1969.

Murphy, R. E. *The Dialectics of Social Life.* New York: Basic Bks., 1971.

Murray, A. "White Norms, Black Deviation" in J. A. Ladner, ed., *The Death of White Sociology.* New York: Vintage, 1973.

Myrdal, G. *An American Dilemma: The Negro Problem and Modern Democracy.* New York: Harper, 1944.

Natanson, M., ed. *Philosophy of the Social Sciences.* New York: Random House, 1963.

Newton, H. P. "A Prison Interview" in Carl Oglesby, ed., *The New Left Reader.* New York: Grove, 1969.

Ofari, E. *The Myth of Black Capitalism.* New York: Monthly Review Press, 1970.

Oglesby, C., ed. *The New Left Reader.* New York: Grove, 1969.

O'Neil, J. *Sociology as a Skin Trade.* New York: Harper, 1972.

Perry, H. *They'll Cut Off Your Project.* New York: Praeger, 1972.

Perry, S. E. "National Policy and the Community Development Corporation," *Law and Contemporary Problems* 36, no. 2 (1971).

Pettigrew, T. F. *A Profile of the Negro American.* Princeton, N.J.: Van Nostrand, 1964.

Pugh, R. W. *Psychology and the Black Experience.* Monterey, Cal.: Brooks/Cole, 1972.

Rainwater, L. "Neutralizing the Disinherited" in V. L. Allen, ed., *Psychological Factors in Poverty.* Chicago: Markham, 1970.

——. ed. *Black Experience: Soul.* New York: Transaction Bks., 1970.

—— and Yancey, W. L. *The Moynihan Report and the Politics of Controversy.* Cambridge: M.I.T. Press, 1967.

Rapoport, A. *Strategy and Conscience*. New York: Harper, 1964.

Rivera, J. "CDC's: A Futuristic View." CCED mimeo, 1971.

Rokeach, M. *The Open and Closed Mind*. New York: Basic Bks., 1960.

Rosenberg, M. *Society and the Adolescent Self-Image*. Princeton, N.J.: Princeton Univ. Press, 1965.

Ryan, W. *Blaming the Victim*. New York: Pantheon Bks., 1971.

Scheff, T. *Being Mentally Ill*. Chicago: Aldine Pub., 1966.

Schramm, W., ed. *The Science of Human Communication*. New York: Basic Bks., 1963.

Sclar, E. "The Community Basis for Economic Development." Center for Community Economic Development, Cambridge, Mass., mimeo, 1970.

Sennett, R. *The Uses of Disorder*. New York: Knopf, 1970.

———. *The Hidden Injuries of Class*. New York: Knopf, 1973.

Shapiro, Evelyn, ed. *Psycho-Sources*. Del Mar, Cal.: CRM Bks., 1973.

Shutz, A. "Concepts, Constructs and Theory Formation" in M. Natanson, ed., *Philosophy of the Social Sciences*. New York: Random House, 1963.

Silberman, Charles, *Crisis in Black and White*. New York: Random House, 1964.

Skinner, B. F. *Beyond Freedom and Dignity*. New York: Random House, 1964.

Skolnik, J. H. *Justice Without Trial*. New York: Wiley, 1966.

——— and Currie, E., eds. *Crisis in American Institutions*. Boston: Little, 1970.

Slater, P. E. *The Pursuit of Loneliness*. Boston: Beacon Press, 1970.

Spiegel, H. B. C. *Citizen Participation and Urban Development*. Vol. 1. NTL Institute for Applied Behavioral Science. Washington, D.C., 1968.

Stein, B. A. *The Community Context of Economic Conversion*. CCED mimeo, 1971.

———. "The Centerville Fund, Inc." *Journal of Applied Behavioral Science*, May 1973.

Stein, D. D.; Hardyck, J. A.; and Brewster Smith, M. "Race and Relief: an open and shut case," *Journal of Personality and Social Psychology* 1 (1965).

Sternlieb, G. *The Tenement Landlord*. New Brunswick, N.J.: Rutgers Univ. Press, 1969.

Stone, C. "Black Politics" in *The Black Scholar* 1, no. 2 (1969).

Sturdivent, F. D. "Community Development Corporations: The Problems of Mixed Objectives," *Law and Contemporary Problems* 36, no. 1 (1971).

Szasz, T. S. *Ideology and Insanity*. Garden City, N.Y.: Doubleday-Anchor, 1970.

Thompson, D. *Discrimination and Popular Culture*. Harmondsworth, Middlesex: Pelican Original, 1964.

Tomkins, S. "Left and Right: Basic Dimensions of Ideology and Personality" in R. W. White, ed., *The Study of Lives*. New York: Atherton, 1964.

Turner, J. "The Sociology of Black Nationalism" in J. A. Ladner, ed., *The Death of White Sociology*. New York: Vintage, 1973. See also *The Black Scholar* 1, no. 2 (1969).

Vitorisz, T., and Harrison, B. "Ghetto Development, Community Corporations, and Public Policy," *Review of Black Political Economy* 2, no. 1 (1971).

Wann, T., ed. *Behaviorism vs. Phenomenology*. Chicago: Univ. of Chicago Press, 1963.

Warren, R. L. *Community in America*. Chicago: Rand McNally, 1963.

———. ed. *Politics and the Ghettos*. New York: Atherton, 1969.

———. "The Model Cities Program," *Social Welfare Forum* 21 (1971).

———. *Truth, Love and Social Change*. Chicago: Rand McNally, 1971.

———. "The Sociology of Knowledge," *Social Science Quarterly*, December 1971.

Weisskopf, W. A. *Alienation and Economics*. New York: Dutton, 1971.

White, R. W. "Motivation Reconsidered," *Psychological Review* 66 (1959).

Wilhelm, S. M. *Who Needs the Negro?* New York: Doubleday-Anchor, 1971.

Williams, R. *Culture and Society*. London: Chatto, 1958.

———. *Communications*. Baltimore, Md.: Pelican, 1968.

Wilson, W. "Rank Order of Discrimination and Its Relevance to Civil Rights Priorities," *Journal of Personality and Social Psychology* 15 (1970).

Wright, R. *Native Son*. New York: Harper, 1940.

———. *Black Boy*. New York: Harper, 1945.

Yablonski, L. *The Tunnel Back*. New York: Macmillan, 1964.

Index